W9-BHK-226

CHASING
the
CHINOOK

On the Trail of Canadian
Words and Culture

WAYNE GRADY

VIKING

VIKING
Published by the Penguin Group
Penguin Books Canada Ltd, 10 Alcorn Avenue, Toronto, Ontario, Canada M4V 3B2
Penguin Books Ltd, 27 Wrights Lane, London W8 5TZ, England
Penguin Putnam Inc., 375 Hudson Street, New York, New York 10014, U.S.A.
Penguin Books Australia Ltd, Ringwood, Victoria, Australia
Penguin Books (NZ) Ltd, cnr Rosedale and Airborne Roads, Albany Aukland 1310,
New Zealand

Penguin Books Ltd Registered Offices: Harmondsworth, Middlesex, England

First published 1998
10 9 8 7 6 5 4 3 2 1

Copyright Acknowledgements. Quotations from the following were used by permission:
A Friction of Lights by Eldon Grier (Toronto: Contact Press, 1963) © Copyright by
Eldon Grier, 1963; *Art as Second Nature: Occasional Pieces* by Michael Hamburger
(Carcanet New Press Ltd., 1975) © Copyright by Michael Hamburger.

Printed and bound in Canada on acid free paper ∞

CANADIAN CATALOGUING IN PUBLICATION DATA

Grady, Wayne
    Chasing the chinook: on the trail of Canadian words and culture

ISBN 0-670-88243-7

1. Canada – Miscellanea. 2. Canadianisms (English).* 3. English language –
Canada – Terms and phrases. I. Title.

FC60.G72 1998   971'.002   C98-931375-1
F1008.G72 1998

Visit Penguin Canada's website at www.penguin.ca

There are words that are the incomparable beasts of our imagination.
—Eldon Grier, "An Ecstasy"

An essay really ought not to be on anything, to deal with anything, to define anything. An essay is a walk, an excursion, not a business trip.
—Michael Hamburger, "An Essay on the Essay"

CONTENTS

INTRODUCTION

This book has had many beginnings. One of them was a conversation I had nearly ten years ago with a friend in New Hampshire. She was (and I hope is) a writer, and she had just bought a small salt-box house that looked perfectly charming to me—a large spray of dried flowers in the fireplace, attractive floral wallpaper above the wainscoting—but that she said needed a lot of fixing up. The wiring was dodgy and the plank floor in the spare bedroom had to be stripped. She wasn't writing at the moment, and she worried about paying for the renovations and keeping up the mortgage. I said something about it being too bad writers couldn't collect pogey. She looked at me quizzically, as though I had changed the subject.

"Pogey?" she said. "What's that?"

"Unemployment insurance," I said. "Don't you have that here?"

"We have unemployment insurance," she said. "But we don't call it pogey."

"What do you call it?" I asked, wonderingly.

"We call it unemployment insurance."

Now, I grew up in Windsor, Ontario (another beginning for this book), where the border between Canada and the United States existed as a kind of fuzzy zone where children sat in the back seat wearing four shirts. It was not a place where the *language* changed.

It didn't occur to me until that day in New Hampshire that Canadians had words for things that Americans did not. I knew that England had different words for things, most of which, for some reason, had to do with cars; the British said bonnet and boot for hood and trunk, for instance, and their tyres sometimes rode up on kerbs. All of that made reading British mystery novels somewhat exotic. I even knew that Americans had words we didn't use in Canada—sophomore, for instance. But the idea that Canadians actually had words not used in either the United States or England was entirely new to me. I began to take notes.

My original idea was to compile a dictionary of Canadianisms, literally a hoard of words that either don't exist elsewhere (like "pogey") or else were first used in Canada before they entered the English language at large (like "puck"). Once I began to look into it, however, I realized that this was not such an original idea after all. There were dozens of such dictionaries already, some of them excellent and exhaustive, some of them idiosyncratic and unreliable; but in any case I had no wish or need to add to their rank. I recalled the words of Samuel Johnson, who, in his own *Dictionary*, defined "lexicographer" as "a harmless drudge." I don't mind being harmless, but I do not want to be considered a drudge. I continued collecting words, however, partly because that is what writers do, but mostly out of a growing fascination with the idea that, quite apart from their interest as individual nuggets of Canadiana—the stuff of dictionaries—collectively they add up to a distinct and self-expressive vocabulary of Canadian culture.

At parties, when people asked me what I was working on, this is the point at which they gulped their drinks and thought they heard their cellphones ringing, so let me hastily say now what these essays are not about. They are not about how we pronounce the words "house" and "about." They are not about how we tack the tag-word "eh?" onto the ends of all our sentences (we don't). They are not about how we call the last letter in the English alphabet "zed"—so does everyone in England, Scotland, Ireland, Wales, Australia and New Zealand. ("Zed" is not a Canadianism; "zee" is an Americanism.) They are not about how we bull-headedly continue to spell "colour" and "storey" like the British rather than like the letter-thrifty Americans. These aspects of our language no doubt reflect something of our culture, but with the possible exception of "eh?" they are all explicable in a sentence or two (my own theory of "eh?" is that it comes from the early Quebec French practice of adding *é* to the ends of sentences, but that hardly justifies a whole essay). "House" and "colour" and "zed" all say more about where we come from than about who we are, and although I recognize that where we come from is inextricably linked to who we are, I prefer to place my emphasis on the latter. For one thing, we all come from different places, and not everyone in Canada says "house" the same way. But we all know what the words "kerosene" and "Sasquatch" mean.

Although we may all know what they mean, most of us don't know where the words come from, and part of what I do in these essays is attempt to be etymologically correct. I am not claiming infallibility when I trace the origin of the word "pogey," for example, to the French *poche*, or even to be ploughing virgin soil; any decent dictionary of word origins, of which there are hundreds (believe me), will do that, although, not surprisingly, many of them exhibit xenophobic blindness when it comes to words that have Canadian origins. Even the mighty *Oxford English Dictionary* misses some Canadian references that predate the American ones it lists as firsts (the little red car at the end of a freight train was called a caboose in Canada some thirty years before the OED says the word first appeared in the United States, for example; and "muskrat" was not first used in New

England and has nothing to do with musk—you'll see why this irks me as you read on).

Tracing a word's pedigree, however, was only a small part of what I wanted to do in these essays, fascinating though that often was. I did the drudge-work mainly to assure myself that the words I chose were indeed Canadian, or at least arguably Canadianish. This was not as open-and-shut as one might suppose. I tried to establish that Groundhog Day was a Canadian term, for example, but had to content myself with proving only that "groundhog" was. And one might think it unnecessary, even tedious, to state that the word "Canada" was Canadian, but the source-word for the name of our country has been attributed to French, Portuguese, Spanish and even Hebrew; to the name of a mountain range, a river, a village, the people in it, and a fur trader. And no one knows why a drink containing vodka and Clamato juice was called a Bloody Caesar, or why Nova Scotians were called bluenoses by American Loyalists. (This left the door invitingly open for my own very plausible suggestions, which I trust will find their way into many future dictionaries of word origins.)

Fun though it was, sorting through all that theoretical etymology was not the main purpose of these essays. To use Michael Hamburger's brilliant metaphor, in which he asserts that an essay is not a business trip but a walk, the Canadian origin of a word was like a shaft of bright sunlight slanting through a library window: it was what drew me outside for these walks, but it hardly ever provided the walk's destination.

Not that the walks all had destinations. Writing an essay is often a matter of clearing the mind of accumulated bits of related information, which is what a walk is mainly good for. But most walks, one will notice, begin and end at the same place, which gives them a sort of rudimentary structure. And as I chose the words I would write about and started writing, I noticed certain recurring images, as though as a walker I was unconsciously taking different paths, all of which took me past the same meadow. After a while I began to look out for that meadow, to wonder what was in it that drew my steps. And it was not until I realized what was in that meadow that I knew I had more than a collection of aimless walks. What I had was a book.

I am going to state the thesis of this book as baldly as I can, so that any debate that follows will at least be posited on solid ground. Canada is a country, and every country has a culture, and a country's culture is expressed in the language or languages spoken by the citizens of that country, and a language is made up of words. This seems to me to be incontrovertible, incontestable and even self-evident. In no other country would such a statement raise so much as an eyebrow; in Canada, it raises hackles, which is to say it touches on issues so contentious that they cut to the very heart and future of the country. I vividly recall the American—one of those involved in negotiating the North American Free Trade Agreement (NAFTA)—who asked a CBC reporter what she thought the difference was between Canada and yoghurt. "Yoghurt has a living culture," was the American's reply. This "joke" sent chills down my spine, because it suggested that if Canadian culture were not on the NAFTA bargaining table—as Canadian negotiators assured us it was not—that was only because no one at the table thought there was such a thing as Canadian culture. I did not find that funny. What was more, the American's joke was frankly racist (in Canada we would call it "ethnocentric"); any other country would have at least demanded that he be removed from the NAFTA negotiating team, if not from polite company. But no one in Canada seemed to notice; hardly anyone I've spoken to since even recalls the incident. And I've even heard Canadians repeating the joke, telling it against themselves the way Newfoundlanders tell jokes about sheep. What is going on here? I wondered.

* * *

"You must learn the American language if you want to understand the American people," wrote Thomas Chandler Haliburton, the patriotic Nova Scotian creator of the Sam Slick stories, in 1838. Although in Haliburton's day "American" could mean anyone living in North America, including British North America, Haliburton and his readers knew exactly what he meant. Americans were those newcomers who had moved into Nova Scotia after the American Revolution and were looking to take over the provincial government in the next election. Nova Scotians, Haliburton was saying, had better learn to speak American if they wanted to understand what was happening around them.

Little has changed in the intervening years. Culturally speaking, Americans are still moving into Canada, still taking over the government and, like Haliburton's clock pedlar Sam Slick, still softsawdering us into wanting things we don't need (like NAFTA and its spawn, the Multilateral Agreement on Investment, or MAI). The irony is that this subtle take-over is possible because we have heeded Haliburton's advice all too well. Canadians have learned the American language so thoroughly that most of us think we speak it. Although some of us can detect differences between the American and Canadian character—we're so polite, they're so pushy—few make the logical leap to assuming that there must also be some difference in the way the two characters are articulated.

The reasons for this linguistic indifference are not hard to find. Only about one in five books sold in Canadian bookstores are written by Canadians. Less than 15 percent of the television hours watched in Canada are Canadian (and that's counting hockey). A full 92 percent of the films shown in Canadian cinemas are American. We know how to speak American. We can detect the difference between a Californian and a Brooklyn accent far more readily than we can distinguish between a Vancouverite and a Torontonian. Most Canadians can identify, even mimic, a country-and-western drawl, but few can say whether a speaker is from Cape Breton or the Ottawa Valley. We are bombarded daily by American English disguised as Canadian. During elections, our newspapers speak of the prime minister's "running mate." The Peace Tower has been known to make its way inexplicably from Parliament to Capitol Hill. Even our knowledge of foreign, non-English literature comes to us (for the most part) via American translations.

And yet most of us speak Canadian. We just don't know it. Every time we pull up to an Esso station, or drive (or curse) a Ski-Doo, or wonder what happened to cabooses, or read a Superman comic, we are participating in a linguistic event that is distinctly Canadian, and some part of our brain is reacting differently than an American brain would while doing those same things. Whenever we peer into a gopher hole, or dump a hockey puck into a corner, or eat *tourtière*, or play shinny, we are participating in Canadian, not American, culture, and every time we use those words we are speaking Canadian.

In 1965 the eminent American literary critic Edmund Wilson published a book called *O Canada: An American's Notes on Canadian Culture*. In it, Wilson remarked that "the relation of Canada to the United States has always been rather peculiar. The constant slight strain it involves is to be felt in the inveterate Canadian habit, always surprising to us, of referring to us as 'the Americans,' as if Canadians were not Americans, too." Reading this sent the same chills down my spine that I felt when I heard the American negotiator's yoghurt joke. Wilson was not being cutely disingenuous; he was articulating the intellectual foundations of NAFTA and the MAI. If Canadians are Americans, what's all this fuss about preserving Canadian culture?

Wilson went on to note a few things that differentiate the two countries. He mentioned our tendency to multiculturalism, although he didn't call it that, by which we allow immigrants to retain the culture of their homelands (whether they want to or not), compared with the American way, which he said is to force "ethnics" to become "melted" into American society. "With us," he wrote, "there is the constant pressure to become 'Americanized.' But is there such a thing as being Canadianized?"

Yes, Mr. Wilson, there is. The problem is that it is Canadians who most need to be Canadianized.

*   *   *

End of diatribe. This is not, despite the foregoing unpaid political announcement, a book of political essays. These are primarily personal essays. Of the hundreds of Canadian words I accumulated over the years, I chose these because I felt I had something personal to say about them; that is, they evoked some visceral response within me that I wanted to explore. I write about the game of crokinole not only because crokinole was invented in Canada, but because I remember playing the game as a child and know that crokinole was, for me, not only a game but also part of the whole intricate web of memories and associations that together form a culture. I write about ice not because ice is a peculiarly Canadian phenomenon (it isn't), but because I have experienced ice in a multitude of its forms, from fresh ice in hockey arenas to multi-year sea ice at the North Pole, and I think my experience of ice says something about me as an individual and as a Canadian. Many of these essays, then, are not simply vehicles for expressing a culture, but are also examples of that culture, of how certain words play through the fabric of a life and take their places in it to create a pattern, and how that pattern defines that life.

So mostly I just set out for walks and write about where those walks take me. Sometimes they take me back to my own experiences, sometimes they take me into Canadian history. Quite often they took me past that American meadow, since so much of Canadian history has been played out against American history—which is why Northrop Frye once defined a Canadian as "an American who has rejected the Revolution." And since a great deal of my life has involved writing and literature, most of the walks took me into the virtual bookstore I carry around in my head. I have of course expressed some strong opinions in these essays, and have even on occasion presented informed opinions as though they were known facts—a very un-Canadian thing to do. My aim has always been to stimulate, which is to administer a series of mild shocks. My hope is that they will be shocks of recognition.

ACKNOWLEDGEMENTS

In any collection of essays written over a period of six years, there will be a large number of people to thank, far too many to acknowledge individually. Many of them are mentioned in the essays themselves, as writers or friends or both, and they include, in no particular order, Brian Brett, David Homel, Diane Schoemperlen, Jon Whyte, Sid Marty, Cal Bailey, Tom Carpenter and Arnie Gelbart. Other friends who were consulted and whose counsel informed my thinking, whether they knew it or not, include Merrily Weisbord, Susan Musgrave, Stephen Reid, Pam Green, Daniel Poliquin, Norman Levine, Rudy Wiebe, Zal Yanovsky, Rose Richardson, Jamie Swift and Bart Robinson. I am also grateful to my agent, Bella Pomer, for her infectious enthusiasm.

Perhaps the person I thought of most often while writing these essays has been Robin Mathews, whom I knew first as a professor at Carleton University and later as a friend. Robin was one of the first Canadians to point to the pervasive influence of American culture in Canada, and in many ways these essays are a tribute to his teaching and his integrity.

The title of this collection, *Chasing the Chinook*, was inspired by a line from Sid Marty's book *Leaning on the Wind: Under the Spell of the Great Chinook* (1995), about the science and lore of the chinook wind that sweeps the Canadian prairies and American Midwest. In one chapter Sid writes about an excursion he took into Montana to collect chinook stories, and he describes the trip as "chasing the daemon chinook." I dropped the "daemon" because part of my point in the Chinook essay is that the wind is not universally regarded as daemonic, but also because I didn't want to give the impression that my entire book was about the chinook. At any rate, I thank Sid for lending me his words.

The title of the essay on the word "Canada," "Here There Are No Maps," is the first line of Margaret Atwood's poem "Oratorio for Sasquatch, Man, and Two Androids," published in *Poems for Voices* by Al Purdy et al. (Toronto: Canadian Broadcasting Corporation, 1970), and is used here with her kind permission.

I would also like to thank Katherine Romba, whose diligence as a researcher has enriched many of these essays and saved me from at least one lawsuit; and John Sweet, who caught more literary lapses in the manuscript than even I thought I was capable of. Meg Taylor took time off while editing this book to get married, for which I congratulate her warmly.

My wife Merilyn Simonds appears frequently in these pages; she is always half of the "we" in the essays, as she is in my life. She is an important part of the "I" as well.

Finally, I am grateful to the Writers Reserve Program of the Ontario Arts Council, which provided invaluable financial support during the writing of these works of creative nonfiction. Embarking on a writing project is a perilous venture at the best of times, and these are not the best of times.

CHASING
the
CHINOOK

Acadia French territory in NE Canada and the United States, ceded to Great Britain in 1713.

—*Webster's Dictionary*

THIS IS THE FOREST PRIMEVAL

Buctouche is a small town at the mouth of the Buctouche River in New Brunswick. It is also the summer home of Antonine Maillet. I had just translated Maillet's short novel *Christophe Cartier de la noisette, dit Nounours*, and was about to embark on her monumental allegory *Le huitième jour*, and I wanted to get the lay of the Acadian landscape. I had a literary sense of the Buctouche area, but I wanted to see it and hear it for myself. I stopped outside a low brick building, one of those five-and-dime stores that sell cheap clothes and expensive souvenirs, including small Acadian flags—the French *tricolore* with a yellow *Stella maris* in one corner. When I went up to the cash, I asked, in my best French, which house belonged to Antonine and received a long, friendly reply. To my complete astonishment I could not understand a word of it. I had entered a private realm, a kind of hidden valley that had its own customs, its own flag and its own language. Some call this place the Republic of Madawaska, but for more than 350 years it has been known as the land of Acadia.

The name comes from the Greek "Arcadia," a district on the Peloponnesus sacred to Jupiter's son Arcas, and also the abode of Pan (another son of Jupiter, by a different marriage), the god of forests, pastures, flocks and herds. It was first applied in the New World by Italian navigator Giovanni da Verrazano, who sailed up the east coast of the New World from Cape Fear to Cape Breton in 1524 and gave the name Arcadia to the territory now known as Massachusetts.

When practically all of eastern North America, including Massachusetts, came under French influence in the seventeenth century, Arcadia became l'Arcadie and eventually l'Acadie. Antonine Maillet believes the "r" was lost sometime around 1632, when three hundred families from the Breton region of France arrived in Port-Royal (now Annapolis Royal), the colony founded by Champlain in 1604. The Breton dialect flattened the "a" in l'Arcadie and likely turned the "d" into a "dg," making the new country l'Acadgie. In the 1671 census there were 380 Acadians in what is now southern Nova Scotia. They spoke the French of their ancestors and lived pretty much as their ancestors had lived; they received little help from France and required even less.

Father Pascal Poirier, author of the authoritative (because unique) *Glossaire acadien*, would have the name of his country derive from Native rather than Greek roots. The Act conveying what is now New Brunswick, Nova Scotia and part of Maine to the Sieur de Monts in 1632 referred to the region as la Cadie, not l'Acadie, much less l'Arcadie, "because of something it knew," he wrote. And what it knew was that "Cadie must have been the original name for the territory," taken from the Malecite and Micmac word *cadic,* meaning "the country." And Cadie ought still to be in use because Cadiens still speak "the language of Touraine and du Berry, the language our forebears spoke when they first stepped off the boats at Port-Royal." He found the presence of such Aboriginal place names as Passamaquoddy, Subenacadie and Tracadie "proof that the name Cadie or Cadic was very frequent" before the arrival of the French. He also saw "stronger proof . . . in the fact that the Acadian people have always called themselves Cadgiens," not Acadgiens. To him, l'Acadie is merely a mistaken way, adopted by "ignorant sots," of writing la Cadie.

It's true that the Act conceding the vast territory to the Sieur de

Monts called it la Cadie, but it is also true that every document before and after that referred to the land as l'Acadie, and it seems much more likely that the administrators in France who penned the 1632 Act got it wrong than that everyone else did. The oral echo of Verrazano's Arcadia is too strong to dismiss. Besides, it's fitting that Acadian land remain linguistically tied to Massachusetts, because it certainly is historically.

*　*　*

"Acadia is a history, a legend, a tale," writes Maillet. "Yes, yes, a real tale, complete with ogres and fairies. You've heard of Colonel Lawrence, haven't you? And the Virgin of the Assumption, who guided her people out of the land of exile? And Gabriel and Evangeline, the unfortunate Tristan and Iseult of Acadia?"

She is referring, of course, to the central legend of Acadia, the event that sits at the heart of the land like a great symbolic mountain: Le Grand Dérangement of the Acadians in 1755, one of the most scurrilous and complex chapters in Canadian history. Some English translators tended to soften the incident by rendering it as a Deportation, as though it were simply a matter of sending some illegal immigrants back to where they came from. A more accurate translation would be the Great Disruption, or the Great Uprooting. I'm going to keep calling it the Derangement; we must not lose sight of the sense of madness, or derailment, in the use of the French *dérangement*.

Maillet is right in referring to the event as a fairy tale. Most of what we think we know about the Derangement comes from Longfellow's poem *Evangeline*, or at least resembles that poem in most of its details, even to those who have never read it. And yet, in turning the Derangement into the backdrop for a love story—much as film director James Cameron did with his Hollywood version of the *Titanic* disaster—Longfellow took some wild liberties with the truth. We can read *Evangeline* (or watch *Titanic*) as fiction, but we must remember that it is American fiction, and the historical facts tweaked to make the fiction work were directed at an American audience.

The historical background to the poem is fairly straightforward. When New France was ceded to Great Britain by the Treaty of Utrecht in 1713, some two thousand Acadians were living in southern Nova Scotia. There were other French settlers living in northern Nova Scotia as well, but they were relative newcomers; they were French, not Acadian. Nothing was done about either group until 1755, when England began preparing for the upcoming Seven Years' War (1756–63). It was then realized that the French in northern Nova Scotia represented a link between two colonies that still belonged to France: Prince Edward Island and Cape Breton Island. The English decided to remove these northern French from Nova Scotia. Somehow, the southern Acadians got mixed up in this scheme, and thanks largely to Longfellow's poem we tend to think that they were the targets all along.

In August 1755, without warning, the Acadians were herded onto transport ships by the British Navy, forced to watch their lands and houses put to the torch, and then resettled in other British colonies, like Boston, Virginia, Maryland and Pennsylvania. Families were split up, lovers torn from each other's arms; it was a terrible cultural upheaval. Antonine Maillet compares it to the Diaspora of the Jews. Thousands of Acadians were rounded up. Maillet, in her 1980 study *Rabelais et les traditions populaires en Acadie*, records that "the list had risen to 4,397 by 1763, distributed as follows: Boston, 1,043; Connecticut, 666; New York, 249; Maryland, 810; Pennsylvania, 383; South Carolina, 280; Georgia, 185; Halifax, 694; Rivière St-Jean, 87." Others followed the Mississippi

River south to Louisiana. Many died: nearly half of the 3,500 Acadians returned to France drowned on the way. Most of the rest were turned away when they reached France, and sought refugee status in England. Those who were accepted in France—about seventy-seven families—settled in Brittany, and their descendants still call themselves Acadians.

This much is true, but there is much to even this part of the story that Longfellow changes. To begin with, his heroine, Evangeline, began life as a woman named Gabrielle, the central figure in a tale called *The Acadian Exile* by a certain Mrs. Williams, who was related to Thomas Chandler Haliburton, the Halifax lawyer and author of the Sam Slick stories. In 1838 the story of Gabrielle somehow fell upon the ears of Reverend Horace Lorenzo Conolly, the rector of St. Matthew's Episcopal Church in Boston. It's possible Conolly picked up a copy of *The Acadian Exile* in a used bookstore. However he came upon it, he told it to Nathaniel Hawthorne, thinking Hawthorne could make a novel out of it; perhaps Conolly believed that writing about the almost unbelievably virtuous Gabrielle would redeem Hawthorne for having celebrated an adulteress in *The Scarlet Letter*. Hawthorne didn't like it: he didn't think there was enough stuff in it for a novel. He wrote in his *Note-Books*:

Heard from a French-Canadian a story of a young couple in Acadie. On their marriage day all the men of the Province were summoned to assemble in the church to hear a proclamation. When assembled, they were seized and shipped off to be distributed through New England, among them the new bridegroom. His bride set off in search of him, wandered about New England all her lifetime, and at last found her bridegroom on his deathbed. The shock was so great it killed her likewise.

The reference to "a French-Canadian" suggests that Conolly really may have heard it from a descendant of a deported Acadian living near Boston, since towns like Lowell, Massachusetts, and Fitchburg, New Hampshire, were (and still are) predominantly French. But the rest of the entry is a fairly accurate thumbnail of *The Acadian Exile.* Hawthorne took Conolly along to Cambridge, Massachusetts, where Longfellow was living, and Conolly told the story to Longfellow, who apparently immediately saw its potential for poetry. For some reason he changed the heroine's name to Evangeline and gave the name Gabriel to her betrothed—and the rest, as they say, is history.

The poem was an instant success when it appeared in 1847, although some critics found its alexandrine quatrains somewhat heavy going. As Longfellow later complained to Hawthorne, "You didn't want to write a poetical novel, and now I'm accused of having written a novelistic poem." It isn't exactly sure-footed: when Van Wyck Brooks once said that Longfellow "is to poetry what the barrel-organ is to music," he might have been thinking of *Evangeline*:

> List to the mournful tradition, still sung by the pines of the forest;
> List to a Tale of Love in Acadie, home of the happy.

Home of the happy? I find the translation by the Quebec poet Pamphile Lemay, first published in 1902, more mellifluous:

> *C'est un poème doux que le coeur psalmodie,*
> *C'est l'idylle d'amour de la belle Acadie!*

But the real problem with Longfellow's poem is that it completely misrepresents what happened in 1755. The tragedy that befell the Acadians was not a simple (-minded) story of perfidious British soldiers falling upon hapless farmers and carting them off. The Derangement was the result of a conspiracy, or at least a collusion, among the three powers vying for control of Nova Scotia: France, England and New England. Particularly New England, the original Arcadia and home of the happy Longfellow.

At first the deportation scheme was not intended to involve the Acadians, who were determinedly neutral in the conflict between England and France. In 1754, William Shirley, governor of Massachusetts (which was still a British colony), approached Colonel Charles Lawrence, commander of His Majesty's troops in Nova Scotia, with a scheme to get the French out of northern Nova Scotia. His plan fell on willing ears. To Lawrence, Fort Beauséjour, on the north side of the Missisquash River across from his own Fort Lawrence, was a constant reminder that British authority in Nova Scotia was extremely tenuous, a matter of gentlemen's agreements and governmental lethargy. With a war against France on the horizon, Fort Beauséjour had to be taken and Nova Scotia made entirely and indisputably British.

Sequestered in Fort Beauséjour was the mystifying Abbé Le Loutre, the heart of French resistance in Nova Scotia. Even his name is mystifying, at least to me: *un loutre* is an otter, a very strange name for the son of a Paris papermaker. At any rate, Le Loutre was the parish priest of the village of Beaubassin and a missionary of uncommon zeal among the Micmacs. It had become his personal crusade to defend the Catholic faith in the New World, and one of the ways he intended to do that was to persuade the Acadians in English territory to move north into the French-held lands above the Missisquash. He had been given a quasi-military position by Quebec as a spy and an *agent provocateur*, and he stirred up the French and the Micmacs against the redcoats.

With Beauséjour as his base (after he had torched Beaubassin to keep it out of British hands), he deployed the Micmacs to harass

English troops and the Acadian settlers, apparently with the enthusiastic if clandestine approval of the French court. Everywhere south of the Missisquash it was dangerous for any white person, settler or soldier, to venture out of doors at night. In 1749 the fishing village of Dartmouth was wiped out and its inhabitants scalped. A British officer was shot under a flag of truce because he had once made a disparaging remark about the Virgin Mary. Le Loutre was well financed: in 1753, after returning from France, he paid a Micmac raiding party 1,800 livres—three times his own living allowance—for eighteen British scalps. And he threatened the Acadians with punitive raids by Micmac warriors if they signed any kind of oath of allegiance to the British. This was the real reason the Acadians were reluctant to sign the British pledge—not because they mistrusted the British, but because they feared reprisals from Le Loutre.

It may well be that Lawrence extended Shirley's original plan of evacuating the northern French to include the Acadians in order to diminish Le Loutre's power and remove a potential fifth column from his back as he stared across the river at Fort Beauséjour. Edward Cornwallis, governor of Nova Scotia, called Le Loutre "a good for nothing Scoundrel as ever lived." And when, in June 1755, the British crossed the river and took the fort, Le Loutre was found to have escaped.

The two battalions engaged in the siege of Fort Beauséjour had been raised in Massachusetts, even though Lawrence had British troops already in Nova Scotia. The British soldiers stationed in Annapolis had become half Acadian themselves; many of them had married Acadian women, had become Catholic, and had refused to participate in the plan to uproot the Acadians from their land. Perhaps they knew that the raid on Le Loutre's stronghold had been executed without orders or authority from England. It was American colonial troops, therefore, not British soldiers, who rounded up the Acadians and distributed them throughout New England. Some of those deported may even have been British soldiers.

Will R. Bird, in his *Done at Grand Pré*, published in 1955—the bicentennial of Le Grand Dérangement—sets the record straight:

> The extremists who always picture burly redcoats beating old women into boats at the water's edge should examine the records. The truth is that there was not a redcoat on the scene except at Annapolis. All were blue-coated New Englanders. The redcoats at Annapolis had been there for years, had married Acadian wives, had had their children baptized by the priest. They would do nothing to aid in the expulsion and Lawrence had to order his New Englanders there to gather the Acadians and load the ships. So much for the flaming hate of the redcoats!

All of which makes Longfellow's patronizing poem particularly galling. I don't object to his ignoring or changing a few facts in order to jerk a few tears (again, like *Titanic*), but the facts that Longfellow manipulates are suspiciously damaging to what Acadians still refer to as the Boston states. The expulsion of the Acadians was first proposed by the governor of Massachusetts, the raid was conducted without orders by Massachusetts troops under the command of Lieutenant-Colonel Winslow, a Massachusetts officer. Acadian lands were expropriated by Winslow for the use of future New England settlers, should New England settlers ever have need of such land— as they would twenty years later, when the American Revolution pushed many New Englanders who wanted to remain under British rule into Nova Scotia, where they took up exactly the Acadian land that had been made vacant in 1755, as Longfellow well knew.

Longfellow writes about the whole incident as though it had taken place in some far-off, exotic and not particularly civilized place. The first line of the poem—"This is the forest primeval"—establishes what for his American audience was a familiar, even nostalgic setting. Anything could happen here, he is saying: expect the worst. Annapolis wasn't the forest primeval in 1755; it was well-cleared and tended farmland, much of it painstakingly reclaimed from tidal flats, and some of the most fertile land in Nova Scotia. The forest primeval was where James Fenimore Cooper had set his highly successful Leatherstocking series: *The Last of the Mohicans* (1826) and *The Deerslayer* (1841). Could Longfellow have been hoping that his readers would respond to the perils of Evangeline as they had to the exploits of Natty Bumppo?

Bacteriophage A virus that infects bacterial cells, often causing their dissolution.

—*Aristotle to Zoos,* 1983, P.B. and J.S. Medawar

OF THINGS VISIBLE AND INVISIBLE

In Sinclair Lewis's 1925 novel *Arrowsmith*, the central character is a young American bacteriologist who stumbles upon a virus that eats bacteria. He names it "the X Principle," and quickly realizes that such a virus could be used to treat all kinds of human diseases caused by bacteria. Simply inject the X Principle, which is supposedly harmless to humans, into our bloodstreams, he imagines, and such scourges as scarlet fever, dysentery, botulism, even bubonic plague, would disappear forever. Fame and fortune dance hand in hand around his tiny laboratory. Before he can announce his discovery to the world, however, he learns from his boss that another scientist, working in France, has made a similar breakthrough.

"Good Lord, Dr. Gottlieb," Martin Arrowsmith tells his not particularly sympathetic informant, "it would mean that all I've done, all these weeks, has just been waste, and I'm a fool—"

"Vell. Anyvay," shrugs Gottlieb, "D'Herelle of the Pasteur Institute has just now published in the *Comptes rendus, Académie des Sciences*, a report—it is your X Principle, absolute. Only he calls it 'bacteriophage.' So."

So. Martin Arrowsmith was fictitious, but his competitor in France was not. Louis D'Herelle was a young bacteriologist from Quebec who, in 1917, left l'Université Laval and went to Paris to work at the Pasteur Institute, which at the time was investigating an outbreak of dysentery. In the journal of the *Académie des Sciences*,

D'Herelle describes pouring a fluid containing a virus into a test-tube filled with cloudy staphylococcus bacteria—the microbe responsible for dysentery—and watching as the bacteria suddenly disappears and the liquid becomes clear (exactly as in Arrowsmith's vial in Lewis's novel). "In a flash," D'Herelle records, "I had understood: what caused my clear spots was in fact an invisible microbe . . . a virus parasitic on bacteria." He did indeed name the viruses "bacteriophages"—literally, "bacteria eaters."

D'Herelle too had his scientific nemesis. Isaac Asimov, in his *Encyclopedia of Science and Technology*, attributes the discovery of bacteriophages to Frederick William Twort (1877–1950), a professor of bacteriology at the University of London who, in 1915, discovered a virus that killed bacteria, although it did not eat them. D'Herelle's claim was made two years later, and it appears he was unaware of Twort's work. Thus D'Herelle was himself a kind of Martin Arrowsmith, beaten to the main punch by a researcher in England. As Asimov notes, "there were some rather unsavoury disputes concerning precedence, but it was the bacteriophages themselves that proved important, whoever discovered them." And whoever discovered them, it was D'Herelle who named them.

So, we have viruses eating bacteria. It's hard to know which side we should be on, because both of them eat us. At least bacteria behave like other organisms. The word is the plural of the Latin word *bacterium*, which means "a small staff," from the shape of the microorganism. Actually, it comes in three shapes, identified in 1853 by the German botanist Ferdinand Cohn. He categorized bacteria as bacteria (short rods), bacilli (long rods) and spirilli (rods arranged in spirals). Bacteria are the oldest form of life on Earth; the so-called blue-green algae that covered the Earth a few billion years ago were probably bacterial, and they produced the oxygen that made more complicated organisms, like us, possible. Bacteria are everywhere on the planet and they are largely beneficial. They break things down; in our digestive systems they turn what we eat into nutrients, on our roadsides they turns dead squirrels into soil. If they get into the wrong places, however, such as our stomachs, they break the wrong things down and we die.

A virus, on the other hand, is something altogether different. It is the Latin word for "slime," or anything that is viscous and usually deadly. It came into the English language in Elizabethan times, meaning "snake's venom," and it hasn't changed in connotation much since then. A virus is bad news. "Viruses are like aliens," says Malcolm Ramsay, a biologist with the University of Saskatchewan in Saskatoon. Malcolm usually concerns himself with larger predators, notably polar bears, but he turns his brilliantly fertile mind to whatever is at hand. And viruses are always at hand. "They are like no other organisms on the planet," he says. "We understand bacteria. In a sense, we *are* bacteria. But viruses," he says, shaking his head, "they are not like anything else we know. They're not even like each other. One of the many curiosities about viruses is that, after they enter a host, they take on so many of the characteristics of the host DNA that they soon resemble the host more closely than they resemble other viruses. That is biologically weird."

That is why it was so startling to discover a virus that actually seemed to be beneficial to humans. D'Herelle was quick to realize the significance of his find, but he was also a little suspicious of it. Before the widespread availability of antibiotics, there was no effective medical defence against bacterial diseases—which included many of the most common causes of human death, including (in addition to those mentioned above) pneumonia, tuberculosis, typhoid and typhus fevers and cholera. Hospitals used sulfa to cut down on infections in open wounds, but sulfa didn't have any effect on internal diseases. Still, doctors turned to bacteriophages almost reluctantly—and used them mostly in the Third World—and got to work inventing antibiotics.

The first antibiotic, penicillin, was discovered in 1928, but it couldn't be produced in quantity until Howard Walter Florey discovered an inexpensive way to isolate it in 1938, just in time for the war (thus making him Sir Howard Walter Florey). This took the pressure off bacteriophage researchers. My wife's mother, who trained as a nurse in Woodstock, Ontario, in the early 1940s, remembered the first time penicillin was used in her hospital. "It was a ruptured appendix," she said, "a real mess. Normally, we would have cleaned up as best we could after the operation, sprinkled in some sulfa and hoped for the best, knowing that the patient probably wouldn't make it. This time we sprinkled in penicillin powder and it worked like magic. The patient was sitting up and obviously recovering within a few hours. After that, we knew that we had a fighting chance against infection."

Penicillin's miracle-working led to the introduction of a wider range of antibiotics, and before long many of the major bacterial diseases appeared to have been conquered. Interest in bacteriophages declined altogether, which is why bacteriophage is not a household word and penicillin is. In recent years, however, antibiotics have lost much of their potency. New strains of such dangerous bacteria as streptococci, staphylococci, salmonella and *E. coli* have turned up that are resistant to most of the drugs traditionally used against them. These new bacteria are bringing back scores of diseases that once were under control: food poisoning, strep A, tuberculosis. People are picking up infections in hospitals at a rate reminiscent of the days before Louis Pasteur.

A recent issue of *Business Week* magazine pointed out that "more than 30 dangerous new infectious agents have been discovered in the past two decades. The death rate in the U.S. from infections

jumped nearly 58 percent between 1980 and 1992." A new strain of
E. coli, the bacterium that lives benignly in our colons but can kill
us if it gets into our stomachs, has been found to be present in three
out of ten American restaurants and is thought to be responsible for
several outbreaks of food poisoning—one of which killed a baby in
New York City in 1997. Most alarming, this new *E. coli* is unfazed
by the antibiotics we've thrown at its predecessors. The *Business Week*
article focused on efforts of major American drug companies to come
up with newer and more powerful antibiotics, but there was nothing in the report to suggest that bacteria—the oldest and most tenacious life form on the planet—won't simply mutate and adapt to
the new drugs as well.

As a result, bacteriophages may be coming back. According to
Peter Radetsky in "The Good Virus" (*Discover*, November 1996):

> Some fifty years after antibiotics heralded the end of bacterial dis-
> ease, their golden age is waning. Disease, of course, remains—it may
> even be on the upswing. More and more microbes are developing
> resistance to our arsenal of antibiotic drugs, and scientists are again
> searching for miracle treatments. Some are looking to the past, to
> the almost forgotten bacteria eaters.

The return of bacterial diseases is disturbing, partly because we may
have to turn to viruses to help us overcome them, and we don't know
very much about viruses. Viral diseases are just as deadly as bacterial ones, and they too seem to be making a comeback. D'Herelle
discovered bacteriophages in 1917, and the next year an outbreak of
Spanish influenza—a viral disease—killed 20 million people worldwide in a matter of weeks. Viruses mutate and resist treatment as
fast as bacteria can, and viral diseases too are rapidly increasing in
frequency, right along with the bacterial ones. New forms of influenza,

yellow fever, dengue, AIDS and even some forms of cancer—all caused by viruses—are killing millions of people every year. And just as bacteria are developing resistances to antibiotics, so viruses are becoming more powerful than the serums with which we inoculate ourselves against them. In 1997, when more than three hundred people in Toronto came down with a disease that attacked their facial muscles, doctors at Mount Sinai Hospital at first suspected an outbreak of Bell's palsy, although Bell's is rare and is not known to be contagious. They eventually traced the disease to a virus, possibly an enterovirus (related to the virus that causes polio, a disease we thought we had licked), which weakened the victims' immune systems and allowed a new herpes-like virus to get into their DNA. Then the herpes-like virus mutated and reproduced so fast that, before doctors could detect it, it was almost identical to the cells of its host.

Elsewhere in the country, new viruses are turning up all the time. In 1995 a new form of hantavirus (which causes victims' lungs to fill up with blood in a matter of hours) began moving north from the American southwest, transmitted by deer mice. Hantavirus is now found in Alberta and Ontario; so far, sixteen people have been affected by it in Canada, and three of them have died. Two women have died in British Columbia after contracting a mysterious virus that attacked their hearts. "Viruses," wrote Carl Sagan, "built like hypodermic syringes, slip their DNA past the host organism's defences and subvert the reproductive machinery of cells." And once they do that, they become virtually undetectable until the autopsy. They become what they eat.

Malcolm Ramsay thinks things are likely to get worse before they get better, at least on the bacterial front. The Americanization of the Canadian medical system—which has meant cutbacks in Medicare and the closing down of hospitals—has resulted in fewer doctors seeing more patients, and people are being discharged from over-crowded hospitals long before they are fully recovered from what-ever put them there in the first place. As a result, drugs replace human attention. "The standard procedure is to give patients a hand-ful of antibiotics and send them home," says Malcolm, "where there is little or no follow-up because home-care nursing has been cut back too." The overprescription of antibiotics has been the main cause of the return of many killer bacterial diseases. Doctors often hand out antibiotics for viral diseases, against which antibiotics are useless, and even patients who need them for bacterial diseases take them without regard to the directions. Both abuses allow bacteria and viruses to mutate and develop resistances.

While Americans are busy making stronger antibiotics with which to treat the new strains of bacterial infections, Canadians are quietly developing new bacteriophages. The *Canadian Journal of Microbiology* reported on two Canadian projects in 1997, aimed at altering the DNA in bacteriophages to make them more effective against the new *E. coli* strain. And at the University of Guelph, a microbiologist named Mansell Griffiths is working on a bacteriophage that can detect bacteria in raw meat before we eat it. He takes the gene that causes the firefly to glow—it's called the lux gene—and graphs it into a bacteriophage. Then he introduces the bacteriophage to a meat sam-ple. If there is bacteria in the meat, the phage will eat it and, thanks to the lux gene, begin to glow. The glow can be picked up by a spe-cial scanner attached to a computer. Treated meat is simply run under the scanner, and any bits that glow are diverted away from the pack-aged meat section of your local supermarket into a stream destined to be made into canned meat. Yum.

While I am not sanguine about either solution to the renewed threat of microbial disease—developing more powerful antibiotics or creating smarter bacteriophages—it is interesting to view the different approaches in cultural terms. The antibiotics buildup is a Cold War-style strategy, staving off the enemy invasion by coming up with bigger and more powerful weapons. Even the vocabulary is militaristic: according to *Business Week*, "the war" between us and the microbes "is still raging," but researchers are "rearming" to "knock back the microbial hordes." Bacteria and viruses are ganging up on us, creating a double threat, and our only defence is to retreat into a medical stockade and repel the attacking savages, as one researcher put it, "with everything we've got."

Bacteriophage research, on the other hand, seems distinctly Canadian, and not only because it was a Canadian who initiated it. With bacteriophages we simply set two old enemies, bacteria and viruses, against each other and let them thrash it out between themselves—ignorant armies clashing by night on some internal darkling plain. Is that not very like encouraging the Iroquois–Huron wars and hoping they'll fight their battles in some distant part of the forest, out of sight?

Balm of Gilead The balsam poplar, found throughout the forested areas of Canada.

—*A Dictionary of Canadianisms on Historical Principles*

A TREE GROWS IN BAMAGALIA

On one of those bright, cool Sundays in mid-March we decided to walk back to what we called our heron rookery, a small swamp walled in on three sides by granite cliffs and on the fourth by the raised bed of a disused railway track. Rising out of the swamp were the grey, weathered trunks of trees, probably cedars, though they had the smoothness and roundness of red elms. Atop each tree, perhaps fifty feet above the frozen water, was the nest of a great blue heron, one of the most beautiful and elegant of birds. Some trees had two or three nests, each one an engineering marvel of twigs and grass woven and jammed together in the cleft of a long-gone branch. Some nests nestled into the crotch formed where one tree had fallen against another and stayed there. All the nests were empty, since it was still early in the season, but in our mind's eye we could see the herons gliding home over the cliffs or standing in perfect profile, one to a nest, like a giant living Egyptian hieroglyph of life.

On the way back we met two neighbours who had also been lured onto the tracks by the strengthening spring sunshine. We stopped to compare our bootmarks in the snow for a while, and the talk came around to trees.

"Have you seen the bamagalia yet?"

I looked at my neighbour blankly for a moment. "The which?" I asked.

"Balm of Gilead," she repeated more slowly. "It's a kind of tree.

We have one on our property, been there for more than a hundred years. My grandfather remembers it being there when he was a boy."

"It's thirteen feet around at the base," said her husband. "Last week, three busloads of school kids came to look at it."

We asked them for directions and the next Sunday set off to have a look. They owned some lakefront land on which they'd built a cottage, and another sixty-five acres of woodlot, swamp and rock cornered by the old railway tracks and a dirt access road. We walked along the tracks a while, past one of the places we go in the fall to pick wild grapes and juniper berries, then turned up the road looking for a trail marked off by red plastic ribbons. We didn't, in the end, need the ribbons, a path made by three busloads of school kids being pretty easy to find. So was the tree. It was one of the largest living things I had ever seen. It dwarfed the birches and soft maples that crowded around it. Its bark was deeply grooved and shaggy, not unlike that of the ancient locusts that lined the main street of the hamlet, escapees from the mash belonging to a distillery that had operated there in the 1820s. Looking directly at the bamagalia's trunk was like looking down from an airplane on a muddy, labyrinthine floodplain.

We could see the tree was very high, but some arithmetical itch within us made us want to find out exactly how high. I had brought a tape to measure the tree's girth—it was actually fourteen feet around at chest height—and we used it to cut a thin length of deadwood six feet long. Then, laying the stick down in the snow with one end touching the tree and the other end pointing along a flat expanse of frozen swamp, we flipped the stick over twenty times, marked the spot, then flipped it over once more. At the twenty-one-stick mark I lay down on the snow and sighted the top of the tree through the stick that was upright at the twenty-stick mark, and Merilyn marked the spot on the stick where my sight-line crossed it;

that mark was exactly five feet, four inches from the ground. Using what little we knew of Euclidean geometry, we calculated that the vertical side of the right-angled triangle formed by the tree was one hundred and twelve feet high. We felt inordinately proud of these calculations, as though by defining the tree numerically we had made it our own.

We felt like explorers. I later learned that Alexander Mackenzie, exploring the upper reaches of the Peace River in 1793, noted in his diary the names of the trees he encountered there, and one of them was a Balm of Gilead, although he didn't call it that. He made a peculiar list, unsettling in its dreamlike mingling of the familiar and the totally alien: "Spruce, red-pine, cypress, poplar, white birch, willow, alder, arrow-wood, redwood, liard, service-tree, bois-picant." Being Highland Scots and therefore from a landscape not noted for its forests, he had evidently relied on his French Canadian voyageurs for information about the trees that were new to him. His paddlers were as new to the area as he was, and gave him French names for trees that looked familiar to them. There is no true cypress in Canada, for example. Mackenzie's cypress (from which the Cypress Hills of Alberta and Saskatchewan get their name) was actually the jackpine (*Pinus banksiana*), for some reason called *cyprès* in Quebec (perhaps because they grew so close; in colloquial French, *ci-près* is "near"). Neither was his "arrow-wood" the American arrowwood (*Oxydendrum arboreum*), since that species does not grow west or north of Indiana; what Mackenzie (or his paddlers) meant by arrowwood is an arboreal mystery. His *bois-picant* ("spike wood"?) was later called devil's club in English (*Oplopanax horridus*). As for "service-tree," if he had asked his Indian hosts instead of his voyageurs, he might have been the first white man to correctly identify *Amelanchier ainifolia* as the saskatoon-berry (from the Plains Cree *Mis-sask-quah-too-min*, the red berry they mixed with dried buffalo meat to make pemmican).

Mackenzie got the word *liard* from his French companions as well, even though he ought to have known it by one of its common English names: balsam poplar, tacamahac (Sir Joseph Banks, botanizing in northern Newfoundland in 1766, had "found one tree only of Takamahaka") or Balm of Gilead. Though now rare in the south, the balsam poplar (*Populus balsamifera*) was once one of the most widely distributed trees of the Canadian forest, found coast to coast and as far north as the tundra. Its French Canadian name comes from the Old French *liard*, meaning grey (liard pears are grey), possibly because the bark turns from greenish-white to grey as the tree matures.

Liard is an adjectival form of the verb *lier*, meaning "to tie or fasten." In the sixteenth century, branches of the liard (the black poplar in France) were used instead of osiers to make withes (*liens*), those long lengths of flexible branches twisted or plaited into a kind of rope (if there is a "lien" on a house, it means it is tied up, usually in red tape). In western and southern Quebec the balsam poplar is still called *liard*, which suggests to me that the basketwork in those folksy, rattan-like chairs and tables now so popular in antique and crafte shoppes was originally made with the pliant shoots of the balsam poplar, Canada not being the natural home of the osier.

Though a hundred years old, our neighbours' balsam poplar was not at its full height; they can reach a hundred and fifty feet in the deep bush. They have upward-pointing branches that begin forty feet from the ground. *P. balsamifera* is a northern version of the eastern cottonwood (*P. deltoides*), ranging from Nova Scotia up through Newfoundland and Labrador, across Quebec and Ontario, through western Canada and, as Mackenzie discovered, down the Peace and Liard Rivers (so named by Mackenzie: the Tacamahac River would also have served) in British Columbia, where it achieves its greatest size. Simon Fraser, another Scot, following partially in Mackenzie's footsteps, reported in 1806 that "the Liard [near Stuart Lake, above the Fraser River] is the most stupendous I ever saw." Since it is related to willows, alders and cottonwoods, it grows best in moist, rich, low-lying soil, but in the dry, rocky and ridged terrain of eastern Ontario (where it has mostly been logged out, my neighbours' bamagalia being a rare oversight) it does at least as well as the mixed hardwoods clustering around it. There is a Bamagalia Beach on Lake Wasi, a few miles south of North Bay, Ontario, so it must have once been plentiful enough up there to impress the settlers who encountered it.

The "bam" is obviously a corruption of balm, as "cam" is of calm. In Genesis, the Ishmaelites carried a medicinal ointment, called balm, from Gilead into Egypt, where its resin was used in preparing the dead for eternity, as is suggested by the word "embalmed." Balm is itself an ancient corruption of balsam; anything healing or soothing is "balsamic" or "balmy." Balsamic vinegar was originally taken as a tonic by those who couldn't afford to travel in balmy climes. The balsam poplar of Canada is not the true balsam of Mecca, the original Balm of Gilead (*Commiphora opobalsamum*), which now grows only on the banks of the Red Sea, a calming gift to King Solomon from the Queen of Sheba. Nor is it the ornamental Balm of Gilead poplar, *Populus candicans*, which was introduced to Canada from Siberia and has since broken away from its urban confines and is found growing wild, although seed houses still sell it. This has a much broader crown and darker upper leaf than the balsam poplar, although in some northern areas feral *P. candicans* may have mixed with *P. balsamifera* to form a tree that has no name of its own and weird characteristics of both parents.

It must be said that, despite its noble ancestral name, the balsam poplar is a weed tree. It is extremely invasive and was, ironically, vexatious to Ontario settlers, who did constant battle to keep their tiny clearings from being reclaimed by the bush; balsam poplar is what they usually had to keep pulling up. It did not begin to decline as a species, however, until someone discovered that its white, pulpy wood made fine magazine-quality paper. Otherwise, its lumber was used mainly for crates and boxes, things that didn't need to last long or cost much, and later it was valued as a veneer for cheap plywood. It is most familiarly seen now as the wood used to make those flimsy baskets we take berry-picking.

Father Marie-Victorin, in his *Flore laurentienne* (1935), notes that the balsam poplar was introduced years ago in France, where it was planted along the avenues and boulevards of cities and along the roads between towns, to replace the dying plane trees that Napoleon had ordered to be planted in the early 1800s so that his troops never had to march in the sun. The balsam poplar rather quickly hybridized with the native black poplar (also called *liard* in France) to form a species whose official name is now *Populus canadensis*. For some inexplicable reason the French call it the Carolina poplar, or simply *le carolin*. I don't expect them to call it the bamagalia, but they could at least call it the Canada poplar.

Bloody Caesar A number of excellent cocktails are closely associated with vodka: Black Russian, Bloody Mary, Bull Shot, Moscow Mule and Screwdriver being the best known.

—*An Encyclopedia of Drinks and Drinking*, 1978, Frederick Martin

SO SET 'EM UP, JOE

One doesn't like to quote oneself as an authority, but in this case I am something of an expert. In my book *The Quiet Limit of the World* there appears the following exchange between me and an American customs officer, conducted during a torrential rainstorm:

"Are you bringing any agricultural products into the United States?" she yelled.

"I don't think so," I yelled back.

"No citrus fruit? Oranges, lemons, grapefruit?"

"Well," I said, "I do have a few lemons in the cooler." Along with a bottle of vodka, a jar of Mott's Clamato Juice, and two cans of Campbell's Beef Bouillon. No one in the States, I knew, had heard of Bloody Caesars. "Do you want them?"

She looked at me. "No, thank you. Just don't peel them until you leave the country."

It's a true story. Being Canadian, I didn't peel the lemons; I punched holes in them, squeezed the juice into my drink, and put the peels back in the cooler until I got home. I like Bloody Caesars. I remember being in the bar of the Algonquin Hotel in New York and ordering a Bloody Caesar. The waiter asked me what it was, I told him, and he brought me a Bloody Mary. Being Canadian, I drank it.

A Bloody Caesar is a drink involving vodka, beef bouillon, Clamato juice and assorted spices on the Bloody Mary principle (see recipe below) that was first concocted in 1962 in the Toronto Press Club, which was then housed in the Prince George Hotel on King Street East. I learned of this one memorable afternoon in one of the Press Club's subsequent locations on Wellesley Street, when I ordered a Bloody Caesar and watched as the bartender, whose name was Joe, opened a can of Campbell's Beef Bouillon and poured a slug of it into the glass. I had had Caesars before, but had never seen anyone adding soup to them. When I asked Joe what he was doing, he said he had been a waiter at the Press Club in the Prince George when Eric Dobson was the bartender. One of the club's specialty drinks was a Bullshot—an ounce of bouillon and a shot of vodka, good for hangovers (both for curing them and getting them)—and one of its regular patrons was Alvin Cook, then owner of the A&P grocery chain. One day Cook brought in a case of Clamato juice, a mixture of tomato and clam juice that his store was introducing, and gave it to Dobson, saying, "Here, see if you can make a drink out of this." Dobson combined a Bullshot with a Bloody Mary, using Clamato instead of tomato juice, and came up with the Bloody Caesar.

Joe then gave me the following recipe:

Combine in a tall glass over ice:
1 oz. vodka
1 slug beef bouillon
1 wedge lime
1 dash Worcestershire sauce
1 small dash Tabasco sauce
Clamato juice to fill.

"Please note," Joe said, leaning towards me over the bar sink as though imparting a great secret, which he was: "No ring of celery salt around the rim of the glass, and no celery stalk sticking up like a stir stick in full foliage." But what I noted most was the beef bouillon: it was delicious. It gave the Clamato juice a deep, rich, inviting colour. And even without the celery it was wholesome. A couple of Bloody Caesars at lunch contain all the major food groups, including meat. I've checked the label on many cans of Mott's Clamato Juice since then; they always give a recipe for Bloody Caesars, but they never mention beef bouillon. The label on a jar of President's Choice Clamato Cocktail gives a recipe for something the President calls a Caesar Cocktail; it too eschews beef bouillon. I think the Canadian Cattlemen's Association should look into this.

When I asked Joe why Dobson had called it a Bloody Caesar instead of a Bloody Khan or a Bloody Ethelred the Unready, he shrugged. "Maybe the Clamato juice reminded him of the anchovies in a Caesar salad," he suggested. But the question nagged me. Why, for that matter, Bloody Mary? The drink was actually named for Queen Mary I of England (1516–58), who was called Bloody Mary because of her persecution of early English Protestants: she martyred three hundred of them. The first Bloody Mary was made by Ferdinand Petiot, a bartender at Harry's Bar in Paris in the 1920s. Petiot called it a Red Snapper, but someone—maybe Morley Callaghan—must have told him that a Red Snapper was a fish, and so the name was changed to Bloody Mary. "Bloody" by itself is what is known as a taboo intensive: "You bloody moron!" is a more intensive expression than "You moron!" "Bloody" is a contraction of "By Our Lady"—as, analogously, "goodbye" is of "God be with ye"—and so Bloody Mary makes perfect sense.

Bloody Caesar does not. But I think I know where the association of bloody and Caesar came from.

There is a wonderful British comedy album called *Beyond the Fringe* that contained sketches by four of England's top comedians—Alan Bennett, Peter Cook, Jonathan Miller and Dudley Moore. The show was first presented at the Edinburgh Theatre Festival in 1960, opened in London the following year "and immediately became the talk of two continents," according to the album jacket. In the fall of 1962—the year of the first Bloody Caesar—the show came to North America. It played in Toronto in September of that year, and for months afterwards people were going around misquoting from it—"Oi'd rather be a judge than a miner," "Loif is rather like a tin of sardines," and so on. It was especially popular among journalists because one of the skits was about Lord Beaverbrook, the Canadian who owned Fleet Street, in which a pair of news hounds attend a cocktail party at "the Beaver's" and drink as much free booze as they can in order "to break him from within." There was also a skit in which the Company take the mickey out of Shakespeare's history plays. After a particularly clamorous sword fight, Peter Cook apostrophizes: "Oh, saucy Worcester, dost thou lie so still?"

The line Cook parodied is from *Julius Caesar*. It's the first thing Mark Antony says upon seeing Caesar's slain body: "O mighty Caesar! Dost thou lie so low?" I've often heard it misquoted, usually in bars, as "O *bloody* Caesar, etc.," probably because throughout all of Act III, in which Caesar is stabbed to death by the conspirators, the name Caesar is constantly linked to the word "blood." Caesar himself says, "Be not fond / To think that *Caesar* bears such rebel *blood* . . ." Immediately after the conspirators stab Caesar, Brutus cries, "Stoop, Romans, stoop, / And let us bathe our hands in *Caesar's blood*." During his famous crowd-swaying scene, in which he turns the fickle plebeians against the conspirators, Antony says that if the Romans knew of Caesar's generosity towards them in his will, "they would go and kiss dead *Caesar's* wounds / And dip their napkins in his sacred *blood*." He shows them the hole in Caesar's knife-torn garment where Brutus withdrew his dagger: "Mark how the *blood* of *Caesar* followed it." And he makes his final, triumphant plea by pointing out that "Even at the base of Pompey's statue / (Which all the while ran *blood*) great *Caesar* fell."

So what we have is a bunch of journalists standing around a bar watching a man mix a new drink. One of the ingredients is Worcestershire sauce, so some wit who has just been to *Beyond the Fringe* declaims: "O saucy Worcester! Dost thou lie so low?"

"No, no, old chap," says another. "It's 'O *bloody* Worcester!'"

"You're both full of Bullshots," says a third, possibly having just returned from Stratford. "It's 'O bloody *Caesar*'—and make mine a double!"

Blue nose 1. A New England colonial name for a Nova
Scotian; 2. A rigorously puritanical person of Spartan habits.
—*Good Words to You,* 1987, John Ciardi

SOT DOWN IN NEW YORK

I have sailed on many ships and have always found it curious that,
even though we may be aboard a 13,000-tonne iron vessel pow-
ered by five electric diesel engines delivering 30,000 horsepower to
three stern propellers, we still call it "sailing." Some seafarers refer
to it as "steaming," which is slightly more modern but seldom more
accurate. At sea, old terms and traditions die hard. Seamen still learn
a bewildering number of knots, even though the only remaining
rope on board might very well be the one they are learning the
knots on.

When a thing does change, it is sometimes for the better. I was
instructed by the first mate on a Coast Guard icebreaker that releas-
ing a ship's hawsers from a dock is no longer called "casting off." It
is now called "letting go," a term I like very much. "It's time to let
go," he said, and our ship eased away from Ogden Point, just outside Victoria, and turned as slowly as a compass needle until it
pointed north, for Bering Strait, the Arctic Ocean and, with luck,
the North Pole. We had let go.

When the long, sleek schooner *Bluenose II* docked in Kingston harbour a few years ago, word went out that lubbers were to be allowed
on deck to have a look at her, and so I went down and joined the
line-up. *Bluenose II* is a replica of the original *Bluenose,* which was
designed by Nova Scotia boat-builder Bill Roue and launched in
Lunenburg in 1921. She won the International Fisherman's Trophy

that year and for the next three years running, in a race that was restricted to working ships. She was the fastest schooner in the world until she sank off Haiti in 1942. According to Silver Donald Cameron (in *Schooner: Bluenose and Bluenose II*), "Roue called her 'Design #117.' Smith and Rhuland [the builders] called her 'Hull #121.' Some of her owners wanted to call her *Cavendish*, in honour of the governor-general, the Duke of Devonshire. But the name chosen was the old, sardonic nickname for Nova Scotians themselves: *Bluenose*."

Nova Scotians were first called "blue noses" in 1785 by United Empire Loyalists who moved to the Annapolis region of Nova Scotia, refugees from the American Revolution. They took up land that thirty years before had belonged to Nova Scotia's Acadians. The Yankee population in the colony, struggling for pre-eminence in the 1785 provincial elections, coined the phrase as a term of derision for the Nova Scotians who had been there before them. Perhaps the best known fictional Loyalist, Thomas Chandler Haliburton's Sam Slick, has no time for blue noses: "I wish one of those Bluenoses," he says in *The Clockmaker*,

> with his go-to-meetin' clothes on, coat-tails pinned up like a leather blind of a shay, an old spur on one heel, and a pipe stuck through his hat band, mounted on one of these limber-timbered critters that moves its hind legs like a hen scratchin' gravel, was sot down in Broadway, in New York, for a sight.

Haliburton thought the term was first applied to a type of potato cultivated in Nova Scotia, which grows into the shape of a nose and has a bluish tinge at one end, and you'd think he'd know. But as Dorothy Duncan, who married Halifax native Hugh MacLennan in 1936, says, "the last person to tell you why he is so called is a Nova

Scotian." And certainly MacLennan never once mentions the term in all his writing. Duncan herself, in her lively book *Bluenose: A Portrait of Nova Scotia* (1946), favoured the derivation offered by Sir Charles G.D. Roberts, who claimed, she writes, that "a famous Nova Scotia privateer in the War of 1812 had a cannon in her bow which was painted bright blue. She made a great deal of money for the province by intercepting United States vessels, and she was called the 'blue nose' by those who had occasion to keep out of her way."

Yankee immigrants, however, had been calling Nova Scotians blue noses for twenty-seven years before the War of 1812, and so the piratical cannon, like the later schooner, most likely took its name from the epithet rather than the other way around. Another theory has it that the name derives from the noses of Nova Scotia fishermen, rendered blue either by the cold North Atlantic wind or (in a variant I once heard from a Cape Bretoner) from being constantly wiped on the cuffs of their blue pea-jackets.

I have my own bluenose theory. To me, the fact that no one seems to agree on a single origin for the word suggests that it meant something to the New Englanders who moved into Nova Scotia and nothing at all to the Nova Scotians to whom it was first applied. This is where Ciardi's second definition—"A rigorously puritanical person of Spartan habits"—comes into the picture. Nova Scotians were a fiercely conservative lot; they lived conservatively and they voted Conservative. Northrop Frye (in his essay "National Consciousness in Canadian Culture") observed that when Haliburton, late in his life, went to England and became involved in politics there, he "joined the Conservative party because he thought it was conservative, though by his Bluenose standards of conservatism it was practically a Communist front." When the Loyalists arrived from colonial New England, their politics were much more tinged with liberalism. They weren't exactly republicans, because that's what they were running away from, but compared to the Nova Scotians they were decidedly radical. The Yankees would have seen the Nova Scotians as puritanically conservative, and they would have derided them for it.

In New England, to be of strictly conservative views on everything from politics to dress to who pours the tea was to be a blue nose. This term would not have meant anything to Nova Scotians and so would not register as an insult. If anything, they would have thought of it as an Americanization of the British term "bluestocking," which would have been quite familiar to literate Nova Scotians like Haliburton. "Bluestocking" had come into use in England in 1653 and referred to Oliver Cromwell's "Little Parliament," whose members dressed in Puritanical plainness right down to their blue worsted (instead of black silk) stockings. It came back into general use in 1750 to apply to several literary groups that met at fashionable London houses to discuss (conservative) politics and other matters of the day, and that were known for their informal way of dressing—including blue worsted instead of black silk stockings. Boswell noted in his *Life of Johnson* (1791) that "these societies were denominated Bluestocking Clubs." The term was used with a degree of derision (the OED calls it "contemptuous"); but it was adopted with some pride by the bluestockings themselves.

It's my guess that, coming up to the Nova Scotia elections of 1785, the Yankees would have cast about for a derisive term to apply to the archly conservative Nova Scotians, and they would have come up with "blue noses." The Nova Scotian candidates, not familiar with that term, would have equated it in their minds with "bluestockings," and would have taken it almost as a compliment.

Whatever its derivation, "bluenose" has indeed been taken up as a badge of honour by those it was intended to insult. And as I walked along the beautifully trimmed deck of *Bluenose II*, ran my hand along its gleaming wooden rails, looked up into the precision of its rigging,

I could almost hear the pride in her builders' voices as they worked: "Yes, by God, we may be bluenoses, but if we can build a ship that will beat the hell out of anything you Yankees can put afloat, what does that make *you?*"

Caboose A car usually placed at the rear of a train, which provides an office and quarters for the conductor and/or trainmen while in transit.

—*Car and Locomotive Cyclopedia of*
American Practices, 1906

TRAINSPOTTING IN WINNIPEG

"She's down in the caboose," says a character in a short story by Cal Bailey. The character is not on a train. Bailey was writing about the Interlake district of Manitoba, where he grew up, and by "caboose" he did not mean the conductor's office and observation car at the end of a freight train, but rather "a kind of hut or shack," he said, when I asked him about the word. "For example, a person might go ice-fishing with a sleigh that had a house on it, and the house was called a caboose. Or the thresherman might arrive on the farm in the fall with a threshing machine and a trailer behind, which he parked by the barn and slept in and cooked his meals in, and we always called the trailer a caboose." Although the Interlake includes the Icelandic settlement at Gimli, where Bailey was born, the word "caboose" was also used by Scottish and Métis inhabitants around the town of Marquette.

In Saskatchewan, the word caboose has been in fairly general use for most of this century. Novelist Rudy Wiebe remembers using it in northern Saskatchewan in the 1930s to describe a "horse-drawn sleigh with a cabin on it. We'd put a woodstove in the cabin, and the reins would come in through a small slit at the front, where there would also be a kind of sliding window. This was what we called a caboose. We thought of it as a Low German word, but the

English-speakers in the area called it a caboose, too. It was just the word we all had for that thing we drove in the winter."

What distinguishes a caboose from an ordinary shack or shanty is the fact that it can be pulled around, on either skids or wheels. Florence Page Jaques, an American nature writer who visited the Interlake with her husband, wildlife artist Francis Lee Jaques, in 1947, recalls in her book *Canadian Spring* meeting Albert Hochbaum at the Delta Waterfowl Research Station, the first wetland conservation project in Canada. Hochbaum had been working at the Delta Marsh since 1938, and had turned a threatened marshland into one of the most productive bird sanctuaries in North America. When Jaques and her husband arrived, Hochbaum

> showed us to our room—two small fishing shacks, or cabooses, as they are called in Manitoba. I had always longed to live on a house-boat and these were closely akin, for they could be pulled anywhere across the marsh. They were tiny things, one a kitchen and one a bedroom; living in them was like keeping house in a couple of shoe-boxes. Our windows looked out on the marsh, and in the blue air above our roofs the ducks flew over.

Of the two buildings described by Jaques, the one that was a true caboose was the kitchen. The word comes from the Old Dutch or Low German *kabuis,* or *kaban-huis,* literally a "cabin-house," and first came into English simply as "cabin." In Late Middle English, a cabin was still a cave or grotto; Langland, in *Piers Plowman* (c. 1377), writes, "Ac thou . . . crope in to a kaban for colde of thy nailes." By Shakespeare's time "cabin" had taken on its present sense of a low, somewhat temporary dwelling made of unsophisticated materials; in *Twelfth Night*, Viola, disguised as a man, tells Olivia that she (he) would "make me a willow Cabine at your gate" to prove her (his) love.

By the late eighteenth century, English had turned *kabuis* into *caboose*, the cook's cabin on the deck of a ship in the merchant marine. The caboose was placed on the foredeck, set on a square of timbers filled with sand that prevented the cook's stove from accidentally setting fire to the ship.

After that, three languages seem to have dovetailed to form one word: *kabuis* also provided the French language with *cambuse*, or storehouse, especially one on a ship, not to be confused with the English caboose, or cookhouse, especially one on a ship. In Canada, *cambuse* came into English from Quebec as *camboose*, the cook's shack in a logging camp and, by extension, the cook's shanty aboard a log raft; the camboose, to bring the etymology full circle, was built on a square of logs filled with sand for the same reason the Old Dutch *kabuis* was. Even in the camp itself the camboose was built on sand, because the ground in a logging camp was usually under several feet of sawdust and wood chips. "To the lumbermen," writes Audrey Saunders in her history of the lumber camps in Ontario's Algonquin Park (*Algonquin Story*, 1947), "the camboose was the central fireplace in the log shanty . . . The camboose shanty was more than a store room in the early lumber camps, since this one building served as dining, sleeping and recreation centre, throughout the winter's bush operations." These lumber camps were referred to as "camboose camps."

The first recorded use of the last car on a train as a conductor's lodgings was in the 1840s, by conductor Nat Williams of the Auburn & Syracuse Railroad. Williams simply commandeered an empty boxcar, kept his flags and lanterns and tools in it, installed a wooden crate and a barrel on which to write his reports, and ate his lunch in it as well. He didn't call it a caboose, though. He probably didn't call it anything. Before long most freight trains designated the last car for the crew's use; by 1875 this was called the waycar, the crummy, the van, the brake van or, in Canada, the cabin-van.

According to the *Encyclopedia of North American Railroading* (1981), the first time the word "caboose" was used was in 1885, "when it referred to conductors' cars on the Buffalo, Corning & New York line." The OED records an American citation from 1881. But the *Dictionary of Canadianisms* provides an earlier reference from the Winnipeg *Daily Times* for April 12, 1879: "A locomotive train with a large amount of freight and a caboose full of laborers left for Cross Lake from the St. Boniface station of the CPR."

But cabooses were in use in Canada, and were called cabooses, long before that. According to Omer Lavallée, CP Rail's "Corporate Historian Emeritus" in the 1980s, when he wrote a regular column in the *CP Rail News*, crew cars were introduced in Canada in 1859, when the Great Western Railway in Ontario put thirty-three "conductors' cars" into service. This innovation came in response to complaints from train crews that riding on the roofs of freight cars, waiting for a whistle signal from the engineer that it was time to apply the brakes, was not fun in foul weather, which along the routes of the Great Western was fairly frequently. These conductors' cars proved so popular (they were really just empty boxcars fitted with benches and wood stoves) that the Northern Railway of Canada, a precursor of the Canadian National Railway, put seven "freight caboose cars" on the tracks the following year, and after that cabooses, called cabooses, were regular features on most long-distance freight trains.

In 1985 the CNR and CPR sought permission to phase out cabooses from their trains because the railways were phasing out train crews, replacing live brakemen with computerized boxes at the ends of freight trains (you might say they were replacing conductors with semi-conductors). The boxes were called End-of-Train Information Systems (ETIS). Little lights went on in the locomotive cab, where the "head-end crew" rides (the other crew was called the "rear-end crew" in polite company), when a journal box overheated or when pressure in a hydraulic line dropped. "This display unit," reported *CP Rail News* in 1985, when testing began, "eliminates the need for tail-end monitoring from the caboose." It also eliminated the need for the caboose, and in December 1987 the Canadian Transport Commission gave the railways approval to work towards "caboose-less trains."

Despite heavy opposition from the United Transportation Union, which saw caboselessness as the first step towards conductorless-ness (correctly, as it turned out), the first cabooseless train left Winnipeg for Swift Current on December 14, 1989. This was a sad day for trainspotters. The railway companies say they save $60 million a year not having to maintain cabooses; I say sitting at a level crossing counting boxcars is not as much fun as it used to be. If you get to the end of the train and do not see a caboose, you sit there for a while thinking the rear end of the train must somehow have broken off. It's rather like seeing half a worm; you begin to wonder where the other half is. Long after the barrier is lifted and the red light stops flashing, you're not sure you should cross the track. A freight train without a caboose seems endless, like a sentence without a period

Canada "There is no geographical necessity to justify the existence of a political unit specifically called Canada. Nevertheless, the political unit exists."

—*Le Canada,* 1937, André Siegfried

Note: second-largest country in world (after Russia); strategic location between Russia and US via north polar route.

—*The CIA World Factbook,* 1995—96

HERE THERE ARE NO MAPS

"*Va au Canada!*" impatient parents would say to their children in seventeenth-century France. Go to hell. On December 26, 1632, a young Ursuline, Marie de l'Incarnation, while sleeping in her monastery in Tours, France, dreamed that she had entered "a very difficult place." She and a companion, she wrote in her diary the next morning, "did not see the obstacles that hindered us, we merely felt them." The two women entered "a large and spacious place that had no roof but the sky. The pavement was white as alabaster but spotted over with vermeil. There was a wonderful silence there." As they walked through this empty wasteland, they came upon a huge house or lodge, "at the foot of which were great spaces, and in these spaces there was a church enveloped in such heavy mists that only the summit of its roof . . . could be seen." The Virgin Mary was sitting on the church roof, and below them a road descended "into the vast spaces"; there were "terrible rocks" on one side of the road "and awful and unguarded precipices on the other." When she awoke, she recounted her dream to her Mother Superior, Françoise de Saint-Bernard, and asked her what it meant. Her Mother

Superior told her the dream could only mean one thing: God wanted her to go to Canada.

"Canada" seems like such an innocent word to have evoked such violent images in the minds of Europeans who had never seen it. What is it about its three monochromatic syllables that seems so alarming to some or so negligible to others? Voltaire, for example, begged the Marquis de Chauvelin in 1760 "to rid the government of France forever of Canada: if you lost it, you lose almost nothing." It is, admittedly, a strange name. Canada. We know that "England" means "land of the Angles," France is the place whence the Francs swooped down on the Romans, who were from Rome. But what, if anything, did the word "Canada" mean?

In his *Histoire du Canada* (1951), Jean Bruchesi writes that the two Gaspé Hurons taken to France by Jacques Cartier in 1534 told him that the word "Canada" was by origin an Iroquoian word meaning "a collection or country of huts," and referred to the land bordering the Saint Lawrence from Quebec to Trois-Rivières, inclusive. Later it was applied to all the land discovered and explored by the French. At the beginning of the 17th century, the word became interchangeable with the name New France, and meant the territory bounded by Hudson Bay, the Atlantic Ocean, Maine and the Great Lakes.

Marius Barbeau, in *Canadian Folk Songs*, says the word applied not to the villages but to the people who lived in them: "The name Canada, itself, which means 'village dwellers,' was that of the Huron-Iroquois, who ranged from the lower St. Lawrence to the bottom lands around the Great Lakes." In the *Jesuit Relations* this territory—renamed New France—is given more specific and much vaster definition. Father Bressani, writing in 1653 (twenty years after Marie de l'Incarnation's arrival) records that by New France is commonly understood the space of land and water which extends from 36 degrees of latitude, which is that of Virginia, to 53, where, nearly, begins the great River of Saint Lawrence; others locate it from 32 to 54. It extends in longitude from 325 degrees to 295, as known to us,—or, to speak more properly, without any limit toward the West.

There have been many attempts to find smaller origins for the word. Jacques Cartier himself described Canada as "the land God gave to Cain," except that he said it in French: "La terre que Dieu a donné à Caïn." This prompted religious utopians to equate Canada with the biblical Canaan, which is not what Cartier meant at all. Thomas Morton, writing about Canada in *The New English Canaan* (1632), thought that Cartier's phrase should be taken much more literally: "From this lake [Oneida] Northwards is derived the famous River of Canada [the St. Lawrence], so named of Monsieur de Cane, a French Lord, who first planted a colony of French in America."

Monsieur de Cane is probably Guillaume de Caën (close enough to Caïn in those days). De Caën was a French Huguenot captain and shipowner (not a lord) who was granted a monopoly of the fur trade in New France from 1621 to 1636 on condition that in each of those years he supply Samuel de Champlain with ten men, six Récollet missionaries (galling for a Huguenot) and six families—510 settlers over the fifteen-year contract—to colonize the new country, an arrangement that would have established Quebec as a Protestant stronghold in the New World (if you don't count the Récollets) had he been allowed to fulfil the terms of his contract. In 1627, however, when Cardinal Richelieu came to power, the Catholic Compagnie de Cent-Associés was founded, the Compagnie de Caën was disbanded, and de Caën himself was forbidden to trade or even to travel in New France "under pain of death." It would be interesting if "Canada" meant "the land God gave to Caën," but it almost certainly does not.

Nor is it likely that the theory proposed by C.H. Wrangler, a correspondent from Gondar, Ethiopia, writing in *Windspeaker* in 1992, bears any more weight. Wrangler quotes Spanish and Portuguese scholars to the effect that "the Spaniards wrote '*Acqui esta nada*' (here there is nothing) on their early maps of northern North Amercia. This was shortened to '*Acqui-nada.*' The equivalent phrase in Portuguese is '*Ca-nada.*'"

This is a version of the idea first mentioned by John Long, in his *Voyages and Travels of an Indian Interpreter and Trader,* published in 1791:

> When the Spaniards (who first discovered this northern clime) sailed past Cape Rosiers at the entrance of the River St. Lawrence, the mountains, now called the Mountains of Nôtre Dame, were covered with snow. Such a prospect, in the summer season, gave them a very unfavourable opinion of the country, and they were deterred from going up the river, supposing the land to be too barren to recompense their labours at present, or afford any future advantages; and the same impressions induced them to call it Capo di Nada, or Cape Nothing, by which name it is described in their charts, and from whence, by corruption of language, it has derived its present name of Canada.

If I were to believe that there is anything Portuguese or Spanish about the word "Canada" at all, which I don't, I would prefer to recall that my wife, during a research trip to Palenque, Mexico, stayed in a Hotel Cañada. *Cañada* is an old Spanish word for a dale between two mountains, and is a much more fitting description of the gentle Nôtre-Dame Mountains, which are actually in New Brunswick at the mouth of the Restigouche River (not in the Gulf of St. Lawrence, as Long supposed), than Cape Nothing. Even in winter. Welcome to Cañada.

There were those who, before Confederation in 1867, thought seriously about naming the new country something else. It had been called Canada for ages; why not try something new? This bold thought was propagated largely by the editors of newspapers. For two or three years they ran a series of "Name This Country" contests, inviting readers to send in suggestions, much as new major-league cities nowadays run "Name This Baseball Team" events, and with much the same—i.e. unusable—results.

From 1865 to 1867, hundreds of amateur nomenclaturists bombarded editors with names. The proposals varied from the lacklustre to the downright lunatic. A survey of them appeared a few years after Confederation in the *Canadian Magazine* (the very name of which is a hint at how the contest turned out). The three most common suggestions were Laurentia, Niagarentia and Ursalia. If Canada had been named by popular vote, in other words, it would have been called one of these. Laurentia survives in things like Laurentian University, which is on the Laurentian Plateau. Niagarentia has mercifully vanished. Ursalia simply means North Country—the country under the constellation Ursus Major. "Let Ursalia," wrote one proponent of the name, "be the name of our coming Empire, and old Grizzly himself our crest, a warm hug for our allies and a death grip for our foes. Then we need not fear comparison with lion, wolf-dog, red dragon or white elephant, raven, cock or eagle, double- or single-headed." The Ursulian flag would consist of a depiction of the Big Dipper (Ursus Major), with one star for each of the four provinces and a few left over for future acquisitions.

Borealia was a popular entry, but can you imagine the jokes that would have ensued? "Come for an exciting vacation in Borealia. Bring a book." Someone could write a long, laboured epic in unrhymed pentameter about the repatriation of the Constitution, and call it *The Borealiad*. Then there was Norland, which, it was thought, "would sound familiar to ears accustomed to England, Scotland and Ireland." Not to mention Greenland, Iceland, Finland and Somaliland. Others less gifted with imagination suggested North America—a little too formal, perhaps, or too egocentric (what would the Americans think?). Then how about Western Britannica? No? Albona? Albionora? OK, try Victorialand. Or Albertoria.

Suggestions from Lower Canada also arrived. These had a particularly Gallic ring: Champlain, Cabotia, Acadia, Hochelaga. One entrant thought Colonia would be a good name because "the Viceroy of Colonia is a dignified, well-rounded phrase."

My favourite suggestions came from further out in left field. Tupona, for example. It was an acronym of The United Provinces of North America, on the United States of North America model, one supposes. A bit forced, but to my mind it beats Mesopelagia ("an interocean territory") hands down. Aquilonia was defended as "a short, expressive and smooth-sounding name, most appropriate to the latitude of our country." Sounds like a beer commercial. Vesperia, "the territory towards sundown," has a sort of resigned sigh in it, as though the entire country were sitting on a suitcase waiting for a westbound train.

And then there was Efisga, which stood for England, France, Ireland, Scotland, Germany and Aborigines. I wouldn't have minded being an Efisgan. "O Efisga, we stand on guard for thee." We would have had the Efisgan Broadcasting Corporation, we would fly Air Efisga, receive reams of useless information from StatsEf, protest the selling of Efdu nuclear reactors, buy PetroEf gasoline and cook with efola oil. But the problem with Efisga, as no doubt immediately seen by the Fathers of Confederation, was that we would have had to prohibit immigration from any place other than the British

Isles (minus Wales), France and Germany. Or else keep adding letters to the name. A wave of immigration from the Ukraine and we become Efisgau; a boatload of refugees from Viet Nam, Efisgavun. And so on until, well, imagine the consternation down at the Efisgavunchibawpsajian embassy when the group from Zaire shows up.

No, all in all, I think we are better off with Canada. It has a certain finality to it. An end place. Go to Canada. In the 1920s and 1930s, British mystery writers like Margery Allingham and Ngaio Marsh routinely sent milquetoast nephews to Canada when they were no longer needed to further the family plot in England, and Canada remains a handy place for novelists to get rid of characters that have become superfluous. In Virginia Woolf's 1925 novel *Mrs. Dalloway*, for example, which is in part an examination of the viciousness of human nature, Lady Bruton throws her energies into a "project for emigrating young people of both sexes born of respectable parents and setting them up with a fair prospect of doing well in Canada." Which would be all very well were it not that by "young people of both sexes" she meant the walking wounded returned from the Great War, people like the Shakespeare-quoting, shell-shocked Septimus Warren Smith, whose war experiences left him believing that "human beings have neither kindness, nor faith, nor charity beyond what serves to increase the pleasure of the moment. They hunt in packs. Their packs scour the desert and vanish screaming into the wilderness." Oh sure, fill Canada up with characters like that and see what kind of literature we get!

Canada's reputation in the European imagination hasn't changed much since the 1600s. In John Osborne's play *The Entertainers*, when an actor complains to his agent that he hasn't had any work for months and desperately needs something to do, the agent replies impatiently: "Well, you could always go to Canada."

Carriole In France a wheeled vehicle. Here, a winter conveyance with one or two seats, consisting of a box placed on
two runners, very low and of solid wood.

—*Glossaire Franco-Canadien*, 1880, Oscar Dunn

JINGO BELLS, JINGO BELLS

Nathaniel Hawthorne, in his *Twice-Told Tales* (1837), has one of
his characters climb into "a four-wheeled carry-all, with a
round half-dozen of pretty girls" in it. Hawthorne's carry-all had
wheels and was pulled by a single horse, but the word was borrowed from the Quebec *carriole*, the familiar one-horse open sleigh,
and "carry-all" was used in English in Quebec long before it was
appropriated by the Americans. The OED gives 1837 as the first use
in the United States, but an article published in 1868 in the Montreal magazine *New Dominion Monthly*, entitled "The Holidays Forty
Years Ago," has the word "carry-all" in use in English Montreal as
early as 1828:

On Christmas-eve, in the year 182— [rocket-science math gives
1828: no wonder the writer wanted to remain anonymous], a number of men of Montreal hired two or three *Marche-doncs*, to go down
to *la Messe de Minuit*, or Midnight Mass, at Pointe aux Trembles,
then a favorite sleigh ride. One of the party had arrived that fall
from the "Old Country," or "Home," as Britain was affectionately
called, and the others were bent on showing him the wonders of
this French country, with which a residence of some years had
made them familiar. The *Marche-donc* was the common name for
the small but comfortable cariole of those days, usually pronounced

by old-country people, "carry-all"; but the pronunciation was inappropriate, for, so far from carrying all of a party, it would carry two passengers comfortably in the low, wide seat behind, though, in case of need, a third might sit on the high, narrow seat in front with the "charretier," or driver. These carioles were well provided with straw in the bottom, and buffalo robes; and the great-coats, muffling shawls, and huge fur caps with ears, usually worn in those days, rendered the upper part of the body safe from even the cold of a Canadian mid-winter night.

Carry-all and carriole are more closely linked etymologically than our anonymous Montrealer knew. In eighteenth-century France a carriole (from the Italian and Provençal carriola) was a small farm wagon used for carrying hay or wood. The word is rooted in the Latin carrus, the Roman baggage wagons used during Caesar's campaign against the Gauls, from which all our words with the root-word "car" in them, denoting some kind of load or conveyance, derive: carriage, cart, chariot, Pélagie's Old French and Acadian charrette, the modern Québécois char (which is the modern English car), cargo and charge (when it means to load up to the absolute limit, as in, "Charge this to my father's account"). The verb "to carry" is from the Latin carricare, which means "to load onto a cart." Thus, Gary Carter carried the Expos for several seasons, even when he didn't. A carry-all and a carriole are thus rooted in the same word. And presumably a carry-all, meaning the hand luggage, is what one would pack for a dash through the snow in a carriole, just as a Pullman bag was taken on the Chattanooga choo-choo and a steamer trunk was suitable for a tramp on a steamer.

A carriole is not to be confused with cabriolet, a light, two-wheeled gig (from the French cabrioler, meaning "to dance a jig"), from which we got the word "cab" in 1830, but not the word "gig," which means to twirl around quickly, like a whirligig or the wheels of a cab. How a "gig" became a professional engagement, as when we hear a rock musician say, "I got a gig down at the Stoned Owl Café," is unknown to me, but I suspect it derives from one of the obscurer senses of the word given in the OED: "Gig: a squeaking noise."

In Quebec, the French *carriole* occasionally lost an "r" and permanently lost its wheels, gained runners and sometimes an enclosed box, and became a winter conveyance too rustic to be called a sleigh (which was *un traineau*) and yet too dignified to be a sledge (which was also *un traineau*). It was already a fixture, and called a carriole in English, in Quebec City when the city was under siege by Benedict Arnold's army during the American Revolution, the Americans trying to force their independence on Canada. Captain Thomas Ainslie, a British soldier defending the newly won colony from American attack, noted in his diary that on December 8, 1775, a cannonball fired by the "Yanky Rebels" took off the head of a horse "and shattered the Cariole in which he was tackled in a thousand pieces."

In 1808, another British sojourner in Canada, Hugh Gray, described the cariole as

a sort of sledge [that] passes over the snow without sinking deep. It is placed on what they call runners, which resemble in form, the irons of a pair of skaits, and rise up in front in the same manner, and for the same purposes. The cariole is generally from nine to twelve inches above the snow. Some, called high runners, are about eighteen inches. The body of the cariole varies in shape, according to the fancy of the owner. It is sometimes like the body of a phaeton, sometimes like a vis-a-vis, and sometimes like a family coach or chariot. The cariole, in short, is the name for all sorts of vehicles used in winter, from a market cart to a state coach.

Even, he might have added, to a dog sled. When the Canadian artist Paul Kane travelled o'er the fields of western Canada in the 1840s, he was sometimes bundled in a "cariole" that seems to have been a cross between a dog sled and a toboggan. In Edmonton, for example, he records (in *Wanderings of an Artist*) that after a Methodist wedding the dogs were harnessed to "sledges and carioles" and the group set off on a wedding party. "The cariole," he writes,

> is intended for carrying one person only; it is a thin flat board, about eighteen inches wide, bent up in front, with a straight back behind to lean against; the sides are made of green buffalo hide, with the hair scraped completely off and dried, resembling thick parchment; this entirely covers the front part, so that a person slips into it as into a tin bath.

In Quebec the carriole may have been the original "shaggin' wagon." Frances Brooke, in *The History of Emily Montague* (1769: the first novel to be set in Canada), has Miss Fermor write to Miss Rivers from Sillery, Quebec, saying that she liked "the winter carriages immensely; the open carriole is a kind of one-horse chaise . . . set on a sledge to run on the ice." The next line hints at the true nature of the carriole's appeal: "The covered carrioles seem the prettiest things in nature to make love in, as there are curtains to draw before the windows."

If there had been bumper stickers in the 1860s as there were in the 1960s, one of them might have read: "If the carriole's rockin', don't be knockin'."

Chinook winds Warm and pleasant winds which sometimes prevail on the eastern slopes of the Rocky Mountains . . .
thus modifying the winter climate of Alberta.

—*Western Canadian Dictionary and Phrase Book*

CHASING THE CHINOOK

We came down through Denmark Strait, between Greenland
and Iceland, and met the storm as we entered the North
Atlantic. Captain Grandy had considered riding it out in one of the
protected coves on Greenland's eastern coast, but in the end he
must have decided that the best way to meet a hurricane was head
on. We were on the *Louis S. St. Laurent*, a 400-foot, 35,000-tonne
icebreaker; it was top-heavy and had a rounded hull, well suited for
breaking ice but not designed for open water. As we rounded the
southern tip of Greenland, we were hit by a solid wall of green water,
a succession of walls, each one washing over the decks, burying our
bow, forcing entry under the maindeck doors. We rolled and pitched
like a melon in a millrace. Everyone on board was sick—the crew,
the cook, even the nurse—some lying on their bunks or on the car-
peted deck of the after lounge, as close to the ship's centre of gravity as they could get. The ship's weight was all under the foremast;
in such heavy seas it seemed we could slide down the windward
side of a wave and just keep going when we hit the trough.

I have always enjoyed bad weather, which is fortunate because we
get a lot of weather in Canada and much of it is bad. When storms
hit, I want to go outside. I have been told that this is a death wish,
an urge to hurry on the inevitable capsize, but I don't believe it; I
feel it more as a life wish, a desire to be in the full moment. Here

in the raging North Atlantic I was not, like King Lear, calling on the elements to "Rage, blow. / You cataracts and hurricanoes, spout / Till you have drenched our steeples, drowned the cocks." My soul was not in any anguished turmoil that I knew of, requiring outward expression in the form of foam about the crow's nest. It's just that there *was* foam about the crow's nest, and you don't get to see that very often, so I thought I'd like to see it.

I staggered up to the wheelhouse to get a better view. The captain was alone at the controls, having sent the watch below to secure the cargo—two months' worth of scientific research in the High Arctic. He was occupied in trying to keep the ship's nose pointing into the wind. Green water was breaking just below the wheelhouse windows, fifty feet above sea level, which made it difficult to see. But the main problem was that the wind was coming at us from one direction and the waves were coming at us from another. If he kept us heading into the wind, the waves broadsided us; if he pointed into the waves, the hurricane blew us horizontal; halfway between the two and we got hit from both sides. When the ship rolled, the cross-trees on the foremast nearly touched water.

I did have one concern. Just before we rounded Greenland, I had called Merilyn on the Inmarsat phone and told her we were due into Halifax in five days, hoping she might fly down to meet us. But the storm had stopped us in our tracks; with the wind gusting to eighty knots, we may even have been losing headway. Captain Grandy, braced into the starboard corner, looked grimly out at the grey sea, one hand on the throttle and the other gripping the wooden railing that ran along the bulkhead.

"Will we still make it to Halifax on Friday?" I asked.

He looked at me as though seeing me for the first time, as though wondering where I had come from. "O Fool," I could almost hear him thinking, "I shall go mad."

He gave a kind of disbelieving laugh. "Jesus, Wayne," he said. "Wrong question. We're in what's known as a perfect hurricane, two storms hitting us at the same time. Don't ask me about Halifax. If this keeps up, we're as likely to be blown back to Iceland."

*   *   *

In 1793, Alexander Mackenzie, exploring in the Peace River district in the Rocky Mountains, was overtaken by a wind he described in his journal as "a perfect hurricane." He was writing about a wind we now call a chinook. Sid Marty, who lives in southern Alberta, refers to it as "the daemon chinook": in January 1996, he says, a chinook wound his anemometer up to 150 kilometres an hour and "gusted up to 209 kilometres an hour near the summit of Crowsnest Pass."

The current definition of a hurricane is a wind that maintains a steady velocity of 140 kilometres an hour and gusts upwards from that, so Mackenzie was not exaggerating. This is a wind that blows sea water through doors and snow through solid walls, tips icebreakers and shifts buildings off their foundations. Marty has seen a chinook tip over a tractor trailor and heard about one that lifted a freight train off its tracks. A chinook, at least in the higher mountain passes, from where it comes screaming down the slopes to spread out over the open prairie, is a land-based hurricane.

But, as the *Western Dictionary* says, there is also a gentler chinook, a soft, zephyr-like wind that sighs through the branches of the tamaracks and lodgepole pines, melts snow and ice in a matter of hours and brings thoughts of spring to winter-bound Calgary residents in December. It is a wind as famous as the *mistral* that blows down the Rhône valley in France every fall, rattling shutters and sandblasting window glass but otherwise not doing much damage. A wind like the breath of El Niño, which blows over the mountains of Chile into central South America and brings ice storms to eastern Ontario and western Quebec.

Whether gentle or demonic, the chinook makes itself felt most noticeably in southern Alberta and Montana but blows as far north and east as Battleford, Saskatchewan. It takes its name from the Chinook Indians, who occupied territory at the mouth of the Columbia River, in the present state of Washington (the direction from which, if you're in Alberta, the winds seem to come). Washington Irving, who, as far as I know, never left New York while writing *Astoria*, his account of the attempt by John Jacob Astor to found an American empire on the Pacific coast in 1810, noted that "the Chinooks resided chiefly along the banks of a river through a low country studded with stagnant pools, and emptying itself in Baker's Bay, a few miles from Cape Disappointment." In fact the Chinooks were a great trading nation, controlling most of the fish and seal industry along the Pacific Coast as far north as Alaska before and after the coming of Europeans. A Chinook chief, Concomly, supplied Fort Astoria with almost all of its provisions, and was such a powerful figure that McDougal, chief factor at Astoria, married Concomly's daughter to secure the relationship.

As with the Phoenicians, where the Chinooks traded they carried their language with them. Diamond Jenness observes in *The Indians of Canada* (1932) that

> in pre-European times contact between tribes was so frequently hostile that no one language gained the ascendancy; but during the more peaceful era that succeeded the first colonization by white men a degraded form of the Chinookan language spoken in the state of Washington became the usual medium of intercourse between the different tribes, like the jargon of broken English current in many parts of the South Seas.

Pidgin Chinook.

Although 80 percent of the Chinook people were wiped out by
scarlet fever in 1829, they and their language continued to dominate
trade on the coast to such an extent that, in 1859, Chinook became
the official diplomatic language of the northern courts. If, as Gary
Geddes writes in the introduction to his anthology of western writing, *Skookum Wawa*, "Chinook is a rough-edged tongue with the whiff
of money, or commerce, about it," it is also responsible for whatever peaceful relations Native nations had with one another and with
white expansionists for more than two hundred years. Several Chinook words are still common on the West Coast: Geddes chose a
Chinook title, meaning "strong talk," for his anthology, confident
that most readers in western Canada would know what it meant
and readers in the east would pretend that they did. During a recent
stay with my friend Brian Brett, a poet and farmer living on Salt-
spring Island, I heard Brian use *skookum* to describe the kind of fence
needed to keep the horse out of the truck garden; the ravens that
continually raided his henhouse, carrying out his chickens' eggs del-
icately and intact in their beaks as they flew off; and the kind of
whisky he preferred to drink in the evenings after a day of repair-
ing fences and chasing ravens.

There are a lot of French and English words in the Chinook jargon
as well. According to a *Dictionary of the Chinook Jargon or Indian Trade
Language*, published in Victoria in 1899, a candle was *shandel*. Table
was *la tahb*. As in Acadian, an American is a *Boston*. As if, before contact, the Chinook had had no word of their own for sick or unhappy:
sick was *sick* and unhappy was *sick tumtum*. Curiously enough, the word
for wind was *wind*—a chinook in Chinook would be *skookum wind*.
But *wind* was usually gentle to the Chinook, more in the sense of
"breath." *Halo wind* meant "to be out of wind"—that is, dead.

The first European to describe a *skookum* wind, though he did not name it a "chinook," was probably Anthony Henday, a Hudson's Bay Company explorer who was one of the first to penetrate the Canadian interior. Henday left York Factory in June 1754 and travelled west along the North Saskatchewan River to Fort Saint-Louis. In December, arriving at the south branch of the Saskatchewan, he found that region so astonishingly mild for the time of year that he made a note of it in his journal: "The weather has been so warm today that we have gone without anything over our bodies and felt no cold . . ." This was obviously a gentle chinook. On the same day thirty-nine years later and higher up in the mountains, Mackenzie encountered the chinook in its more demonic guise:

> On the 29th [of December], the wind being at North-East, and the weather calm and cloudy, a rumbling noise was heard in the air like distant thunder, when the sky cleared away in the South-West; from whence there blew a perfect hurricane, which lasted till eight. Soon after it commenced, the atmosphere became so warm that it dissolved all the snow on the ground; even the ice was covered with water, and had the same appearance as when it is breaking up in the spring.

Mackenzie welcomed the wind for several reasons, not least among them his deduction that it came from the Pacific Ocean, which he was seeking and which he believed must therefore be close at hand: "These warm winds come off the Pacific Ocean, which cannot, in a direct line, be very far from us; the distance being so short, that though they pass over the mountains covered with snow, there is not time for them to cool." Mackenzie was right about where the winds originated, but way off in his estimate of how far they had travelled, since he was still more than a thousand kilometres from the coast.

As J.G. MacGregor explains in *The Land of Twelve-Foot Davis* (1952), an anecdotal history of the Peace River country, chinooks blow in from the Pacific carrying a heavy load of moisture. When they rise to get over the Rockies, they condense and drop a lot of that moisture on Vancouver, and this condensing causes them to warm up. "The heat given off by the condensation is carried over the mountains," and then "the rapid descent of the air on the east side compresses it, and more heat is given off." By the time the chinook reaches Calgary, it is hot and thirsty, and has been known to raise the ground temperature by eighty degrees in a matter of hours.

Although most dramatically associated with winter, in fact chinooks blow year round. As R.M. Patterson records in *The Buffalo Head* (1960), it was a summer chinook that fanned a small forest fire in British Columbia into the huge "Phillips fire" of July 1936, which eventually destroyed 900 million board feet of timber, one-third of the province's annual production. The wind, writes Patterson,

> blew day and night out of the southwest, and it blew strongly as in the fall or wintertime. The Chinook Arch, even, formed in the western sky—that curious standing arch of heavy, streamlined cloud that, in any normal year, is never seen in summertime. The Arch stayed still over the mountains, and through it streamed the Chinook; it was as if the gates of hell had been flung open. The blistering wind sucked dry what little moisture was left in the country; only in the deep woods and on the northeast slopes did any green grass remain. Even the poplar leaves began to wither.

The chinook in both its gentle and demonic forms has been the stuff of legend in both western Canada and Montana, the two regions together known as Chinook Country. Edith Fowke gathered some of them in *Folklore of Canada;* she cites Herbert Halpert, the American who established folklore studies at Memorial University in Newfoundland, who observed that "sober descriptions of the effects of the 'chinook' strike the newcomer as the wildest flights of imagination." Sober descriptions, however, are not what folklorists usually collect. A lot of the stories in Fowke's collection come from the McDougall family. John, a missionary, and his two sons were among the first settlers around Banff and were well known for their tall tales. "Dave McDougall," Halpert reported,

> lived at Morley, which is about fifty miles west of Calgary, on the Bow River. He started to town with a team and bobsleigh. He was travelling east. A foot of snow was on the ground when he left his home. On the road he was overtaken by a chinook. It was a particularly warm chinook, and, fearing that he wouldn't get to town before the snow melted, he whipped up the horses to a gallop. The snow melted so fast that the front runners were on snow but the back runners were in the mud. Try as he might he could not go fast enough to get the back runners out of the mud and up on to the snow.

In *Leaning on the Wind: Under the Spell of the Great Chinook* (1995), Sid Marty writes about hearing this same story from his friend James Riviere, who lives near Twin Butte. Riviere says he got it from a man named Windy Paul Cyr, and Windy Paul always added the kicker: "And when I got to my gate, that's where the chinook caught up and passed me by; it left me stuck in the mud. I stood up, and looked back; and here come my poor dog, a-swimmin' up the road behind me."

When Marty drove south into Montana to gather more stories about the chinook—he calls it "chasing the daemon chinook"—he says he began for the first time to understand the differences between the two countries. Marty had grown up in Alberta thinking there was little difference between his home province and Montana: "In my mind," he writes, "there was no fence between the nations." If asked, he might even have described himself as a Montanan. But during this trip, along with stories about the big wind, he acquired a few distinctions between the two halves of Chinook Country. Some of those distinctions favour Montana—their names, for instance. "Alberta," he writes, "is an imposition, a whalebone corset of a word that will not fit our rolling plains and exuberant mountains." He likes the word "Montana," derived from the Spanish word for mountainous country; it is "a happy name that rolls from the tongue." And Alberta is more densely populated than Montana—2.7 million people compared to Montana's 800,000—a decided disadvantage for Marty, who loves the solitude and ruggedness of the mountains. Alberta seems almost urban to him: there are nearly as many people living in Calgary as in all Montana.

Both places are swept by the mighty chinook. On the highways near Livingston, Montana (which has a street named Chinook Street), there are signs reading "Chain Up Here," and Marty meets a trucker who tells him, "When you look in the rear-view mirror and see your trailer wheels starting to lift off the ground, it's time to pull over." Winds at the Livingston airport often hit 115 miles (185 km) per hour, and the temperature in Helena can go down to minus 58 degrees Fahrenheit. One story Marty dug up was of an old rancher who says he has to get home to unfreeze his lantern. When told that kerosene doesn't freeze, the rancher replies, "It isn't the coal oil that freezes, it's the flame."

Although Montanans tell Marty that they and Albertans are "the same people, you know," Marty doesn't buy it. He'd spent too many nights in hotel rooms watching things like shoot-outs in Waco, Texas, on one channel and "machine-gun festivals" on another, and he knew there would never be Canadian draft dodgers hiding out in the hills of Montana. The difference is also discernible in the chinook stories he heard. In Montana the big wind seems less benign than it does in Alberta. It's always windy in Montana; it just gets windier when there's a chinook. And although, as in Canada, Montana chinooks are associated with warm weather, they are more often harbingers of hazard: overturned trucks, derailed trains, roofs torn off buildings. In Canada, chinooks bring warmth to a frost-bitten land. In Montana, glass from a plate-glass window is blown across a living room. A dog is held by a chinook against a barn wall and starves to death before the wind stops. The wind "blows the highways bare of snow one day, and coats them with black ice another day." Called "Snow Eater" in Alberta, it's called the "Black Wind" in Montana, or, since it blows from the northwest, the direction of Canada, the "Klondike Chinook." The only good thing Marty hears about the chinook in Montana is from a Blackfoot elder, who tells him that his people "always welcomed the chinook wind. It cleared the snow and allowed us to get out, move around, go hunting." To most of the whites Marty talked to, however, the chinook was a scourge.

Gentle and relentless winds can be scourges too. In a story called "Tramontana," Gabriel García Márquez writes about the tramontana wind that blows in the fall along Spain's Costa Brava, "a harsh, tenacious wind that carries with it the seeds of madness." Diane Schoemperlen, a short-story writer who lived in Canmore, Alberta (about where Morley would be) before moving to Kingston, says that the worst thing she's heard about chinooks is that when a chinook blows "it supposedly does something to the ions in the air that makes people act funny. This is sometimes cited as an excuse for eccentric behaviour, often eccentric behaviour involving alcohol." One such story (a version of it appears in Schoemperlen's short story "Railroading," but I heard it first from the late Jon Whyte, a long-time Banff resident and storyteller) is of retired railwayman Bruce Beattie, who, when a chinook started blowing at the tail end of an eight-day drinking binge, decided he had to get to Canmore in a hurry, so he stole a train—just walked down to the CPR yard, fired up a locomotive and drove it, along with forty-seven boxcars and a caboose, down to Canmore. He was arrested for theft, of course, but (and here it was Jon who added the kicker) the judge threw the case out of court because, as Beattie pointed out, the train never left CPR property.

At the end of his trip Marty was told by an elderly couple north of the Canadian border (in which he now believed) that the chinook was a good wind because it blew down all the TV antennas and kept the greenhorns in the cities, where they belonged. I guess that means I'm not a greenhorn. As I said, I like stormy weather. Once when I was in Edmonton and had to get to Drumheller, normally a two-hour drive south, I started out in a gentle snowfall that some Alberta friends warned me could turn into a perfect blizzard in a matter of minutes. I said I didn't mind, and by the time I was halfway to Red Deer, the snow was so thick I could barely see my windshield wipers. I couldn't stop for fear of being rammed from behind, so I drove on, caught in a swirling whiteness that was like driving with my eyes squeezed shut. Sid Marty heard of a man who drove in a snowstorm like this one, steering and straining to see through his windshield, not knowing that his car had stalled three hours before. In order to check if I was still on the road, I had to open the car door and follow the tire tracks below me. This felt fine until I realized I was following the tracks of my own front tire. Then I just laughed and closed the door and kept on driving. It took me six hours to get to Drumheller. Shortly before I got into Drum, the blizzard changed into a chinook and as if by magic the snow disappeared and the road became bare. By the time I eased down into the Badlands, there wasn't a flake of snow on the ground. I was disappointed.

Colcannon Night Almost universal in St. John's, Nfld.,
for Hallowe'en (used by those who eat colcannon on that night).
—*Dialect Notes of the American Dialect Society*, 1895

BUBBLE AND SCREECH

A year or so ago, a Kingston hotel owner brought over an Irish pub—literally. He had an entire pub dismantled beam by beam in Dublin, shipped to Kingston and reassembled inside the Prince George Hotel, complete with scarred tables, Harp beer pulls and bar mats, and two old geezers who wouldn't give up their bench seats in the snug. Even the cooks and wait staff were sent to Ireland to learn how to draw a proper Guinness (though they don't make the shamrock in the foam) and to make such traditional Irish culinary delights as Figgy Duff and Apple Grunt. The menu features a side dish called colcannon, which turns out to be boiled potatoes and cabbage mashed together with butter to form a kind of paste, with bits of corned beef chopped up in it and everything all stirred up. It is quite delicious. The City Hall clerks from next door eat it with ketchup; the geezers in the corner won't touch it. Everyone feels happy and authentic.

Colcannon is a traditional Irish dish, made by boiling potatoes, cabbage (or curly kale) and leeks in separate pots, then mashing them together until the whole doings is a uniform pale green. It is served in a deep dish; a dent pressed in the centre with a spoon is filled with melted butter. Colcannon came to Canada with Irish set-tlers, first to Newfoundland, where various other things were added to it—Newfoundland colcannon can contain up to seven vegetables, as well as a bit of pork or rabbit—and later to Nova Scotia, where

Scottish settlers modified the traditional dish by boldly adding carrots to it, and the Germans in Lunenburg County threw in turnips, sauerkraut and sausage.

It was not long confined to the coast, however. Irish lumbermen in Upper Canada also ate colcannon and introduced it to the Scotch, or the scotch to it, more like. Samuel Thompson, in *Reminiscences of a Canadian Pioneer* (1884), recalled his experiences in Ontario logging camps in the 1830s, when loggers participated in tree-felling contests along the Scotch Line in Simcoe County. Two teams would chop "until the harsh sound of the breakfast dinner horn would summon both to the house to partake of the rude but plentiful mess of 'colcannon' and milk, which was to supply strength for a long and severe day's labour."

Now, colcannon is not a rude mess. Haggis is a rude mess. My mother, who was born in Newfoundland of English stock, does not remember eating colcannon. She thought I might be thinking of Bubble and Squeak or a Jigs' Dinner. But Bubble and Squeak is cold potatoes and cold boiled cabbage fried on a dry skillet, and the thought of it is like the sound of fingernails on slate. A Jigs' Dinner is also called a boiled dinner and has much the same ingredients as colcannon, but everything is cooked in the same pot (even the corned beef and the cloth bag filled with pease-pudding), which makes it a true concoction (from the Latin *con*, together, and *coquere*, to cook) but does not make it colcannon. It is called Jigs' Dinner, according to my mother, after the popular newspaper comic strip of the 1920s, *Maggie & Jigs*, featuring the tuxedoed but down-to-earth Jigs and his lah-dee-dah wife Maggie. Jigs, a sort of wealthy Andy Capp, was always trying to sneak out for a feed of corned beef and cabbage, and Maggie was always ready with a rolling pin to stop him. It should be mentioned, however, that Newfoundlanders once did a lot of jigging for cod, and a jig-house was a boarding house for seamen—where, presumably, corned beef and cabbage was a fairly common feature at mealtime. Corned beef has always been popular in Newfoundland, along with barrels of bacon preserved in its own lard. My mother's oldest sister, who lives in Paradise—now a suburb of St. John's—forgoes the bacon but has eaten a lard sandwich for lunch every day of her life, and she's 86. Newfoundlanders will go a long way to avoid eating fish.

The OED is vague about the origins of the word "colcannon." It acknowledges that "col" refers to the cabbage but suggests that "cannon" must mean "that spinach was formerly pounded with a cannon ball." Canadian food writer Mark Morton, in his book *Cupboard Love*, repeats this spurious bit of etymology: "The compound arose," he writes, "when Irish peasants turned cannon balls into kitchen implements by using them to pound vegetables into a paste; by so doing, they effected a transformation rivalling the United Nations' mandate to turn swords into ploughshares."

This is wild and intemperate surmise, and could not have been made by anyone who has ever actually tried to mash spinach with a cannon ball. My grandmother, who was born and lived all her life in Renews, a small fishing village south of St. John's, kept two or three cannon balls in her house; they had evidently rolled down the hill above her garden from an old artillery post placed there in the 1700s to protect Newfoundland from invasion by the Dutch. The cannon is still there, a pitted, black shape half embedded in the ground, lurking up through the grass like a crocodile in a swamp. My grandmother dug up the cannon balls in her garden and took them inside to use as bedwarmers, but as far as I know she never pounded vegetables into paste with them. No, the word "colcannon" comes directly from the Irish *cál ceannfhionn*, which simply means white-headed cabbage.

Cál, of course, is *col*, the Latin for cabbage, the root word for almost all of our brassicas except, oddly enough, cabbage, which comes from the French *chou cabus*, or great-head cole. We call cabbage salad "cole slaw" from the Dutch *koolsla* (the Dutch did eventually invade Newfoundland, and their language crops up in many intriguing ways). *Col* is retained in kohlrabi, kale, cauliflower, broccoli and collard greens. (Cole Porter, the songwriter, might have been a cabbage head, but he took his name from the French *colporteur*, which meant a distributor of religious tracts. His "cole" is cognate with collar, not with cole slaw.)

In Ireland, colcannon was always served on Hallowe'en, which was an ancient Celtic witches' festival, along with a form of potato pancake called boxty. In Newfoundland, especially in St. John's, the tradition was kept up (minus the boxty and the witches) and Hallowe'en was called Colcannon Night. Often a button was sequestered somewhere in the colcannon dish: if a young woman got the button, it meant she would marry that year; if a man got it, it meant he would never marry at all (it was thus called a bachelor's button). Variations on the theme had cooks sequestering a wide range of tooth-shattering items: in some places, a penny meant marriage; a matchstick or a thimble meant spinsterhood; a ring meant money; a button meant poverty. And a cannon ball, no doubt, meant disagreement, and no future as a cook.

Common gallinule Chicken-foot coot (an allusion to the
lack of webs connecting the toes of this atypical water bird. Ont.).
—*Folk Names of Canadian Birds*, 1959, W.L. McAtee

WHERE NESTS THE CHICKEN-FOOT COOT

There are lots of coots around. My first view of one, puns aside
for the moment, came a few years ago. My wife and I were
watching birds in the Hanalei National Wildlife Refuge, on the Hawaiian island of Kauai—the fabled Land of Hanalei, where Puff the
Magic Dragon is supposed to have frolicked in the autumn mist with
Little Jackie Paper. We were easing along a path between two rows
of large, paddy-like fields filled with various wading and swimming
birds, following the struttings of a black-necked stilt, when another
bird came into our binoculars' field of vision. It was black, had a
white beak and looked like a chicken. It quickly vanished back into
the reeds, giving us time to riffle through our *Bird Life in Hawai'i*.
By the time it reappeared from the reeds and swam out into the
open pond, we knew what it was: the Hawaiian coot, or Alae
Ke'oke'O, *Fulica americana alai*, "a nonmigratory subspecies of the
American coot."

It is not unusual to see a very rare subspecies of a common bird
before seeing the common bird itself. Life often vouchsafes us an
exquisite pleasure that we are too inept to appreciate. It is what
makes us cocky. On my first visit to Point Pelee, that birders' mecca
in southwestern Ontario, the first warbler I saw was a Kirtland's warbler. Someone had to identify it for me, and I ticked it off my list
as casually as though it had been a starling or a house finch. Only
later did I learn that the Kirtland's is one of the rarest birds in North

America, and having already seen one I thought I might as well continue birding. So with the Hawaiian coot. There are only a few hundred of them in existence, and although American coots aren't as numerous as they once were, they aren't exactly on the Audubon Blue List, and I have since seen many. The first was in our home town—Kingston, Ontario—a year or so later. This time we were watching a lesser yellow-legs pick its way along a dried-up stream bed when a black chicken-like bird with a white forehead darted suddenly out of the tall grass, looked around nervously, and then dashed back into the grass. American coot.

The late Helen Quilliam, whose *History of the Birds of Kingston, Ontario* (1973) is a wonderful example of the invaluable contributions amateur birders have made to the science of ornithology, notes that the American coot's presence in Kingston is "something of an enigma." Very few nests have been found, and only small flocks of a dozen or so birds have been seen heading north during spring migration. But huge flocks stop over in the fall on the way back to Mexico and Panama. "Where do these large flocks come from in the autumn?" Quilliam asks. The question has been resolved by observation farther north: small flocks of coots congregate in northern staging areas and head south *en masse*. At one time they must have migrated all the way to Hawaii, and after a few tiring commutes some of them must have decided to stay and the rest decided never to go back. Birds are a lot like people.

There are European coots as well. The word "coot" was first applied in Europe to the guillemot, but the name was later given to something called a bald coot that was neither bald nor a guillemot. Actually, "bald" meant "balled," which in Celtic was a white patch, usually on a forehead, which certainly describes an American coot (and a bald eagle). The origin of the word "coot" is not known; it was around in Middle English, is probably from the Low German or

Dutch *koet*, meaning short-tailed, and is possibly related to "scoot" and "scout," two other early names for the guillemot.

In Canada the American coot is also known as the baldface or whiteface duck, for obvious reasons, and as the black fish-duck, the fool hen, the hell-diver and the louse bird, for not-so-obvious reasons. In the words of Paul Ehrlich et al., authors of *The Birder's Handbook*, it is "conspicuous, noisy, and aggressively territorial," which is probably why crotchety old men are often called coots. Eric Partridge, in his *Dictionary of Slang*, says "coot" simply means "a simpleton." American coots may be simple but they are also crotchety, and their territoriality often makes them vicious: they will swim over to another bird that happens into their purview and jab at it with one clawed foot while trying to tip it upside down and drown it with the other. We have not observed this behaviour—in fact it has appeared to us to be a somewhat cautious creature—but we believe Ehrlich et al. when they say it exists.

Coots on either side of the Atlantic are not particularly endangered, partly because no one has ever found them good eating. Percy Taverner, in his definitive *Birds of Eastern Canada* (1922), says "they are sometimes shot by the hunter, who later finds them indifferent eating." In Europe, not even Alexandre Dumas, in his vastly entertaining *Grand dictionnaire de cuisine*, published posthumously in 1873, could find much of a savoury nature to say about coots. Dumas was as well known in his lifetime as a cook as he was for being the author of *Les trois mousquetaires*; it was he who provided the delightful information that when Louis XVIII ate chops, "the chops were not merely grilled; they were grilled between two other chops." In his *Dictionnaire*, Dumas recommended coot only because, like teals and flamingos, they could be eaten on meatless Fridays.

"The coot is like a fish," he wrote. "It looks like a duck and lives out its life on the sea, plunging to the bottom for little shellfish on

955 LD MONTREAL RD
OTTAWA, ON, CA

DATE   TIME   #BR
03/09/04 14:29 #401025S

CARD NUMBER
SEQUENCE # 3614

DEPOSIT $ 1303.14
TD SAVINGS II

CURRENT BALANCE

Protect your PIN
Protégez votre NIP

which it feeds." The male, he thought, was edible, but "the finest cooks have been defeated in the attempt" to cook a female coot that would be fit to eat. "Their best try, coot with chocolate, though a masterpiece of the art, has few admirers." If one were desperate for meat on Friday, he recommended parboiling the plucked coot first, then broiling it on a spit, basted with butter, salt, pepper and vinegar. He advised serving it with a sauce made of its own liver chopped with mushrooms and nutmeg, with the juice of an orange added just before serving.

Dumas was not writing about the American coot; he was probably describing a European relative, *Fulica atra*. The best recipe I've heard for American coot is as follows: Bring a large pot of water to boil; to the boiling water add the coot and a one-foot length of driftwood. Allow both to boil until the driftwood is soft, then throw away the coot and eat the driftwood.

As it turns out, the chicken-foot coot is no coot at all, but a northern Ontario name for the common gallinule (*Gallinula chloropus*), which is itself something of an enigma since the gallinule is seldom if ever found in northern Ontario. It is most often seen along the Great Lakes. It looks something like the American coot, swims with the same head-jerking motion, and is in fact a member of the same family (the rails, or Rallidae). American coots and Canadian gallinules are often mistaken for one another when travelling abroad. But there are differences, and we should note them. The term chicken-foot is a reference to the gallinule's toes, which are smooth and scaly, unadorned with the fleshy, scalloped webs of the American coot. The gallinule speaks a similar but distinct language, and its beak is bright red rather than white. In Hawaiian legend, an American coot felt sorry for human beings because they had no fire, and so it flew to the home of the gods, stole a glowing ember from their fire and returned to Maui with the ember in its beak. On the way, the ember scorched the coot's white beak, turning it red, and it thereby became the gallinule. This legend may also explain why a white forehead patch is called a "blaze."

The gallinule is also less aggressive than the American coot, less individualistic—and here I am tempted to press the national characteristics to their limits. Gallinules are more community-minded. American coots will often be seen swimming alone out in the open part of the marsh, claiming the entire wetland as their own, looking for intruders to drown, whereas gallinules stick closer in among the reeds, "confining themselves," says Taverner, "to the small pools in the marsh or to the clear leads or passages that thread them." When an intruder is detected, gallinules don't fly at it with intent to kill; rather, one of them will begin to make its *kek-kek-kek* sound, and this will be answered by the *kek-kek-kek* of another, and then another, until the whole marsh is alive with indignation and alarm. Then the noise will stop abruptly and things will go on pretty much as they were before the intrusion.

Chicken-foot coot is only one of the gallinule's folk names. It is also called the blue rail, the rice bird and the mud hen. In Quebec it is *la poule d'eau*, which means water-hen. Gabrielle Roy's novel *La petite poule d'eau*, which has been translated as *Where Nests the Water Hen*, perhaps ought to have been called, less euphonically but more accurately, *Where Nests the Chicken-foot Coot*.

Crokinole The most popular indoor game of all.

—*Eaton's Catalogue, Fall/Winter,* 1918

HUSTLING CROKINOLE

Crokinole is a hard game to describe to someone who has never seen a crokinole board, but then it's hard to imagine anyone, at least in Canada, who has never seen a crokinole board. It's that big, round, polished-wood thing with a hole in the centre that you find at lawn and garage sales, country auctions and, increasingly, antique stores specializing in Canadiana. Knowledgeable purchasers will check to make sure the pegs are still there—eight of them, arranged symmetrically around the hole, creating a kind of clearing with a shallow well at the centre—and that there is a full set of twenty-four flat, round, wooden pieces that come with it, twelve blond ones and twelve black ones.

To me, and I suspect to many of my generation who lived in rural Canada, crokinole will always be associated with coming of age, a kind of unstated rite of passage. I grew up in Dalston, Ontario, a small farming community north of Toronto. To someone passing through on Highway 93, Dalston was little more than a thickening concentration of farms between Crown Hill and Craighurst, a crossroads with a general store and gas station, a two-roomed red-brick schoolhouse, a United church and one or two grand houses close to the corner. But to those of us who lived there, Dalston was as complex and intriguing a collection of individuals as anyone could hope for. I lived there only four years; my father was in the Air Force and had been stationed to a base nearby, but he opted to live in Dalston rather than on the base itself because, if you can imagine, it was cheaper. But it seems to me that almost everything useful that I know now I learned in Dalston, from my ninth to my thirteenth year.

Every Friday evening during the winter, the school caretaker, a farmer whose name was (no kidding) Mr. Handy, would push back the desks in both rooms of the school, pour an extra bucket of water down the holes of the two outhouses, and sweep the wooden floor with Dustbane in preparation for the weekly Euchre Party. Euchre is a card game, a (very) simplified form of bridge. The origin of the name is not Canadian—it's from the Dutch *Jucker* and thus related to the English *Joker*—but it is curiously entangled in my mind with the word "eucharist," which gives some idea of how significant these weekly card parties were to rural communities. Going to them was like going to church. The men shaved and combed their hair and dressed up in fresh checked shirts and Sunday pants, and the women wore their second-best dresses and the rather showy brooches their oldest sons gave them two Christmases ago. They brought their own card-tables and folding chairs and set them up in two rows running the length of the main schoolroom, from the teacher's desk at the front to the woodstove and bell rope in back, and they sat four to a table playing euchre and drinking tea out of fine, dainty cups with saucers. And, because euchre is not a particularly challenging game— there are only five cards to a hand, and once you get the hang of it, it's pretty hard to play them in the wrong order—they talked. They talked about the weather and hog prices, they talked about their kids' piano lessons and the Cuban Missile Crisis. They agreed to help Lorne Jory cut his firewood in the fall if he'd lend Allen Brown a couple-three dozen spiles so he could tap a few more maple trees in the spring. They pre-elected Mrs. Ward the next president of the Women's Auxiliary and learned that young Carl Forbes was taking his retainer out of his mouth and putting it in his lunch pail on the way to school.

Kids who came to the euchre parties with their parents were relegated to the other room (Grades 1 to 3). This room was set up like the main room, but instead of playing euchre we played crokinole. We were the older kids—old enough to be left alone in the next room but not old enough to be left alone at home. There was magic in crokinole: the sight of those card-tables, each with its own dark board, the sound of the crokinoles being gathered into piles, like poker chips. It was almost a violent game. If an opponent's crokinole was on the board, you had to hit it with your own crokinole, that was the rule; and if you hit it hard enough, it would slam against the little retaining wall at the edge of the board with a satisfying snap. You could also send a crokinole flying so fast that when it hit the centre hole it would take off like a UFO and slam into your partner's chest. Crokinole existed in an imitation adult world. Like the adults in the next room, we talked about the things that were important to us: schoolyard politics, chores, other kids. We learned about our community as well as about ourselves, we learned how to play as partners rather than as individuals, we learned how to win with dignity and, more importantly, how to lose with grace.

As we grew older, our attention was drawn more and more to what was going on in the next room. Sudden bursts of male laughter would make us look up, finger poised over a crokinole, until it stopped; a shriek from someone's mother told us she had just slapped a bower on her opponent's ace, maybe her husband's. Our bodies were still playing crokinole, but in our minds we were holding the five highest trump cards (called in euchre a jamboree) and drinking tea. We began to regard crokinole as a kind of apprenticeship for euchre, just as later, when we were old enough to move into the next room ourselves (as, one by one, we somehow knew not to go into the crokinole room but nervously to take a seat at one of the card-tables) euchre was to be a proving ground for life.

According to Wayne Kelly of Lucan, Ontario, a founding member of the Lucan Crokinole Club, author of *The Crokinole Book* and owner of the world's largest collection of crokinole boards (fifty-three at last count), "the origin of crokinole is a mystery." When I played Wayne at Toronto's annual Harbourfront Games Fair a few years ago, he told me that the game is a hybrid of the British game squails (a form of shove-ha'penny played on a board instead of a bar) and the Anglo-Indian board game caroms, in which small wooden discs are sent flying into little net pockets at the four corners of the board. "But whereas squails was a pub pastime and caroms was played for money," writes Merilyn Simonds Mohr (my wife in a former incarnation) in *The Games Treasury*, "crokinole was a game of impeccable moral character, associated with neither gambling nor drink." Quite right: in Dalston we neither gambled nor drank. In fact, Merilyn tracked down a reference to crokinole in the 1918 *Eaton's Catalogue* that promoted the game as having "no objectionable features whatever."

Which is, of course, the joke behind the title of Doug Bowie's 1970 television drama *The Krokinol Hustlers.* The play is about a young man who has applied for a job in an obscure corporation and thinks everything that happens to him from then on is part of a test he has to undergo in order to get the job. He doesn't know what the job is, or what the corporation does, or who is testing him; he just knows he has to do whatever he's asked to do—or maybe not. When an old geezer challenges him to a game of crokinole, for example, he agrees, but is then unsure whether he is supposed to win or lose. When he wins, he's accused of being "one of those crokinole hustlers," and he doesn't know whether that is good or bad. "It was all supposed to have a vaguely Kafkaesque feel to it," says Bowie, "the idea of being on trial but not knowing what for. That's why I spelled it 'krokinol,' even though no one got it at the time—they just thought

I didn't know how to spell 'crokinole.' But I wanted the two k's, as in Kafka, and the Kremlin-like associations. It was supposed to be ominous and funny, the idea of someone being accused of hustling crokinole."

The game seems to have been invented in the late nineteenth century by Mennonites in southwestern Ontario, which explains its impeccable moral character. There are no written rules because they are so easy to remember there is no point writing them down. The object is to get your opponent's pieces off the board and to leave yours on. If your opponent has a piece on the board, you have to hit it. If you hit one of your own pieces instead of your opponent's, both your pieces are taken off the board. A piece in the centre hole is worth twenty points (and is removed from the board); a piece inside the ring of pegs is worth fifteen, outside the pegs is ten and around the perimeter of the board is five. After each player has had six turns, add up your scores and the highest score wins. The only debatable rule I know of has to do with whether you can get up out of your chair to get a better angle for a shot, and the rule on that is no, you can't: some part of your seat must remain seated. This is known as "the one-cheek rule," and it results in so much leaning and contorting that some have suggested that crokinole should be elevated from a game to a sport, as ping-pong was when it became table tennis. But most sports I know inhibit conversation, and crokinole does not do that.

According to Wayne Kelly, the game spread from southwestern Ontario into Manitoba when Mennonites did, and also down into New England, possibly on one of the Conestoga wagons that traded between the Pennsylvania Dutch and the Mennonites around Kitchener. The oldest extant board in the United States was made by the M.B. Ross Company of New York; it was made in 1880 and now belongs to Lee Dennis of Massachusetts. But the oldest board Wayne knows about was made in Perth County, Ontario, by a wagonwright named Echardt Whettlanger, who presented it as a birthday present to his five-year-old son Adam in 1875. The difference is that Whettlanger didn't patent his board, and the M.B. Ross Company of New York did.

The name is from the French *croquignole*, which means "a fillip" (the proper word for the flick of the finger that sends a crokinole piece gliding across the board); it also means "a small, round biscuit made of sweet pastry, cut into flat, round discs and deep-fried in fat"—in short, a cookie. In Manitoba, crokinole pieces are still called "cookies," although in Ontario they are usually known as "buttons." As Michael Webster has written in *Harrowsmith* magazine, "it looks as though no one will ever know how it came about that German immigrants crossed a British pub game with an Indian board game, gave it a French name and then thought the story too uninteresting or too unimportant to record. In retrospect, it's hard to imagine an attitude more typically Canadian."

I found my crokinole board at a yard sale on the lawn of a farm-house a few miles north of Kingston. It's a beautiful piece of work: the playing surface is cherry, the trough and octagonal sides distinctively dented but still solid, with square-headed nails holding them together. There is no date on it, but it is quite old. The edges of the hole at the centre have been rounded out by generations of finger-nails picking out the twenty-pointers, and the pegs around the hole are old screws whose rubber sheathing has long since worn away. Playing crokinole on it is like playing a madrigal on an old Martin guitar: you are participating in an ancient and honourable occupation using the right instrument. The pieces are worn and smooth, like pebbles or old coins.

Merilyn and I play on it often, usually out at the cabin, in the winter, when the nights are long and the light is failing. When I am absorbed in lining up a particularly difficult shot, I sometimes look up half expecting to see someone else across from me, someone younger, my brother maybe, waving an egg salad sandwich in the air with one hand and riffling the crokinoles in his trough impatiently with his fingers as he waits for me to take aim and shoot. I am tempted to aim at his fingers. Then I notice there is no chalkboard behind her, and that through the closed cabin door there is no murmer of adult conversation, no clinking of china plates, no triumphant, eucharistic shout. I look at Merilyn oddly for a second or two, or so I'm told, before returning my attention to the board.

Documentary The creative interpretation of actuality.
—John Grierson

ART AS HAMMER

The trouble started before the ship even left the dock. I was preparing for a two-month voyage on the Canadian icebreaker *Louis S. St. Laurent,* to take part in a scientific expedition into the western Arctic Ocean. We were to go from Victoria, through Bering Strait and eventually, weather permitting, to the North Pole. Along with the American icebreaker *Polar Sea*, we would be sailing through the world's largest and most impenetrable icefield, and if we made it, we would be the first ships to reach the Pole from the west. We would be making history. I was along to make a record of the voyage—two records, actually: one in a video documentary and another in a book, the kind that blends science, nature, travel and personal observations, a genre known in Canada as literary nonfiction or sometimes creative documentary. It would be an enormous task, making a film and writing a book at the same time, and the more I thought about it, the more I realized I couldn't do it.

I had thought I'd be able to take along a camera and videotape the expedition—ship ploughing through ice, crew swabbing decks, scientists looking anxious or pensive in their lab coats—while at the same time making notes for the book. In fact, I secretly thought the film footage could *be* my notes. What better way to write a book than to have a filmed record of the trip? The camera and film were being supplied by Galafilm of Montreal, a production company run by my friend Arnie Gelbart. When I got back with umpteen hours of tape, Arnie would get someone to cut and splice it down to a two-hour TV documentary, with script and narration by me. Piece of cake.

Two weeks before the trip, Arnie arranged for me to take a crash course on making a "video diary," a type of film that had become popular in Britain. The BBC handed out Hi-8 video cameras to people doing interesting or wacky things—stalking the Loch Ness Monster, or catching a mining company in the act of dumping toxic waste, or trying to start a community theatre—and the people went around for the next few months or a year filming and filming and filming. Every few weeks they would bring in their spent cassettes and pick up fresh ones and then go back at it. In the end, someone at the BBC would take all the cassettes, edit them down to an hour or two of dramatic documentary, and air them. They were wildly popular. They told real stories. And they looked fun to make.

They also represented an incredible amount of work. None of the video diarists, I noticed, was also writing a book. After the first day of the course Arnie gave me a camera to take back to my hotel room for the night, and the next day I was to bring in a half-hour tape of myself. Me eating. Me brushing my teeth. Me stopping someone on the street and asking directions. Me going into a store and buying a newspaper. People used to making films might find that sort of thing easy, but I found myself becoming extremely annoyed with my own tiresome and self-conscious face. I resented how much time I had to spend thinking about myself. How unnatural it was to try to look natural. And how different from writing a book! To write a book a writer has to disappear, to become a kind of positive void, like a black hole into which all the pertinent information is drawn and rests. Everyone had to forget I was a writer and just talk as though to themselves. I couldn't do that with a camera attached to my face. To make a documentary, I suppose a filmmaker has to disappear too. But a filmmaker disappears by becoming so obviously and constantly present that everyone forgets he is there, like white noise. I had to become merely inconspicuous; I couldn't disappear both ways at once. There suddenly loomed the unnerving prospect of me coming back from the North Pole with neither a film nor a book. A week before we were to leave, Arnie decided to send a real cinematographer along with me. I think the many admirers of Canada's international documentary reputation ought to be extremely grateful to him.

*   *   *

Canada owes its regard as a country particularly adept at producing film documentaries to John Grierson (1898–1972), the first director of the National Film Board. Grierson was born in Scotland, the son of a Calvinist schoolmaster. He studied moral philosophy at Glasgow University and was possessed of a fanatical conviction that if art had any value at all, it was as an instrument for social change. "I look on cinema as a pulpit," he said, "and use it as a propagandist." He came to Canada in 1939 to head up the fledgling NFB, which had been established by Prime Minister Mackenzie King (at Grierson's suggestion) to make films that would bolster morale in Canada for the war effort. Grierson came filled with admiration for Soviet propaganda films like Sergei Eisenstein's *Battleship Potemkin* (Grierson had arranged for its distribution in the United States in 1926) as well as for nonfiction films like Robert Flaherty's *Nanook of the North*. He was keen to carry out the Canadian government's mandate to produce patriotic short films to counter the propagandist newsreels coming out of Nazi Germany. "Art is not a mirror," he once wrote; "art is a hammer." And during his stay in Canada he used that hammer to forge a conscientious film community centred in the NFB.

Grierson considered the documentary film to be a work of art; the best propaganda, he believed, was a film that convinced viewers of its moral integrity by also having artistic integrity. His own first film, *The Drifters* (1929), was a poetic tribute to the Scottish fishermen he had grown up with. "The camera is moving around a very slippery deck," Grierson said in 1933, describing what he did in the film, "noting detail after detail, and part of the time it is poised perilously up on top of the wheelhouse trying to get the swing of the ship." None of this was haphazard; Grierson knew what he wanted and took his time to make sure he got it. He didn't just shoot everything and hope for the best, as I thought I could do in the Arctic. Grierson wanted his film to be "a sort of demonstration . . . of the camera's power of natural observation, taking all the little bits and pieces and binding them together." It's the binding together that makes the bits and pieces a film.

Grierson first used the word "documentary" to describe a film in an anonymous review of Robert Flaherty's *Moana* that appeared in the *New York Sun* in 1926. He applied the term almost disparagingly: he praised the film as "a soft breath from a sunlit island washed by a marvellous sea as warm as the balmy air," and only secondarily acknowledged its "documentary value" as "a visual account of events in the daily life of a Polynesian youth and his family." In later essays he used "documentary" as a noun: "Beyond the newsmen and the magazine men," he wrote in "First Principles of Documentary" in 1932, "one begins to wander into the world of documentary proper, into the only world in which documentary can hope to achieve the ordinary virtues of an art." When he defined "documentary" as "the creative interpretation of actuality," he was leaving the door wide open for art. (Though not for fiction, which he abhorred in film. He never called fictional films "films," but always, somewhat contemptuously, "movies," much as Aldous Huxley, in *Brave New World*, referred to "feelies," and he discouraged the Canadian government from establishing a feature film industry in Canada to counter the influx of movies from the U.S.)

Combining art and social realism has a long literary tradition, and filmmakers before Grierson had recognized the potential of film for bringing about social change. Grierson borrowed the word "documentary" from the French *documentaire*, a category of film that had its roots in French military footage of the First World War. Crews of filmmakers literally collected filmed "documents" of battles and manoeuvres, and these were kept as archives just as still photographs and paper documents were. They weren't propaganda and they weren't art, but they were important sources of information about how the real world worked, or in some cases didn't work, and as such laid the foundations for the more artistic "interpretations of actuality" projected by Grierson.

The military *documentaires* were logical extensions of the very first uses of moving pictures. Louis Lumière invented the moving picture camera, which he called the *cinématographe*, in 1895, and ushered in the ability to create a realistic record of the world around him, a kind of living document. Lumière said he filmed nature *sur le vif*, which differentiated his work from *nature morte*, the still life captured by the box camera. At first he recorded what was literally around him: his first film was of workers leaving the Lumière factory in Lyons. Grierson recalled seeing Lumière's second opus— Lumière's son eating an apple—in Scotland when he was six, and marvelling at "the fine careless rapture" with which Lumière projected real life onto a two-dimensional screen.

Eventually, though, Lumière began to look farther afield. He sent cinematographers—operators specially trained, in fact exclusively licensed, to use his equipment—around the world to show his films as well as to make more films, which they sent back to France to be shown at home. The first motion picture to be shown in Canada was a Lumière film: on June 27, 1896, two "representatives of M. Lumière of Lyons"—a M. Minier and a M. Pupier—invited the mayor of Montreal and other prominent citizens to a private showing at 78 boulevard St. Laurent, a storefront on the Main a few doors up from the harbour. "Animated photography has arrived," declared the Montreal newspaper *La Presse*. The first film shown was of a train arriving at the Lyons-Perrache station: "Nothing is more life-like," declared *La Presse*. "You are really there at the station." This was followed by a cavalry charge, then by waves crashing on an ocean shore, then a card game between Louis Lumière and some friends in a garden, then two priests gesturing, then a wall being torn down, and circus performers doing tricks on horseback. Although the vibrations of the *cinématographe* "spoiled the clarity," at times giving "objects a vaguely dreamlike quality," the *La Presse* reviewer found the event "truly amazing. All that was needed to complete the illusion was colour and a phonograph to reproduce sounds. That is soon to come, we are to believe." Messieurs Minier and Pupier also filmed the first motion picture in Canada: a documentary of dancers at Kahnawake, a Mohawk reserve on the mainland just off the island of Montreal.

As Isabelle Reynauld, a Université de Montréal film professor, has pointed out (in a paper delivered at the Carpenter Center for the Visual Arts, at Harvard University, in 1995), the Lumière catalogues show that early documentary filmmakers did not simply "spontaneously record whatever happened to pass in front of the camera," as is commonly supposed by most film historians—including John Grierson, who dismissed the Lumière productions as "shimmying exoticisms." According to Reynauld, Lumière's operators "asked themselves the same questions that filmmakers have to address today." They had to find a subject, then decide on an angle, in both senses of the term. The length of their films was restricted to fifty seconds—film was available only in twelve-metre strips—and so, when filming a subject or event that took place over a period of time, they had to decide when to turn the camera off and when to turn it back on again. That forced them to consider such cinematographic problems as selection, dramatic impact, interpretation and even plot. They weren't just depicting scenes, or scenics; they were splicing images together to tell a story. "When you think that they only had fifty seconds to grasp, show and outline a given situation," Reynauld points out, "the pioneers' creative constraints were equivalent to today's."

There is nothing new under the paper moon. IMAX films, for example, have a lot in common with the Lumière revolution. IMAX equipment can be run only by licensed operators in specially constructed theatres. So far, only documentaries have been made in the IMAX format. I remember the first one I saw, at Expo '67 (in Montreal), consisted entirely of what was seen through the lens of a camera strapped to the hood of a bobsled, and the whoozy effect in my stomach must have been very similar to that experienced by Lumière's early audiences watching a train coming straight at them in the Lyons station. And IMAX films are restricted to a maximum of fifty minutes because the large, 70-mm format limits the amount of film that a single reel can hold.

"The Canadian psyche seems better suited to information programming than to drama," film critic Martin Knelman wrote in *Home Movies* (1987), "partly because of the documentary traditions established in this country by John Grierson. The essence of drama is conflict, and Canadians—historically and by temperament—tend to avoid conflict."

I don't believe it. Information programming can be dramatic, for one thing. And there was a documentary tradition in Canada long before Grierson got here; Grierson simply showed us how to apply it to film. Knelman is right in the sense that what we responded to in Grierson's vision was his celebration of realism as a legitimate medium for art, because we have always held realism closer to our hearts than idealism. The rest of Knelman's statement, the bit about conflict and temperament, is the old Canadian myth, which goes something like this: The history of the United States is the struggle of idealism and romanticism against practicality and common sense, with the former winning more often than not. The American Revolution was the imposition of idealistic fervour over political reality; the settling of the American West was the romantic triumph of the individual over the forces of nature. As Northrop Frye stated, "a Canadian is an American who has rejected the Revolution." Canada gained its independence from England not in pitched battles but through a century-long legal process; our revolution is known as "The Repatriation of the Constitution." And when we settled the Prairies, we sent an armed police force out first to make sure law and order would prevail over the chaotic forces of the wild.

There is some truth to this, but the fact is that Canadians have always had a healthy respect for reality; our climate demanded it, and our literature reflected it long before film came along. Documentary film was simply an opportunity to go out and record that reality in a new way. Grierson gave us permission to manipulate reality slightly in order to make it tell the truth. We'd been doing it all along anyway; Grierson and his followers merely pointed out that it is impossible *not* to "interpret actuality" when you create art.

Look at the symbolism. In the early days of the motion picture, two kinds of camera were invented almost simultaneously. In France, Lumière produced the *cinématographe* in 1895; in the United States, Thomas Edison invented what he called the kinetoscope in 1894. The *cinématographe* weighed about five kilograms, could be packed in a small box and operated by one person; it was hand-cranked, the handcrafted wooden box could be used to develop film, and the camera itself could be turned into a projector. A cinematographer could go out during the day, film a local event, develop the film in his hotel room and screen his *documentaire* to an admiring public that same evening. It was a portable, self-contained field unit.

On the other hand, as Erik Barnouw points out in *Documentary: A History of the Non-Fiction Film* (1974), Edison's kinetoscope was "an unwieldy monster." It weighed fifty kilograms, required several people to operate it, worked on electricity, and could only be used in a special building Edison had erected in West Orange, New Jersey —a tarpaper shack that he called "the Black Maria." While the Lumière camera allowed filmmakers to go out and film events as they actually occurred, to film subjects who were not aware they were being filmed, Edison's subjects had to be brought to the Black Maria; his films were studio films and his subjects were intensely aware that they were being filmed. They were acting.

Edison's kinetograph, in other words, led directly to the studio productions and Hollywood; it never caught on in Canada. In Canada it was Lumière's *cinématographe* that conformed most perfectly with what we wanted to do with our films. This had nothing to do with Grierson's heavy-handed influence: we invited him here.

The first film made in Canada—the 1896 film depicting Mohawk dancers at Kahnawake—was a documentary (and it was staged, by the way: it was filmed in summer, but the dancers were obviously told to wear their more colourful winter costumes). The first feature film in Canada wasn't made until 1914, when the Canadian Bioscope Company of Halifax did *Evangeline*, a Canadian story that they based on an American poem and for which they hired American actors, thus establishing another Canadian tradition.

Under Grierson, the National Film Board became one of the most important producers of documentary films in the world. Grierson undertook to carry out the NFB's original mandate, which was "to interpret Canada to Canadians and to other nations, to 'imaginate' the country (create it in the imagination of its people) and to bring it alive to itself as a distinct entity within North America." This was a task so unique that it required the reinvention of the word "imaginate" to express it, and the NFB responded by attracting the best film minds in the world: Flaherty came up for a while, as did Boris Kaufman, Stuart Legg supervised the *World in Action* series that depicted Canada's domestic response to the Second World War, Wolf Koenig and Colin Low (whose *City of Gold*, a 1957 documentary of Dawson City during the Klondike years, narrated by Pierre Berton, won an Academy Award), Norman McLaren, Donald Brittain. The NFB's central role in Canadian film production has sadly declined since the early 1980s, when the Applebaum–Hébert Report called the Board "irrelevant" and the federal government fell in love with American-style feature films, an affair it tried to articulate in its Film & Video Policy in 1984, which recommended the severe cuts in funding that have since crippled the NFB as a creative entity.

Documentary still informs and distinguishes Canadian films, however, and numerous features by Canadian filmmakers contain sudden and illuminating slices of documentary. The recent re-release of Claude Jutra's *Mon Oncle Antoine*, for instance, prompted Noreen Golfman, re-reviewing it in *Canadian Forum,* to call it "a fictional ciné-document of what Lucien Bouchard prefers to identify as a 'people.'" Would that be like imagining Quebec? Golfman also praises Don Shebib's *Goin' Down the Road* "for some of the same documentary-flavoured reasons." Moving out of the realm of art, the recent Hollywood blockbuster movie of all time, *Titanic*, directed by Canadian filmmaker James Cameron, opens and closes with a documentary-flavoured framing device: the supposed efforts of a contemporary salvage company to dredge up the remains of the doomed ocean liner from the bottom of the Atlantic Ocean (in reality, from the bottom of a 17-million-gallon tank Cameron had constructed in Mexico). For reasons that should by now be obvious, Cameron thought it was important to establish documentary veracity for the Cinderella plot line that churns in the guts of the movie, as though he were trying to disguise the fact that he was making fiction. It was galling, nonetheless, to see the *Titanic*'s survivors being taken to New York (the Statue of Liberty raising her torch in welcome) when we know that in fact they were taken to Halifax. But a tradition is a tradition. It's just that culture is memory, and it is a terrible thing when memory clashes with tradition.

*   *   *

The cinematographer Arnie sent along on the expedition to help make the documentary was Stefan Nitoslawski. Stefan did what I could not: he became a fixture on board the ship, showing up at all hours with his camera, filming and filming until his presence ceased to make everyone nervous. He filmed 110 hours of footage, much of it reminiscent of Grierson's description of *The Drifters*—waves crashing over the bow, the yawing of the ship during storms, views from the top of the wheelhouse that give a tremendous sense of space, which is essentially what the High Arctic is. Much of it was also straight newsreel stuff: the coastguard crew swabbing the decks, the scientists looking anxiously at their instruments. As for me, I made scratchy little notes in my notebooks, trying to disappear into the background, still thinking I would use Stefan's film when I got back to refamiliarize myself with the events of the trip that he had documented so thoroughly.

But in the end I wrote the book from my scratchy little notes. I didn't want to review the trip in its actuality; I wanted to imaginate it in my own mind. I found that a couple of sentences scribbled on a page invoked whole conversations, entire afternoons, in my memory, but when I watched Stefan's raw footage all I recalled was what was recorded right there on the film. Nothing existed beyond what was depicted on the screen; the screen was its own reality, its own memory. This is, to my mind, a very curious fact and a serious indictment of television. If culture is memory, what kind of culture is a TV culture?

When we got back to Montreal, Arnie's editors scissored and pasted Stefan's tapes into a two-hour documentary called *By Icebreaker to the North Pole*, which has been shown half a dozen times on American television but has yet to be aired by a Canadian network. The book I wrote, *The Quiet Limit of the World*, has been published in Canada but not in the United States.

Dominion See "dangerous."

Dangerous From OF *dongier*, from LL *dominium*, rule, "subject to the jurisdiction of." If true, this derivation shows how subjects feared their overlords.

—*Dictionary of Word Origins*, 1945, Joseph T. Shipley

THE KINGDOM OF CANADA

"In 1867, Canada became a Dominion," Ralph Connor noted somewhat offhandedly in his autobiography, *Postscript to Adventure*. Ralph Connor was the pen name of the Reverend Charles Gordon, who grew up in Ontario's Glengarry County. "I was seven years old," he continued. "I don't remember hearing a word about this great achievement, even in the manse."

Becoming an independent nation would have been a great achievement, a cause for national celebration. Becoming a dominion was not. Calling Canada a dominion was an act of the baldest cynicism on the part of England and ought to have incited rioting even in the streets of Glengarry, if Glengarry had streets. In law if not in effect, it meant that nothing whatsoever had changed in regard to Canada's legal ties with England, and it underscored the uneasy relationship Canada has had with the United States. It meant that the dream of John A. Macdonald would remain (and remains) unrealized. It is because of this infernal word "dominion" that I grit my teeth every time I visit my daughter.

Canada became a dominion by virtue of the British North America Act of 1867, supposedly to distinguish it from more obviously dependent members of the British Empire—Dominica, for example, which was an out-and-out colony. Canadians supposed at the time that "dominion" signified quasi-equality with the mother country. We should have checked our dictionaries. The word is from the Latin *dominium*, which actually means "absolute possession," and indicates that which is owned or ruled by a despot. In the Bible, man is given "dominion" over the fish of the sea, the fowl of the air, the cattle of the land, "and over all the earth, and over every creeping thing that creepeth upon the earth" (Genesis 1:26)—by which we are not meant to suppose that *Homo sapiens* existed in a state of quasi-equality with any of those things. Man *hath* dominion; the creepie-crawlies *were* a dominion. There is a difference. Canadians celebrating "Dominion Day" were rather like members of the French aristocracy whooping it up on Bastille Day.

One gets a sense of this in the poem "Canada to England" by the very perceptive nineteenth-century Canadian writer Isabella Valancy Crawford. Composed shortly after Confederation, the poem ostensively celebrates Canada's new-found status as England's "warrior kinsman." But note the ambiguity in the second stanza:

The times have won a change. Nature no more
Lords it alone and binds the lonely land
A serf to tongueless solitudes; but Nature's self
Is led, glad captive, in light fetters rich
As music-sounding silver can adorn;
And man has forged them, and our silent God
Behind His flaming worlds smiles on the deed.
"Man hath dominion"—words of primal might;
"Man hath dominion"—thus the words of God.

Crawford was reminding Canadians that being a dominion wasn't the same as being independent. Perhaps she knew that a "dominion" was the last thing the Fathers of Confederation wanted Canada to be. The articles of the BNA Act, drawn up at the Charlottetown Conference in 1864, clearly stated that the new nation would be called the Kingdom of Canada, not the Dominion of Canada. This was the designation favoured by John A. Macdonald, who took it from a proposal put forth by Sir John Beverley Robinson in 1822 and reiterated two years later by Bishop Strachan. In November 1866, John A. and fifteen other delegates from British North America travelled to England to present the terms of this earlier Charlottetown accord to the Colonial Office for ratification. This was done on December 25. In January, after consulting with the colonial minister, Lord Carnarvon, two changes were made in the Resolutions before the Act was read in Parliament: the number of senators could be increased from 72 to 78 by the Queen, if she so wished; and the name of the new nation was changed from the Kingdom of Canada to the Dominion of Canada. The increase in senatorial appointments raised no particular alarm among the Canadian representatives—no one really cared about the Senate even before there was one. But the name change infuriated Macdonald, and for two very powerful reasons—one to do with Canada's relationship to England, and the other to do with Canada's relationship with the United States.

The majority of Canada's Fathers of Confederation were of Scottish descent, and they must have seen in the relationship between Canada and England many of the same problems that existed between England and Scotland. In the nineteenth century many Scottish patriots wished for a return to a separate Kingdom of Scotland, and there were many Scottish patriots in Canada, most of them from the fiercely independent-minded Highland clans. At the time of Confederation, 16 percent of Canadians were of Scottish descent, and Scots controlled virtually every branch of political power, from the leadership of the parties to the editorship of every significant newspaper. There is no doubt that, in wanting this new country to be called the Kingdom of Canada, the Scottish delegates to England knew exactly what they were demanding. And there can also be little doubt that, in inking out the word "Kingdom" and writing "Dominion" in its place, the British Crown knew exactly what it was doing.

The second reason was equally galling. Macdonald must have seen that Scotland's attitude towards the English—whom Sir Walter Scott referred to as "the Southern men"—was similar in its intensity to the attitude towards the United States that was taking hold in Canada. Still fulminating about the name change in 1889, Macdonald explained in a letter to Lord Knutsford that the name was changed "at the insistence of Lord Derby, then foreign minister, who feared the first name would wound the sensibilities of the Yankees." The British colonial office, in other words, feared that the Americans would not be best pleased to have a fully independent nation—a kingdom no less, bigger than itself—as its nearest neighbour; much better to have a semi-subservient colony, a dominion, with which future annexation would be a matter of diplomatic wrangling with London rather than all-out war with Canada. England feared any kind of confrontation with the United States: Lord Derby, who was Leader of the House of Commons, was later described by Benjamin Disraeli as "dwelling in a region of perpetual funk" at the prospect of locking horns with the United States.

The popular belief that it was Sir Leonard Tilley who suggested "dominion" at the London Conference after consulting his Bible and coming upon the phrase in Psalm 72—"He shall have dominion also from sea to sea, and from the river unto the ends of the earth"—is a piece of hokum promulgated by Tilley's son in a letter to G.S. Holmstead dated June 28, 1917, nearly fifty years after the fact. Tilley's biblical excursion may have suggested Canada's motto—*A mari usque ad mare*—which was formally adopted in 1921, but the term "dominion" had been in use to describe British-owned foreign soil for at least three hundred years. Sir Francis Drake envisioned "Dominions across the sea" where displaced Englishmen would dwell, and the American *Journals of the Continental Congress* (1774) record that at that Congress, called to discuss the independence of the Thirteen Colonies (and the possibility of Canada becoming the fourteenth), it was noted that "by another Act the dominion of Canada is to be extended, modelled, and governed" by the new United States. The Americans were calling Canada a dominion more than a century before Canada existed, and that is why we do today. As W.L. Morton observes in *The Kingdom of Canada: A General History from Earliest Times*, "Once more Canadian sentiment and interest were sacrificed to Anglo-American consideration," a sacrifice that "was to cost Canada much confusion of thought over the next two generations."

Canada was the first country to be called a dominion. It was the first of the "old" dominions, along with Australia, New Zealand, South Africa and Newfoundland, to be given sovereign independence with the passing of the Statute of Westminster in 1931. Other dominions enjoying such status now include Trinidad and Tobago, Jamaica, Malta, Barbados, Mauritius, Tonga and Fiji. Former dominions that are now republics include Ireland, India, Ceylon, Cyprus, half of Africa, Singapore and Bangladesh (with Australia in the process of becoming one). Calling a country a dominion simply meant that it enjoyed complete freedom to manage its own internal affairs as well as to negotiate commercial treaties with foreign countries, but that all matters involving political or military relationships with other powers were to be handled by the Imperial government, although usually in consultation with Dominion representatives. As, for example, when Canada was asked to supply troops to the British Expeditionary Forces during the Boer War: Sir Wilfrid Laurier refused at first, blustering "that Canada was a nation perfectly independent, that the lien of the Empire over us did not weigh the weight of one feather, but that we were just as independent today, under the suzerainty of England, as we could be if absolutely independent." But he dutifully sent the troops when England told him to.

According to the Constitution Act of 1982, we are still officially called the Dominion of Canada, although the word has fallen into disuse. Dominion Day is now called Canada Day, the old Dominion Observatory Time Signal—ten short beeps followed by a ten-second silence, then one long beep—which used to be heard on the Dominion Network at one o'clock, is now the National Research Council Official Time Signal and is heard on the CBC.

Have we finally sensed that being a dominion is not quite the same thing as being an independent nation? If so, it may be helpful to note that nowhere in the BNA Act are we actually referred to as the Dominion of Canada; what the Act enacts is "that it shall be lawful for the Queen, by and with the advice of Her Majesty's Most Honourable Privy Council, to declare, by proclamation, that on and after the day therein appointed, the provinces of Canada, Nova Scotia and New Brunswick shall form one and be one dominion under the name of Canada."

Still, Sir John A. would have had it read "one kingdom," and he didn't give a damn what the Americans thought about it. Which is why I grit my teeth every time I visit my daughter. She lives in a small apartment on Wellington Street in Kingston, a building constructed by John A. in 1834 and in which he opened his first law practice a year later. Beside the main entrance to the building there is a bronze commemorative plaque that reads:

In this Building
John A. Macdonald
Father of Confederation
and
First Prime Minister
of the
Dominion of Canada
Began the
Practice of Law in 1835

The inscription is followed by the information that the plaque was manufactured in the United States by the Lake Shore Markers Company of Erie, Pennsylvania.

Filles du roi At first New France was a country of explorers, fur traders and colonists. So few women wanted to come that, to correct the imbalance, certain drastic measures had to be adopted, the most important of which was sending over the "Filles du Roy" in 1665.

> —*La civilisation traditionelle de l'habitant'*
> *aux 17e et 18e siècles, 1967,* Robert-Lionel Séguin

FIGURES IN THE FIRST GARDEN

Jacques Parizeau delivered his career-ending speech immediately after the 1995 Quebec referendum. In it, he implied that if only true Quebeckers had voted, then Quebec's destiny as an independent nation would have been assured. Instead, he said, the sovereigntist or "Oui" side in the referendum had been defeated by "money and the ethnic vote," by which he meant immigrants and Jews. The stunned silence with which these racist remarks were received even by members of Parizeau's Parti Québécois was followed almost immediately by his resignation.

Parizeau should have known better. Earlier that year, another Quebec politician had been bumped from the federal cabinet for having uttered essentially the same sentiment. Bloc Québécois MP Philippe Paré had been removed from two important committees by Bloc leader Lucien Bouchard for having expressed the opinion that only *pures laines* Quebeckers should decide the province's future in a public referendum. *Pure laine* was rendered as "old stock" in the newspapers reporting Paré's remarks—and later, Parizeau's speech—but the phrase literally means "pure wool," or perhaps even "virgin wool." Thus, after the referendum, Mordecai Richler announced that he was sponsoring a new literary prize, which he called the Prix Parizeau, for "the best work of fiction by a Quebec ethnic impure wool person."

Writers continue to chew over the implications of "ethnocentricity"—for which, read racism—in Quebec culture. In her controversial book *L'arpenteur et le navigateur* (*The Surveyor and the Navigator*, 1997), for example, Monique LaRue examines the role of nationalism in literature, quoting a Québécoise writer who laments that "the most recent generation of immigrant writers write works that . . . show none of the linguistic characteristics that have established Quebec literature in the francophone world." LaRue mentions David Homel as an example, a Jewish novelist from Chicago who moved to Montreal in 1986; she also refers to French novelist Louis Ferdinand Céline, whose work has consistently been attacked for its blatant anti-Semitism, as "one of the greatest writers of our time." These and other issues raised in *L'arpenteur et le navigateur* were discussed in *Canadian Forum* in an article called "The Pure Laine Debate."

Who are these *pures laines*, I wondered. As I've said, the phrase means "pure wool," although clothing manufacturers usually render it on labels as "virgin wool," which implies, one supposes, purer than pure (but not, apparently, unadulterated: in nineteenth-century England there was an ointment known as either "virgin barm" or "bastard barm," depending, perhaps, on one's religion). A *pure laine* is a contemporary Quebecker who can trace his or her family history back to earliest times—purer than pure Quebeckers, in other words. One evening I was attending a dinner party in Ottawa and found myself seated next to a charming woman who told me that she had been born in Quebec and was from one of Quebec's oldest families. She had married a lawyer, also from an old Quebec family, and so I asked her if she and her husband considered themselves to be *pures laines*.

In Ottawa, every question has its political connotations, and for a moment she must have thought I was asking whether or not she supported the Parti Québécois, or how she had voted in the referendum. Both questions would have been impertinent. When I assured her that I was interested only in the meaning of the term *pure laine*, she said that yes, she supposed they did, or at least that others probably would.

"How far back do you trace your Quebec roots?" I asked her.

"Quite far," she said. "Several generations. I haven't really checked back all the way."

"As far back as the Conquest?" I asked. The defeat of the French army on the Plains of Abraham was in September 1759, about five or six generations ago—not that far back to a genealogist.

"Yes," she said, pursing her lips consideringly. "Perhaps that far."

I thought I could get away with one last question and still remain within the bounds of polite dinner-table conversation. I was wrong. "As far back, perhaps, as the *filles du roi?*"

Her eyes widened in horror. Colour drained from her forehead into her cheeks. She swung her upper body away from me in her chair and cast an outraged regard in my direction. "*Les filles du roi?*" she nearly shouted. "*Les filles du roi?* Do you know what you are saying, monsieur?"

"Well, I—"

She rapidly recomposed herself and lowered her voice. "I was taught in school by nuns, and from what they told us, *les filles du roi* were nothing but prostitutes! The nuns called them *les filles de joie*. Are you implying that my family and my husband's family are descended from prostitutes?"

"Of course not," I protested, the ignorant *Anglais*. "They weren't all prostitutes, were they? Some of them—"

"Monsieur," she said, placing her hand on my wrist. "If you go around saying that *pures laines* means being descended from *les filles du roi*, you are going to offend a lot of people. A lot of very important people." And she leaned towards me and looked straight into my eyes. "We don't go back that far."

*   *   *

There are a surprising number of Quebeckers who can trace their family histories back to the settlement era. Many of the original families married amongst themselves, and still do, and as a result Quebec's gene pool is particularly unalloyed, so much so that researchers wanting to isolate specific genetic characteristics, such as obesity, or proneness to having twins, or certain heart conditions, or diabetes, conduct their studies in Quebec. Whether this homogeneity extends to voting preferences, as Parizeau evidently believed, is something geneticists cannot determine, but the fact remains that *les pures laines* comprise a compact and definable segment of North American society, which makes for good science if not for good politics.

But, as I learned in Ottawa, not all of them extend back to the small group of women known as *les filles du roi*. These were women sent to New France during the reign of Louis xiv to become wives of what constituted an overabundance of male colonists. The usual translation of the phrase, "the king's daughters," is somewhat misleading. In seventeenth- and eighteenth-century France, *les filles* had several meanings, depending on the context: daughters, girls, loose women, maids or servants, or factory workers. Colonists in New France would have been aware of all of these nuances. Sylva Clapin, the Quebec writer who in 1894 compiled one of the first dictionaries of the Quebec language, noted that in Quebec the word *fille* "doesn't have the usually dishonest sense that one attaches to it in

France." In France, a young man who frequented *les filles* was consorting with prostitutes (in fact, *les filles du roi* may have been a pun on *les filles des rues*). But in Quebec, *fille* was more often used to denote a servant or a maid, or a worker: *une fille de moulin, une fille de factorie*. In seventeenth-century New France, *les filles du roi* would have been understood in all of those senses: the French Crown was sending over women of doubtful virtue or parentage to become wives, servants or workers in New France.

The first census taken in Canada, conducted by Jean Talon in 1666, showed the total population of the colony was 3,215, of which more than 2,000 were unmarried men. There were only 528 families. There were, in addition, 1,200 unmarried troops. Talon offered the troops large grants of land—promising seigneuries to the officers—if they would remain in the colony after the campaign against the Iroquois instead of returning to France. At the same time, he petitioned Louis xiv to send over five hundred colonists a year in order to maintain the stability of the colony.

The King replied that he could not spare five hundred able-bodied men, but that he would send over marriageable women instead, who would eventually produce able-bodied men. Accordingly, the first "bride ship" arrived in 1668 with one hundred and fifty *filles du roi* on board. As I told my dinner companion, not all of them were prostitutes. Some came from rural France, unmarried for any of a number of reasons. Some were from Paris orphanages. But many *were* reformed prostitutes. Whatever their origins, very few *filles du roi* came to Canada willingly. "New France has a bad reputation in the mother country," writes Quebec novelist Anne Hébert in *The First Garden* (1990). "People speak of a 'place of horror' and of the 'suburbs of hell.' Peasant women need coaxing. They have to turn to the Salpêtrière, that home for former prostitutes, to populate the colony."

The Salpêtrière was more than a home for prostitutes, however. It was once a prison for women (many of whom were undoubtedly prostitutes, and not necessarily former prostitutes), but it later became a refuge for aged and indigent women, a kind of poorhouse. Its reputation as a home for prostitutes probably comes from its name. We think of saltpetre as a physic given to criminals and Boy Scouts to dullen the sexual impulse, but in fact saltpetre is simply potassium nitrate and, as the principal ingredient of gunpowder, could just as easily have a reputation for exciting the passions and so should probably not be given to criminals or Boy Scouts. In any case the Salpêtrière in Paris got its name from having begun life in 1656 as a gunpowder factory.

But it is true that a woman chosen to be a *fille du roi* needed a certain amount of urging to come to Canada. Each was therefore given a dowry of fifty livres, a few household items and free transportation to Canada on one of the "bride ships." Quebec poet Alain Grandbois, in his biography of the explorer Louis Jolliet, *Né à Québec* (1933), draws a colourful picture of the arrival of one of the bride ships in the harbour at Quebec City:

Sails idle, furled the length of the stay, the ship slowly swung about, unsure of her mooring. The captain gesticulated.

Suddenly, in the commotion of the manoeuvres, amidst the cries and curses of the officers, came peals of gay, feminine laughter as a lively, colourful group of girls crowded together on the fo'c's'le. In no time a cry arose in the taverns of the fort and spread through all the town. "The King's girls! The King's girls!"

The entire population of Quebec ran down to the river. Shoved by rough hands, boats grated on the rocks. Young men, ill at ease in brand new clothes, were taken aboard. To keep themselves in countenance, some of them tried out gay wisecracks. Already, from the sailing ship, elbows on the gunwale, bantering sailors challenged them. The girls were silent. And now, as the boats nudged the hull of the ship, anxious eyes scanned the fo'c's'le as each young man tried to make out the unknown face of his future bride.

The list of suitors with the names, ages, trades and conditions was read aloud. Then those of the marriageable girls. Hammered upon the silence, the beautiful syllables of French provinces indicated a blonde, a brunette or a redhead. Normandy, the most often repeated. Then Orléans, Poitou, Bourgogne, Touraine. Sometimes Paris. Less often Provence. And blue-eyed girls with wistful faces shivered at the name Bretagne. The young man having the best credentials had the first choice.

This picture has a slightly roseate tint. Many of the unmarried men in New France were as reluctant to marry a *fille du roi* as the *filles du roi* had been to accept the King's invitation. Talon had to resort to the law to ensure that the women were married off as quickly as possible. He legislated grievous fines to any man who refused to marry a *fille du roi*. In Ville-Marie (Montreal), François Lenoir was brought to court and fined 150 livres for his refusal to marry. The urgency of the situation is made clear in a letter from Jean-Baptiste Colbert, the French foreign minister, to Talon:

> I pray you, commend it to the consideration of everyone that their prosperity, their sustenance and all that is dear to them depend on a general resolution, never to be departed from, to marry: youths at eighteen or nineteen, and girls at fourteen or fifteen. Those who may seem to have absolutely renounced marriage, should be made to bear additional burdens, and be excluded from all honours. It would be well even to add some mark of infamy.

The reference to girls of fourteen or fifteen suggests that many of the *filles du roi* were indeed orphans.

Talon responded by decreeing that unmarried men were forbidden by law to spend more than twenty-four hours outside the settlement. Furthermore, "all discharged soldiers, some of them dealing as brigands, will be barred from fur-trading and hunting and the honours of the Church and the religious communities if, within a fortnight after the arrival of the *filles du roi*, they have not married."

As the women debarked from the bride ships that landed in Montreal, they were taken to the home of Marguerite Bourgeoys, who had founded the Congrégation de Notre-Dame de Montréal, a version of the Congrégation's convent in Troyes to which young women were taken for instruction in religious matters and teaching. At Marguerite Bourgeoys's establishment the *filles du roi* were trained for their future role as the wives of settlers. Sewing and knitting they had been taught at Salpêtrière; calving and chicken-dressing they had yet to learn. It was also to Marguerite Bourgeoys's home that young men came to look over the new arrivals and choose a wife. Priests were on hand, and mass marriages of thirty and forty couples were not uncommon.

In all, more than a thousand *filles du roi* were sent over between 1665 and 1672. The number of families in the colony doubled in the first three years, and baptisms rose to 1,100. This means that within six years of the 1666 census the women in nearly two-thirds of the households in New France were *filles du roi*. As one historian has remarked, "there are few French Canadians today who do not own within their veins the blood of some of these King's girls." At any rate, "virgin wool" is probably not the most felicitous translation of *pure laine*; something like "homespun" might be safer.

*   *   *

I certainly had no intention of insulting my dinner companion by suggesting that her family was descended from *les filles du roi*. I was
simply curious about the phrase *pures laines*. Especially coming from
the mouth of Jacques Parizeau. I still find his attitude towards "money
and the ethnic vote" curious. Immigrants to Quebec—known in the
Quebec language as *les allophones*—have played an enormously valuable role in establishing the openness and enthusiasm for life and literature with which I, at least, associate Quebec culture.

There are many examples from which to choose, but I will take
just one: the case of the novelist Alicja Poznanska. Born in Cracow,
Poland, in 1930, she was barely ten years old when the Germans
invaded her country, and she was a runner in the Polish resistance in
Warsaw until she was captured by the Nazis and, although Catholic,
sent to Bergen-Belsen. She escaped from the concentration camp in
1944 and walked back to Poland, where she discovered that her parents were dead, and where she was molested by the Russian army
that had liberated Poland from the Germans. After the war she was
awarded Poland's Iron Cross for bravery in the face of the enemy, and
allowed to go to Paris to study. In 1955 she emigrated to Quebec, married a Québécois and began writing; her novels have titles like *Flight*
(1963) and *Surviving* (1964). For some reason, only one has ever been
translated into English—by an American translator: *The Lilacs Are
Blooming in Warsaw* (1981), which won the Prix Européen and was
called by Eugène Ionesco "one of the best novels I have had the pleasure of reading." In it, she writes about a young woman of thirteen
named Helena who fought in the Polish resistance, was raped by her
Russian liberators, and survived to become a respected and humani-
tarian writer. In the novel, Helena dreams of her grandmother, who,
like Helena, has suffered horribly at the hands of Poland's newcomers. "My dear," her grandmother tells her, "in our day God spoke not
only Polish, but also the language of the Jews. Never forget that."

Under her maiden name Poznanska wrote for Pierre Trudeau's magazine *Cité libre*, calling for a recognition of differences and rejecting the kind of frenzied purist idolatry that gave rise to Nazism and which she, like Trudeau, detected in the Quebec nationalist movement. In an essay published in 1961 about freedom of expression in Gaullist France, she warned that a citizenry cannot be passive about its right to speak out: "Freedom," she wrote, "is not a vague word, or an abstract value, and the greatness of a country depends on the ability of its citizens to reason, to vibrate, to act freely. When people allow themselves to be led by the nose by one man or one party, their national character is always depleted."

The Québécois she married in 1956, and with whom she remained until her death in 1990, was Jacques Parizeau.

Garrison mentality Small and isolated communities surrounded with a physical or psychological "frontier."

—*The Bush Garden*, 1971, Northrop Frye

Garrison (*adj.*) Of, associated with, or having a garrison: *Kingston is a garrison town.*

—*Gage Canadian Dictionary*, 1997

ACROSS THE RIVER AND OUT OF THE BUSH GARDEN

Before going up to Northrop Frye's office to interview him for a profile I was writing for *Saturday Night*, I dawdled for some time in the E.J. Pratt Library. The library is part of Victoria University, the University of Toronto enclave where Frye had been a student and then a professor for more than fifty years. There was a painting in the library that I liked—a dreamy mountainscape, all cobalt blue and icy white, with rivers of glaciers oozing down between jagged peaks. Though it was clearly meant to depict the awesome power of nature, I found it calming.

There was another painting in the library, however, that soothed me not at all. It was Douglas Martin's portrait of Northrop Frye, a piece no less impressionistic than the first, but the impression was more nightmarish than dreamy. This is how I described it in the profile of Frye I eventually wrote:

In the foreground is a fairly conventional representation of Frye sitting, knees together, hands folded on his right leg. The expression behind the rimless glasses and below the shock of once-red hair is one of hard-earned confidence, stony imperturbability, and limitless impatience. But it is the background that attracts attention: Frye is suspended, without even a chair, in the overcast sky above a vast, treeless wasteland of barren cliffs and a wild, divided river, like a modern, rumple-suited Christ transfiguring himself out of a Biblical wilderness.

Martin's painting is brilliant because the landscape stretching out behind the irascible figure of Frye is a perfect representation of Frye's view not only of Canadian nature but also of Canadian literature, which he saw as a barren wasteland dotted here and there with pale green attempts at civilization—failed, for the most part. He once wrote that to be an educated literary critic turning one's attention to Canadian literature was like being a giraffe trying to eat grass.

He was equally appalled by nature red in tooth and claw. To further paraphrase Tennyson, dragons of the prime that tare each other in their slime were never mellow music to Frye. Nature to him was malevolent, chaotic, unformed and demonically opposed to the human struggle towards sweetness and light; nature was the opposite of intellect and civilization. "Anything that isn't bourgeois," he told me when I finally went up to beard the literary lion in his den, "is strictly in the trees." The phrase aptly reflects Frye's attitude both to literature and to trees.

Frye nonetheless wrote a lot about nature, both directly and inadvertently. Many of his literary metaphors—like the one about the giraffe—are drawn from nature. His book on the Canadian imagination, published in 1971 but written over the preceding thirty years, was called *The Bush Garden* (a phrase he says he "pilfered" from Margaret Atwood's *Journals of Susanna Moodie*). In it he likened the Canadian imagination to a vast, undifferentiated forest full of beasts in which is found only the occasional roughly hewn cultural clearing, which always astonished him rather as Conrad was surprised when he came across an illiterate below-decks halfwit mouthing his way through a newspaper. In his preface Frye stated that "it is with human beings as with birds: the creative instinct has a great deal to do with the assertion of territorial rights"; in the same paragraph, "there is always something vegetable about the imagination." And later: "If evaluation is one's guiding principle, criticism of Canadian literature would become only a debunking project, leaving it a poor naked *alouette* plucked of every feather of decency and dignity."

These are images that come readily to anyone born and raised, as Frye was, in Canada (he was born in Sherbrooke, Quebec, and grew up in Moncton, New Brunswick), and are not indications of any particular love for or affinity with nature; they are simply the tools Canadian writers come up with when they delve into their mental toolboxes for metaphors. When Frye wrote directly and deliberately about nature, however, he portrayed it as a menacing presence, a threatening physical reality that he made the very antithesis of art. "One is surprised to find," he wrote as early as 1943, in a review of A.J.M. Smith's anthology *The Book of Canadian Poetry*, "how few really good Canadian poets have thought that getting out of cities into God's great outdoors really brings one closer to the sources of inspiration." In this important essay Frye clearly stated his preference for poetry that depicted nature as a destructive force:

> Canadian poetry is at its best a poetry of incubus and *cauchemar*, the source of which is the unusually exposed contact of the poet with nature which Canada provides. Nature is seen by the poet, first as unconsciousness, then as a kind of existence which is cruel and meaningless, then as the source of the cruelty and subconscious stampedings within the human mind . . . Nature is consistently sinister and menacing in Canadian poetry.

For Frye, nature was always something brutal to be got beyond, some tree to be climbed out of, some satanic force to be repudiated by intellect. In a powerfully visionary paragraph towards the end of the review, Frye extolled the virtue of E.J. Pratt's long poem *Brébeuf and His Brethren*, which he called "the greatest single Canadian poem." In it, Brébeuf, "the man with the vision," is tied to a stake and destroyed "by savages who are in the state of nature, and who represent its mindless barbarity." He equates the Iroquois Jesuit-killers with somewhat more contemporary villains: "However frantically they may try to beat [Brébeuf's vision] off, their way of savagery is doomed; it is doomed in their Nazi descendants; it is doomed even if it lasts to the end of time." (It may be helpful to remember here that Frye, a Methodist minister, was considering a poem featuring Catholic missionaries, written by Pratt, the son of a Methodist minister and Frye's colleague at Victoria, a Methodist college. Earle Birney, reviewing the same poem in *Canadian Forum* in 1940, found Pratt's depiction of "the religious motivations and experiences of the Huron missionaries . . . at best romantically and energetically apprehended rather than emotionally realized." Frye *preferred* intellectional apprehension to emotional realization, and that led him into the ethical quagmire of innocently equating Iroquois defending their homeland with Nazis herding Jews into death camps. This view may have seemed socially advanced in 1943, but it too was doomed.)

It was in his Conclusion to the *Literary History of Canada*, a monumental work edited in 1965 by Karl F. Klinck, that Frye expressed his view of nature and its effect on the Canadian psyche, and therefore on its culture, in a splendidly visual metaphor that once again pilfered from the very nature he was maligning. Noting that whereas early explorers and immigrants to the United States were greeted by a warm, benign, friendly coastline, with luscious trees and tantalizing grapevines, Canada, by way of contrast, "has, for all practical purposes, no Atlantic seaboard. The traveller from Europe edges into it like a tiny Jonah entering an inconceivably large whale, slipping past the Straits of Belle Isle into the Gulf of St. Lawrence, where five Canadian provinces surround him, for the most part invisible." Canadian immigrants, he said, were thereby subjected upon their arrival to a vision of nature as an immense, all-consuming beast: "To enter the United States is a matter of crossing an ocean; to enter Canada is a matter of being silently swallowed by an alien continent."

You can see where this is heading. To Frye, English Canadians were foreigners (either British immigrants or "Americans who had rejected the Revolution") transplanted into a hostile environment; we never really got over our shock and dismay at finding ourselves isolated in this "alien," "inconceivably large," "mindless" wilderness. Rather than come to terms with our new surroundings, says Frye, we barricaded ourselves from it; we built walls, fences, fortresses, enclosures, universities; we dug bush gardens in which to cultivate our vegetable imaginations, we enclosed ourselves within a cultural envelope that sealed us off from the *cauchemar* reality of our natural environment. We formed "small and isolated communities surrounded with a physical or psychological 'frontier' . . . communities that provide all that their members have in the way of distinctively human values . . . yet [are] confronted with a huge, unthinking, menacing and formidable physical setting." Such communities, he says, "are bound to develop what we may provisionally call a garrison mentality. In the earliest maps of the country the only inhabited centres are forts, and that remains true of the cultural maps for a much later time."

A garrison, of course, is a fort or (to use the feminized form of the word) a fortress. The word derives from the Old German *war*, meaning caution—as in warn, wary and beware—which passed into

Old French as *garir*, "to protect" (from which we also get "garage"). The aural connection to *guerre* (war) might also come into it. The leap from caution to protection was made early: George Saville, the Marquis of Halifax, in his *Advice to a Daughter* (1650), warned her that "love is a passion that hath friends in the garrison." Troops were garrisoned (as they were in Kingston); garrisons had walls and provisions and civilization (Kingston has not only Fort Henry but also Queen's University); for Frye, the gates outside which the barbarians waited were garrison gates.

In other words, early settlers to Canada were so dumbstruck by the vastness and malevolence of the nature that surrounded them, so different from what they had been used to in Europe, that they immediately enclosed themselves in garrisons. At first, the walls of the garrison were intended only to keep nature out; eventually, however, the walls also served to keep culture in. We developed a mentality that required walls to give us definition. We ended up liking our walls, losing our ability or even our will to see beyond them. We became what Frye called "a closely knit and beleaguered society" whose "moral and social values are unquestionable"—a society attuned primarily to crisis and defence ("in a perilous enterprise, one does not discuss causes or motives"), in which things practical were prized and things like art, books, painting, pure science, were seen as frivolous and unnecessary. Frye acknowledged that such a society can be "anticultural," fostering "a dominating herd-mind in which nothing original can grow," and leading to "the death of communication and dialogue"; but he preferred to think that there was also "a more creative side of the garrison mentality, one that has had positive effects on our intellectual life." He was just a little unclear about what those positive effects might be. He pointed to the "highly articulate and argumentative society in nineteenth-century Canada" as an example; another was the curious fact that there seemed to be more authoritative literary criticism written in Canada than literature.

To Frye, the best Canadian literature is therefore that which recognizes and accepts this fundamental duality between man and nature. That is, literature that has its source in the garrison mentality best expresses who we are as a people.

The question is: is it true that we are a garrisoned people? Did we respond to the vastness and isolation of the wilderness by huddling together in garrisons? Or did we walk boldly out into it, compelled by its seeming limitless beauty to express our response in a literature that is filled with wonder and respect? It seems to me that some of us did the former while others of us did the latter, and one's view of the nature of the Canadian mentality depends largely on how one defines literature.

Let's be literal-minded for a moment. Quebec is a walled city, granted. But its walls were built not to protect it from nature or Satan's Native envoys, but from other Europeans—specifically, English soldiers. Quebec City is walled for the same reason most of the old cities of Europe were walled—because of man's, not nature's, inhumanity to man. Let us look again at those "earliest maps" of Canada. It is literally true that the "inhabited centres" were forts, but that is a linguistic conceit, because only a small percentage of the population lived in "inhabited centres." Most of the people were either out wandering the woods (voyageurs, *coureurs-de-bois*, fur traders) or farming the clearings (settlers, *habitants*), and they were not living in fortified garrisons. I think Frye would argue that only the forts counted, because that's where the civilized people lived; that's where there was music, and books, and theatres and universities. What was outside the walls didn't count. Anything outside the garrison gates was barbaric, "still in the trees."

After Frye, we read everywhere that it is our fear and mistrust of nature that informs our best literature. Margaret Atwood's *Survival* (1970), intended as a guide for teachers of Canadian literature, picks up Frye's theme and examines the official Canlit canon in its light: "Not surprisingly," she wrote, "in a country with such a high ration of trees, lakes and rocks to people, images from Nature are almost everywhere. Added up, they depict a Nature that is often dead and unanswering or actively hostile to man." The title of Dennis Lee's book of criticism, *Savage Fields*, expresses Frye's nature/civilization dualism (he calls nature "earth" and civilization "world"); he points out that there is much grey ground between them, but he essentially asserts that much of the tension in Canadian literature is derived from the psychotic break that results when writers try to inhabit both earth and world at the same time.

There is no doubt that nature in Canada is harsh, occasionally punishingly so (and at times the punishment seems unnecessary and undeserved), especially for one whose literary sensibilities were formed by a study of English literature. But it does not necessarily follow that as a people we responded to nature with fear and loathing. No doubt some of us did, and the garrison mentality thesis explains much that is good—and much that is bad—in Canadian literature, particularly if we confine our discourse to poetry and fiction. There is no doubt that Earle Birney's poem "David," Pratt's *The Titanic*, Robert Harlow's novel *Scann* and Michael Ondaatje's *In the Skin of a Lion* derive much of their undeniable power from the elemental conflict between human endeavour and the largely antagonistic forces of nature. One could almost choose a work at random. Take down, for example, Ondaatje's superb anthology of Canadian stories, *From Ink Lake*, open it to Joe Rosenblatt's prose piece "The Lake," and read that Eagle Lake evokes "an aquatic mood, as opposed to a human one."

"When Northrop Frye and others who have commandeered his

facile epithet," writes John Moss in his critical work *Patterns of Iso-lation*, "refer to the 'garrison mentality' that permeates the Canadian experience, their observation is accurate . . . but incomplete as a basis for literary analysis." There is plenty of evidence for the idea that not every newcomer to Canada scurried into a garrison. Many early works of nonfiction—nature writing, science writing, settlers' diaries and letters—can hardly be said to have been produced by writers who harboured deep-rooted psychological disturbances when confronted with the wilderness. Here is Samuel Hearne's descrip-tion of the timber wolf:

> They always burrow underground to bring forth their young, and
> though it is natural to suppose them very fierce at those times, yet
> I have frequently seen the Indians go to their dens, and take out the
> young ones and play with them. I never knew a Northern Indian
> hurt one of them: on the contrary, they always put them carefully
> into the den again; and I have sometimes seen them paint the faces
> of the young Wolves with vermillion, or red ochre.

This does not seem to me to express a deep-seated fear of nature—quite the opposite. "It is hard to resist the ministry of the woods," writes Ralph Connor in *Glengarry School Days*. "The sympathetic silence of the trees, the aromatic airs that breathe through the shady spaces, the soft mingling of broken lights—these all combine to lay upon the spirit a soothing balm, and bring to the heart peace."

Catharine Parr Traill, sister of Susanna Moodie, came to Canada in 1832 and experienced her first Canadian winter in a log shanty near Peterborough. "The 1st of March," she wrote in *The Backwoods of Canada*, "was the coldest day and night I ever experienced in my life." Did this send her shivering into the nearest garrison? "I enjoy a walk in the woods of a bright winter day," she continued, "when not a cloud, or the faint shadow of a cloud, obscures the soft azure of the heavens above . . ." Where is the terror, the shaking of the fist against overwhelming isolation and despair? "After a day or two of heavy snow the sky brightens, and the air becomes exquisitely clear and free from vapour; the smoke ascends in tall spiral columns: seen against the saffron-tinted sky of an evening, or early of a clear morning, when the hoar-frost sparkles on the trees, the effect is singularly beautiful."

Anna Brownell Jameson, travelling through the wilds of central Ontario in 1838, also exulted in the very aspects of nature that Frye said ought to have terrified her:

> No one who has a single atom of imagination, can travel through these forest roads of Canada without being strongly impressed and excited. The seemingly interminable line of trees before you; the boundless wilderness around; the mysterious depths amid the multitudinous foliage, where foot of man hath never penetrated,—and which partial gleams of the noontide sun, now seen, now lost, lit up with a changeful, magical beauty—the wondrous splendour and novelty of the flowers,—the silence, unbroken but by the low cry of a bird, or hum of insect, or the splash and croak of some huge bull-frog,—the solitude in which we proceeded mile after mile, no human being, no human dwelling within sight . . .

The idea that we have been raised in garrisons, physical and cultural, has done a lot of harm to our self-image. Frye may not have intended his judgement to be taken quite as literally as it has; in a later essay, "Across the River and Out of the Trees," he wrote that he had "spoken of what I call a garrison mentality and of the alternating moods of pastoral populism and imaginative terror (which has nothing to do with a poet's feeling terrified)," as though someone had thought that it has. Well, many writers have thought that's what he meant, that in order to be a true Canadian one had to tremble at the thought of venturing out of the garrison. Like those poets Frye mentioned who never felt the urge to view nature at first hand, we have become accustomed to thinking of ourselves as a quiet, unassuming, uninteresting society—mild, hard-working, uncontentious, lacking in humour, subtlety and grace. What a pity it would be if that picture of ourselves were formed from a partial rather than an impartial reading of our national literature, or from an intellectual concept of nature imposed upon us from an ivory tower.

* * *

The walkway between the E.J. Pratt Library and the New Academic Building that housed Northrop Frye's tiny office passed through a small clearing fringed with budding magnolias and alive with the chirruping of a dozen house sparrows, ecstatic in the year's first really tangible sunlight. When at last I climbed the stairs to Frye's floor I encountered Jay Macpherson in the hallway, standing by a leaf-scattered bulletin board. She was a tall, thin woman, a long-time friend and colleague of Frye's and one of the finest poets of her generation. I said hello and she smiled at me uncertainly. When I told her who I was and what I was doing, and asked if I could speak to her briefly after I had interviewed Frye, her smile faded and her eyes widened in absolute terror.

"Oh," she said, "oh no," shaking her head and flapping her arms as though to ward off an intruder. "No, I . . . I couldn't possibly . . ."

And turning, she literally ran off down the hall and disappeared into the clattering fastness of her garrison.

Gopher 1. one of several kinds of small ground squirrels.
2. *Slang, Obs.* a member of the North West Mounted Police.
—*Dictionary of Canadianisms*

RODENTS OF THE LOST ARK

Like many people in rural Ontario, I grew up calling ordinary groundhogs "gophers." We knew they were properly called ground-hogs, and we called them by their correct name most of the time. But every now and then we would be walking across a pasture or along a fence row, we would come upon a burrow that we knew full well had been dug by a groundhog, and we would say: "Gopher hole."

This seems to be a national trait, since just about every burrow-ing rodent in North America has, at one time or another, been called a gopher. But true gophers are a western varmint. So numerous are they on the Prairies that you can hardly enter a W.O. Mitchell novel without tripping over one. The gopher that "squeaked questioningly at Brian . . . from its pulpit hole" in *Who Has Seen the Wind* did so on page eleven; Carlyle Sinclair swerves to avoid a gopher on page fifteen in *The Vanishing Point*; and in *How I Spent My Summer Holi-days*, Hugh realizes as early as page eight that "like the badger and the weasel and the skunk and the coyote and the gopher, we were earth creatures."

The gopher is neither a prairie dog (*Cynomys ludovicianus*), which in Canada is found only in southern Saskatchewan's Grasslands National Park, nor a ground squirrel (any of the *Spermophilus* species), which Frederick Wooding (*Wild Mammals of Canada*, 1982) says are "most commonly, though erroneously, known as a gopher." Ernest Thompson Seton, the Canadian nature writer, almost got it right in his book *Wild Animals at Home*, an anecdotal account of the animals in Yellowstone National Park. Seton writes about prairie dogs and ground squirrels, then describes something he calls a mole-gopher (*Thomomys talpoides*), a burrowing rodent "about the size of a rat, but [with] a short tail and relatively immense forepaws and claws." This animal is now known as the northern pocket gopher (Seton may have been misled by the name *talpoides,* which means "mole-like"), and is one of sixteen species of pocket gopher found on the prairies of North America (only two of which, the northern and the plains, *Geomys bursarius*, are found in Canada), and they are the only animal that can legitimately be called "gopher."

The word "gopher" comes from the French *gaufre*, which means honeycomb, the pattern bees make with wax. A *gaufre* is also a waffle, a flat cake pressed with a honeycomb pattern by a *gaufrière,* or waffle-iron. The word *gaufre* was applied by French Canadian voyageurs to the burrowing rodents that riddled the Prairies, because the animals' intricate and labyrinthine tunnels literally honeycombed the earth. In time, *gaufre* was Anglicized to "gopher."

Just when and where this linguistic transformation took place is not precisely known, but we can narrow it down. Alexander Mackenzie, travelling up the river that now bears his name in 1796, noted in his journal on July 17 that he and his party "perceived many ground-hogs, and heard them whistle in every direction." These were probably Arctic ground squirrels (they were definitely not ground-hogs), but if the word "gopher" had existed then, Mackenzie no doubt would have used it, since he usually got the names of things by asking his French voyageurs. Henry Breckinridge, in his *Views of Louisiana 1812*, noted that "the Gopher . . . lives under ground, in the prairies, and is also found east of the Mississippi," so the word came into general use between 1796 and 1812.

By mid-nineteenth century, residents of Arkansas and Minnesota were called Gophers, probably because they lived in sod houses, and in 1869 even inhabitants of Florida were called Gophers, according to the *Overland Monthly*, "on account of all the gophers in that state." Apparently the word, like the animal itself, travelled fast. But it is certain that there was no English word "gopher" before 1796.

Which is why no one quite knows what kind of wood the Ark was made from. According to the King James Version of the Bible, which was translated by various scholars of several denominations between 1350 and 1620, Noah was instructed by Jehovah to "make . . . an ark of gopher wood" (Genesis 6:14). This has confused biblicists, as it no doubt confused Noah, because there was no tree in the Holy Land called gopher wood. Ten generations from Adam, there was no tree anywhere called gopher wood. And at the time the King James Version was being translated there was no word "gopher" in English. The word was simply an English phonetic equivalent of the Hebrew word, which was pronounced *gofer*. No one knows what the Hebrew word *gofer* meant. It could have been a place name. It might have been a local name for some kind of tree. The translator simply rendered it in English as "gopher" and left it at that, hoping no one would notice. Scholars have assumed that what God meant by gopher wood was either (a) any softwood, such as cedar or pine (the French Bible has Noé building the ark from "bois résineux"), or (b) cypress.

Both interpretations present problems. If God had wanted the Ark made from cedar or pine, He no doubt would have said so, because both trees were common in the Holy Land and Noah would have known what the hell He was talking about. Similarly, the Hebrew language already had a perfectly good word for cypress, and it was not *gofer*, it was *tirzâh*. And even this is needlessly problematic, because the *tirzâh* tree was also unknown to Noah; it grew only in the Taurus Mountains in what is now Turkey. Cypress was later used for shipbuilding by the Egyptians, but the Egyptians weren't around when Noah was (it is also unlikely that Noah would have recognized the word "ark," since the Hebrew word for ark is an adaptation of the later Egyptian word for chest—hence Ark of the Covenant). So even if it is possible that the author of Genesis was thinking "cypress" when he wrote "gopher," it is not likely that Noah could have thought *tirzâh* when he heard *gofer* (or thought "big boat" when he heard "ark"). It is hard to imagine what Noah thought when he heard the Voice of God telling him that the fate of the human race depended on his building a sixty-cubit thingamajig out of a kind of wood he had never heard of. No wonder he drank.

Timothy Findley imagined just that in his novel *Not Wanted on the Voyage*. After Findley's Mr. Noah Noyes (a delicious surname, combining "No" and "yes" in English and the French verb *noyer*, which means "to flood") receives his instructions from Yaweh (Jehovah), Findley explains that "gopher wood was . . . a strong, light-textured wood with some of the qualities of cork. Beams and planks were hewn from gigantic trees whose bark was a bilious green and whose flesh was yellow." This has to have been an inspired guess, based on the cypress explanation. Findley's wood-haulers hewed it in a far-off, mountainous region inhabited by giants and dwarves, which may have been the Taurus Mountains, and cypress is strong and light-textured, with a greenish bark and yellow wood. It has, however, none of the qualities of cork, which is bark, and anyway, Noah wouldn't have known cork either. But none of this explains why the wood from which the Ark was built was translated into English as "gopher wood," when there was no such word in English as "gopher." What could the poor translator have thought that he meant?

Being a poor translator myself, I can easily imagine translating Holy Writ at the express behest of the archbishop and being faced with an inexplicable Hebrew word that, when transliterated into English, was equally inexplicable. The translator was thus in exactly the same position as Noah himself, building a ship at the behest of Jehovah and faced with a very important and explicit, but inexplicable, instruction. What is gopher wood? they must both have asked themselves. What in damnation is this "tree of Gopher"? The translator must have reasoned that the biblical reference was probably to the cypress tree; that cypress was used for boat building because it was strong but light in weight, a quality it derived from its honeycombed structure; and that honeycomb in French was *gaufre*, a word that sounded a lot like the Hebrew *gofer*. He must have sat up in bed one night, possibly after eating a plate of waffles for dinner (maybe it was Shrove Tuesday), and said, possibly aloud, "Why don't I just leave it?"

It was a prophetic solution, as it turns out, because there is, now, a tree called gopherwood. It is a very rare tree; it grows only in the southern United States, mostly in eastern Tennessee and parts of southwestern North Carolina. Its scientific name is *Cladrastis lutea*, and it was discovered by the French botanist André Michaux, who spotted it near Fort Blount, Tennessee, in February 1796. He didn't call it gopherwood, he called it yellowwood. He gathered some seeds, planted them in his acclimation garden near Charleston, and sent some of the seedlings to France along with two other new species he had found, magnolia and rhododendron. The yellowwood specimens did not survive. Marie Antoinette sent them on to her father, the Emperor of Austria, and they were lost somewhere on the way, and by the time anyone missed them Marie Antoinette and several of her friends had lost their heads.

Meanwhile, back in South Carolina, Michaux taught American settlers to extract a yellow dye from the yellowwood's roots, and the light, strong, polishable wood became popular for gunstocks, which made the tree rarer still. The trunks have thin, silvery grey bark and bright, clear, yellow wood that darkens to light brown on exposure to sunlight. Its presence in the United States is a profound mystery, because it is the sole New World example of a genus otherwise known only in the mountainous regions of China and Japan, where, you may be sure, it is not called gopherwood. No one knows how it got to North America or why it is now called gopherwood. It just seems to be the kind of tree someone would look at and, knowing full well that what they were looking at was yellowwood, say: "There's a gopherwood." It's as if it were there to fulfil some kind of prophecy, and maybe it is.

Andreas Schroeder's *Dustship Glory*, another Canadian novel about a Noah and his Ark, is based on a true story. Schroeder's Noah is Tom Sukanen, a prairie farmer of Finnish origin who moved from Minnesota (which would make him a Gopher) to Manybones, Saskatchewan, just before the Dirty Thirties. In 1931, Sukanen took it into his head to build an Ark, a huge, tanker-sized steamship, that he constructed in the middle of a prairie grainfield "like a raised finger," waiting for—no, inviting—the torrential rain that finally came in May 1939, just in time for the Second World War.

By then Sukanen had begun winching his ship across the prairie towards the South Saskatchewan River, an epically laborious business: in twenty-five months he managed to move it only four miles, and the effort drove him mad. He lived on "rabbits and gophers he managed to trap in his snares;" in the winter he wore a "gopherskin coat." He frightened children and threatened farmers. He attracted the attention of the police.

In 1941 he was consigned to a mental hospital by the RCMP, whose predecessors were once known as "gophers" because, it was said, they took to hiding at the first sign of trouble. Sukanen never launched his ship. He had made his Ark out of steel and oak planks. It was too heavy to move. If it had been lighter, dragging it across the prairie might not have driven him mad. It's tempting to think that if Sukanen had built his Ark from gopherwood, as the Bible had instructed, he just might have made it to the river.

Grizzly bear An ugly, bad-tempered, hulking legend that has survived time and a thousand campfires that buzz with the tales of his prowess.

—*Wildlife in Canada*, 1970, R.D. Lawrence

EXEUNT PURSUED BY A BEAR

A few years ago, when I was in Yellowstone National Park, everyone was buying little bells at the gift shop in Mammoth and sewing them to their backpacks or threading them into the laces of their Kodiak hiking boots. The whole park was a jingling nuisance. The theory was that bears would hear the bells a mile away and take off in the opposite direction. I declined to adorn myself, having just spent two weeks in Banff with a park warden who told me that grizzly bears were just as likely to be attracted by the tinkling bells as repelled by them; he referred to them as "dinner bells." In Yellowstone, I happened to overhear a park ranger telling a group of hikers about bears. Each hiker had half a dozen bells sewn onto clothing, laced into boots, wired to caps. One couple had even replaced the buttons on their five-year-old daughter's jacket with bells.

"There are two kinds of bears in Yellowstone," the ranger was saying. "We have black bears and grizzly bears. The black bears are harmless, but we really have to watch out for the grizzlies."

There was a pause during which the hikers fingered their bells, somewhat smugly, I thought.

"We'll know when we're getting into grizzly country," continued the ranger, "because we'll see bear sign long before we see any bears—tracks, scratch posts, scat. And it's easy to tell the difference between black bear scat and grizzly scat."

"What's the difference?" asked one of the hikers.

"Well, for one thing," said the ranger with a small smile, "grizzly bear scat has a lot of these little bells in it."

The grizzly or brown bear (*Ursus arctos horribilis*) once ranged over all of North America from Alaska to Mexico, and there is recent evidence that an eastern subspecies of grizzly roamed as far as Labrador and the Ungava. It is now confined to the northern and western mountains of Alberta, British Columbia, Alaska, and parts of the northern United States such as Yellowstone, where it is considered a Canadian incursion. "Problem bears," that is, grizzlies that persist in frequenting parts of their normal range that humans would rather frequent, are routinely live-trapped in Yellowstone and shipped north to Banff and Yoho, presumably where they came from. The animal was first described in the Jesuit *Relations* of 1666 by Father François-Joseph le Mercier, who was quoting a report by Father Claude-Jean Allouez (1622–89) concerning an animal he'd seen in the Assiniboine River area in Manitoba. Allouez does not actually call it a grizzly but simply "a brown bear, very large" that his Native companions treated with a great deal of respect.

The first reference in English is by Henry Kelsey, the intrepid Hudson's Bay Company trader, who wrote on August 20, 1691: "This plain affords Nothing but short, Round sticky grass & Buffalo & a great sort of a Bear wch is Bigger than any white Bear & is Neither White nor Black But silver hair'd like our English Rabbit."

I like the kind of sensibility that can compare a grizzly with a rabbit. The silver hairs are what earned the animal the adjective grizzly—"grisled," from the Old French *grisel*, meant "grey"; Patient Griselda must have gone grey-headed waiting on her husband—though this epithet was not conferred until 1743, when the bear was described by James Isham, the Hudson's Bay Company factor at Churchill, in his *Observations on Hudson's Bay*. Isham was an accomplished natural historian and linguist, though a lousy speller, and he erroneously thought the grizzly to be a salt-and-pepper variety of the black bear. "Black bear's their is pretty many and some Very Large," he noted. "Especially the Grizel bears which will seize a Man if Come in his way having known an Indian tore in a Sad manner with one."

Samuel Hearne gets the species right in his *Journey to the Northern Ocean, 1771*: "Brown bears are, I believe, never found in the North-Indian territories: but I saw the skin of an enormous grisled Bear in the tents of the Esquimeaux at the Copper River, and many of them are said to breed not very remote from that part."

"Grisled" soon became "grisly." Alexander Mackenzie, travelling the Peace River in 1793, noted in his journal:

> We perceived along the river tracks of large bears, some of which were nine inches wide, and of a proportionate length. We saw one of their dens, or winter quarters, called watee, in an island, which was ten feet deep, five feet high, and six feet wide; but we had not yet seen one of those animals. The Indians entertain great apprehension of this kind of bear, which is called the grisly bear, and they never venture to attack it but in a party of at least three or four.

Thomas Drummond, a botanist in John Franklin's company on his journey up the Assiniboine River in 1825, "had a narrow escape from the jaws of a grisly bear" when he was botanizing, and discovered that "the best mode of getting rid of bears when attacked by them was to rattle my vasculum, or specimen box, when they immediately decamp."

Whatever method one chooses, it is always wise to respect the animal now more commonly called the grizzly. With an average male weight of above four hundred kilograms, it is the second largest predator in the world after its close relative the polar bear. Its reputation for unpredictable malevolence towards humans, which has been cited to justify its slaughter, is undeserved: grizzlies do not waste valuable energy needlessly running after tourists, bear-bells or no bear-bells. R.D. Lawrence writes that he has encountered grizzlies in the Rocky Mountains and they just sloped off without a backward glance. They may misinterpret human reactions as acts of aggression or territoriality, and even experienced woodsmen tell tales of unprovoked bear attacks, but by and large such encounters are rare. As Isham noted, you have to come in the way of one to be tore in a sad manner. Mike Gibeau, the warden in Banff who told me about the dinner bells, also told me about a photographer who had wandered into a remote valley in the park and been mauled by a grizzly. "But," said Mike, "the valley had been put off-limits by the park because we knew there was a migrating grizzly going through with her cubs, and the photographer went in anyway to get some photographs." In other words, the photographer was hunting for the bear. Bears can sense this.

The grizzly's decline began almost as soon as the animal was discovered by Europeans. This may have to do with what American nature writer Barry Lopez, in *Of Wolves and Men*, calls "theriophobia," which he defines as "fear of the beast as an irrational, violent, insatiable creature." That would describe the grizzly in the minds of many who have not encountered one. Conjure up the image and there follows an irrational, violent and insatiable urge to wipe the grizzly off the face of the Earth. By the end of the nineteenth century, as William T. Hornaday, then director of the New York Zoo, wrote in *Camp Fires in the Canadian Rockies* (1906), "in the United States, outside the Yellowstone Park and the Bitter Root Mountains, grizzly bears are so very rare that it is almost impossible for a sportsman to go out and kill one." Which is what Hornaday was doing in the Canadian Rockies.

An equally important reason for their decline, however, has been the decrease in their natural habitat. Male grizzlies require enormous home ranges; some males have been recorded ranging over areas of 27,000 square miles. When those territories are diminished by logging or cut through by highways and railway lines, the bears' reproductive rates are affected. Confined now almost exclusively to national parks, the ranges of individual grizzlies have been reduced to a fraction of what they need: in Yellowstone National Park their ranges are as small as 22 square miles; the average in Alberta is less than 457 square miles. Only in the Yukon do grizzlies get anything approaching their original territories, which is why a current plan known as the Yellowstone-to-Yukon Initiative, or Y2Y—which is trying to establish an unbroken corridor of wilderness between the two extremes of the grizzly's range—may be the last hope for the survival of North America's ugly, bad-tempered, hulking legend.

Knowledge is supposed to temper credulity and even incite compassion. Early American settlers, unfamiliar with bear habits, would come across dead and bloated cows in their fields and believe that their livestock had been turned into deadstock by bears. A bear, they said, could pick up a full-grown cow, apply its mouth to the cow's anus, and blow it up like a balloon, separating the skin from the rest of the cow and thereby killing it. At least that's what they told Peter Kalm, a Swedish naturalist who had studied under Linnaeus and travelled through the United States and Canada in 1745. Kalm reports this absurdity with a straight face.

People were prepared to say and believe anything bad about bears. Theodore Roosevelt, the American president who liked to hunt, often travelled to the Rockies and even into the Himalayas to kill bears. The legend is, of course, that he once shot a female grizzly and, finding that she had a cub with her, refrained from shooting the youngster. Roosevelt was rewarded for this act of humanity by having a stuffed toy named after him; thus was born the Teddy Bear. No one seems to have pointed out that if the story were true, then the president was being honoured for killing a mother and leaving her cub to starve to death alone.

We do things differently in Canada. We didn't name a toy after a politician; we named a beer after the bear.

Groundhog A woodchuck.

—*The Oxford Canadian Dictionary*

WHO ARE WIARTON WILLIE?

I magine it is the morning of February 2 in Wiarton, Ontario. A
late January thaw has turned most of the snow into hard, granu-
lar pellets and a sudden overnight freeze has covered the ground with
a crust of greyish ice. Now a warm east wind has come up and is
whistling through the trees and telephone poles. In the parking lot
of the Wiarton Willie Motel, cars and vans glow with a kind of flat
lustre under the yellow lights. The logos of all the major news media,
painted onto the sides of the vehicles, are all but invisible. It is six
o'clock, still dark, and inside the motel the journalists who have
come to Wiarton from Toronto are getting up, fumbling into warm
clothing and stumbling down the covered walkway to the motel
office, where the owner has put out an urn of Tim Horton coffee
and a tray of donuts. Every now and then one of the journalists,
mouth full of glazed sour-cream and holding a large double-double,
ventures over to the plate-glass window and looks out into the
swirling darkness. All words beginning with "f" have been deleted
from the following account of their reactions: "Holy."

An hour later the vans and cars are parked in another parking
lot, this one beside the Wiarton High School. They have been joined
by other vehicles. Some of the journalists have gone into the high
school to check out the pancake breakfast, maybe tape a few inter-
views; others remain in the vans to sort through their equipment.
Exhaust fumes coil out of tailpipes. Windshield defrosters roar into
the darkness. A few technicians venture outside to set up tripods

and test cameras. They have a problem, which they are discussing amongst themselves. If they leave the cameras inside the vans, the lenses will fog over when they bring them out into the cold air. On the other hand, if they leave the cameras outside in the cold, the batteries will go dead. What to do?

It is a problem that has not presented itself in Punxsutawney, Pennsylvania, where an almost identical scene is at this very moment taking place, minus the snow and ice and exhaust fumes, plus about 1,500 extra people. The journalists in Wiarton who have seen the movie *Groundhog Day*, starring Second City graduate Bill Murray and Andie MacDowell, mention this. In the movie, Bill Murray plays a TV weatherman from New York who enters a kind of time shunt in Punxsutawney: every morning he wakes up to find it is still February 2 and he is still in Punxsutawney. Several people in Wiarton blow into their hands and express the fervent hope that nothing like that will happen here in Wiarton. Others take a sip of coffee and think about waking up in the Wiarton Willie Motel every morning beside Andie MacDowell.

A low platform with a painted backdrop has been set up in the schoolyard, and three sections of bleachers have been dragged over from the football field and arranged in front of it. In the grey, presunrise light, people are beginning to fill the bleachers. Some of them have come by Ski-Doo and are wearing brightly coloured snowmobile suits; others drove up in pick-up trucks and station wagons and are less flamboyantly dressed. Members of the high school band are milling about on the stage trying to keep their instruments warm, especially the brass section. As it gets on for eight, the journalists also take their places in the bleachers, the band strikes up a kind of processional, and almost immediately a line of dignitaries—the mayor, the local MPP, a town crier, Mother Nature, Toronto rock star Lawrence Gowan—files out of the school and assembles on the stage. Gowan is dressed in black, but the mayor and the MPP are wearing white tuxedos with pink cummerbunds. Mother Nature is in a long white gown with pink flowers threaded into her hair. There are also two figures dressed up in white groundhog costumes made out of a furry material that used to be called Borg, carrying bottles of pink champagne.

Everyone is waiting for Wiarton Willie to appear. Wiarton Willie is an albino groundhog—white fur, pink eyes—who lives in a little wooden house with tiny glass windows and a small wooden chimney at the Wiarton Willie Motel. Every year at this time, for the past thirty or forty years (no one can remember when it started), people have been coming to this small community on the Bruce Peninsula to ask Wiarton Willie when spring is going to arrive. They want to know the approximate date. Before he summons Willie to the stage, the mayor makes a speech welcoming all the tourists and members of the press who are doing so much to put Wiarton on the map. Then the MPP makes a speech declaring that February 2 ought to be made a national holiday, and that he is going to take the matter up with his colleagues when he returns to Queen's Park. Mother Nature makes a speech reminding everyone that Wiarton Willie symbolizes our lasting and fruitful link with the wild. The band and Larry Gowan play a few bars of Gowan's most popular song, "You're a Strange Animal." Then the mayor says he thinks the weather is beginning to warm up already, and he draws everyone's attention to a small opening cut into the painted backdrop down at stage level, and he conjures Wiarton Willie to come out of his hole and speak to them about the weather.

*　　*　　*

February is called February because in ancient Rome it was the month of februation, or purification of the people by sacrifice. Christianity subsumed that practice into the purification of the Virgin Mary (six weeks after childbirth). In Scotland, a woman would enter the church carrying a candle as soon as she had recovered from childbirth; this was called being "churched." Priests set aside February 2 for the blessing of the candles to be used for that purpose in the coming year, and so February 2 was called Candlemas Day. Groundhogs did not figure largely in the ceremony. Candlemas Day, however, had long been associated with the renewal of spring. It was held in pre-Christian, Celtic Scotland that good weather on February 2 meant a long continuation of winter, and vice versa, the Scots being temperamentally wary of good omens. A Latin couplet by Sir Thomas Browne combined the Roman ritual of februation, the Catholic veneration of Mary, and Druidic scepticism quite nicely:

Si sol splendescat Maria Purificante
Major erit glacies post festum quam fuit ante.

"If the sun shines on Mary's purification, there will be more winter after the festival than there was before it," which is more or less summed up in the old Scottish rhyme:

If Candlemas Day be dry and fair,
The half o' winter's come and mair;
If Candlemas Day be wet and foul,
The half o' winter was gone at Youl [Yule, i.e. Christmas].

Candlemas was one of the four "quarter days" in the Celtic calendar, the others being Old Beltane (May 15), Lammas (August 1) and Martinmas, or Old Hallowmas (November 11), and so probably had more to do with Druidism and witchcraft than with the Catholic business with the candles. Christian holidays tend to involve the sky, whereas

Celtic festivals were usually firmly grounded in the earth. Except for Midsummer Day (June 24), the English quarter days are decidedly Christian: Lady Day (March 25), Michaelmas (September 29) and Christmas (December 25). When England annexed Celtic Scotland, the six weeks of winter surrounding Candlemas became tied up with the coincidence that February 2 came six weeks after the birth of Christ: if there is bad weather on February 2, then the middle of winter was at Christmas; it there is good weather, then midwinter fell on Candlemas and spring would begin around St. Patrick's Day. It must have been the Celtic twilight that introduced the notion of animals into Candlemas. No groundhogs yet, but there is a nineteenth-century German proverb that comes close: "The badger peeps out of his hole on Candlemas Day and, if he finds snow, walks abroad; but if he sees the sun shining, he draws back into his hole."

When the Highland Scots came to Nova Scotia, they brought their own quarter days with them, and Candlemas once again became a popular celebration of spring. German and Dutch immigrants to Nova Scotia and Pennsylvania added the animal element, but unfortunately there were no badgers in eastern North America, and so they had to find some other animal that came out of hibernation in early February. In the United States, groundhogs seem to have stood in for badgers almost from the beginning: an early dictionary of Americanisms compiled by Schele de Vere in 1871 notes that "Candlemas is known as Groundhog Day, for on that day the ground hog comes annually out of his hole, after a long winter nap, to look for his shadow." Punxsutawney got into the act in 1886. In Canada, however, people went out to look for bears, not groundhogs, on Candlemas. "Just a gleam of sunshine enough for the bear to see his shadow," noted Mary Ann King, of Chippawa, Ontario, in 1893. Incredible as it may seem, the practice continued well into the twentieth century: the old Kingston *Daily British Whig* noted on January 31, 1920, that

Candlemas Day will be celebrated on Monday, February second. This is the day on which the bear will either see or he won't see his shadow. Here's hoping he won't see it, for it will mean the turning of the long, hard winter we have had. On the other hand, if Mr. Bear does see his shadow, according to the old saying, we may look for six weeks more of bad weather.

Not until 1938 is there mention of groundhogs in Canadian newspapers.

* * *

The word "groundhog," however, seems to have been used first in Canada. It is an appropriation of the Afrikaans word *aardvark*, which literally means "earth-pig." The Dutch used it to describe *Orycteropus afer*, a large, South African burrowing rodent. "A is for aardvark," as Lister Sinclair used to remind us on the CBC programme *Ideas*, but it was only really for aardvark in Cape Town and Johannesburg. The translation of aardvark as groundhog was (mis)applied by Alexander Mackenzie in 1789 to the burrowing rodent known to the Algonquins and Cree as the *ochak*, and already known to Canadian and American trappers as "wejack," which eventually became "woodchuck." If it hadn't been for Mackenzie, February 2 would be called Woodchuck Day.

Whether called a groundhog or a woodchuck, however, *Marmota monax* is a poor choice for making a scheduled appearance at Candlemas. It is a true deep hibernator. It eats copious quantities of field crops during the summer, storing up fat and annoying farmers, until fall frosts send it down into its burrow, where it hibernates in a sealed chamber three or four feet below the surface. Over the winter its body temperature drops from 35 degrees Celsius to below

8 degrees Celsius, its heartbeat slows from 100 beats a minute to 15, and its oxygen consumption falls to one-tenth the normal rate. It is not, in other words, an early riser. Raccoons would be much better. Raccoons are always up and about in February. There are even lots of raccoons in Toronto. The media scrum wouldn't have to leave the city. Instead of Wiarton Willie it could have Rosedale Rocky or High Park Harry. The good people of Wiarton would not like that, though.

*   *   *

Wiarton's mayor is joined on the stage by Wiarton Willie's handler, who also owns the Wiarton Willie Motel. His name is Brower and he has about half a dozen Wiarton Willies secreted about his place, extras waiting in the wings in case the main attraction dies (as groundhogs tend to do in their third or fourth year). Anyone in the Wiarton area who sees an albino groundhog gives Brower a call. There are a lot of albino groundhogs around Wiarton—albinism tends to work like that.

Everyone's attention is on the little hole cut into the backdrop. The backdrop has been painted to look like a stone fence, and the hole appears to be under one of the stones. Somebody in the bleachers whispers, "Why does that backdrop look so familiar?"

And somebody else replies, "Because it's the same as the one in the movie *Groundhog Day*. Remember?"

"Oh, yeah. Cool."

The mayor says that he and Mr. Brower here are the only two human beings in the world who can speak Groundhog, and when Wiarton Willie finally comes out of his hole, sliding feet first and looking back over his shoulder, the mayor picks him up and speaks to him. Are we going to have an early spring, Willie?

Willie takes a while to respond. Groundhogs are thoughtful crea-tures, not given to rash predictions. In some parts of our range, he tells the mayor, we used to be called "pickets," because we would stand up beside our burrows so straight and so lost in thought that cowboys would tie their horses up to us. Farmers shoot us even after we thoughtfully pile up huge mounds of earth beside our bur-rows to warn cattle not to step in our holes, because the mounds get clogged up in the farmers' cutters during haying season and we dull the blades. Now, I live in a nice frame house and Mr. Brower here takes pretty good care of me and I don't have to worry much about farmers or farmers' dogs or foxes or coyotes, and so I can spend all the time I want just thinking about things like the weather.

But you know how it is when you think too long about some-thing. You second-guess yourself. You lose touch with your instincts in the matter. You go to say one thing and then you bethink yourself and blurt out the opposite. Last year, for example, I told you that spring was just around the corner, and it turned out we had the lat-est, coldest spring in the history of weather observation. This year it's already pretty warm and it's fairly cloudy, with hardly a shadow in sight, and I think we could be in for an early—

The farmers in the audience begin to smile.

—but hang on, is that a faint touch of light over there on the horizon, a small patch of blue poking through the clouds? I believe it is. I think I can see the sun. Is that Mother Nature's shadow stretch-ing out along the platform? I'm not going to take any chances this year, Mr. Mayor; I'm going to go for a late spring.

Six more weeks of winter, everyone, says the mayor. All the spec-tators wearing snowmobile suits begin to cheer.

Ice See *Iron*.

—*Dictionary of Word Origins,* 1945, Joseph T. Shipley

WATER TURNED TO BONE

I am sitting in a high school art class. The teacher, whom we all admire—a tall, thin, sadistic man with a fixed sneer and absolutely no talent of his own—is grudgingly passing out sheets of paper and bits of broken charcoal and telling us to draw something.

"Anything," he says, hopelessly. "Draw shapes. Be abstract, be pure form, be"—he looks around the room for the right word—"original." None of us knows what he wants. "When you finish, I'm going to come around and look, and if I recognize what it is you've drawn, you fail."

I take a piece of charcoal and draw something that I think looks vaguely like a cloud. No, no: it's not supposed to look like anything. I draw the outline of a second cloud behind the first, and join the edges with lines, shading in the bulges and recesses as though light is hitting it low from some invisible source off the page to my right. A thin section of cloud. A slice of white toast. When the teacher comes around and asks me what it is, I look up and shrug, too clever to fall into his trap.

"Nothing," I say. "Just a shape."

"There is a fine but important distinction," says the teacher, "between thinking you've drawn nothing and being too stupid to know what you have drawn."

But I didn't know what I had drawn until thirty years later, when I travelled to the Arctic to join a ship and saw sea ice for the first time in my life. On our first day in ice I recognized with a shock the flat, cloud-like shapes that drifted past the ship, the curiously abstract, solid chunks of pure form that I had imagined all those years ago in high school. I had drawn an ice floe.

* * *

"Ice" is not a Canadian word. It comes from the Sanskrit *is*, which meant "smooth," and also shows up in Old Norse: Iceland was originally called, even in English, Island, which was confusing since England was also an island. There is a tenth-century Anglo-Saxon riddle, a short poem that describes an object or a concept, and the hearer has to figure out what is being described. The answer to this one is "ice":

I saw a creature   wandering the way,
And wonderfully   were her wonders worn,
A wonder on the waves   water turned to bone.

This is ice as both thing and idea, as a mental construct, a subject of scientific study as well as of imaginative power, and it is this word that has come to Canada and stayed. Ice is to Canadians what sand is to Saharans, almost what air is to birds. The Inuit really do have twenty words for snow; Canadian mariners and ice scientists have many more designations for different kinds of ice. Here are a few of them from the *Dictionary of Newfoundland English*, the *Dictionary of Prince Edward Island English* and the *Glossary of Permafrost and Related Ground-Ice Terms*, published by the National Research Council of Canada:

BURIED ICE: ice thrown up on shore or formed on the ground, then covered by subsequent sedimentation. Buried ice that forms after the material that covers it has been deposited is called EPIGENETIC ICE.

CAKE ICE: a large chunk of floating ice, a floe.

FIELD ICE: a large, flat expanse of floating ice. This is an ancient designation: in 1766, Sir Joseph Banks, sailing to Newfoundland, recorded in his journal that when approaching the island the ship was "accompanied by several small flat Pieces of Ice which the seamen call field Ice," which was "Easily seen by its white appearance not unlike the Breaking of a wave into foam." Banks was describing the phenomenon known as "ice blink."

GREASE ICE: ice in the very first stage of forming on the surface of the water; also called FRAZIL ICE or, more recently, PLASTIC ICE.

PANCAKE ICE: first-year ice floes rounded from having collided with one another.

ROTTEN ICE: sea ice made soft by the process of melting, very dangerous to walk on.

RUNNING ICE: ice floes driven by current or wind.

SHELL ICE: a thin layer of ice over a thicker layer, with an air space between, also very dangerous to walk on. Also called TOP ICE, CAT ICE, or DOUBLE ICE.

SHORE ICE: sea ice that adheres to the coastline and extends out to sea. Also called FAST ICE or BOARD ICE.

The ship I joined was the Canadian Coast Guard icebreaker *Martha L. Black*. I met her in Cambridge Bay, was taken aboard by helicopter as she sat in the calm, blue waters of the harbour, and sailed north with her into the western Arctic Ocean. It was my first time in sea ice, the first time I'd really thought about ice. From Victoria Island, although it was August and "a good year for ice," as the captain said, it took us two weeks to work our way through Victoria Strait and Larsen Sound to Bellot Strait, a narrow corridor separating Somerset Island from the Boothia Peninsula, and therefore the western from the eastern Arctic. Normally, ice chokes Bellot Strait for twelve months a year, but that summer, for some reason, the strait was eerily ice-free, a current of dark water drawing us along at nearly six knots. We steered between the high walls of the strait, staring suspiciously ahead as though expecting to be drawn into a cliff of solid ice.

By slack tide we were at Fort Ross, an old Hudson's Bay Company post built on the southern shore of Somerset Island in 1937 and abandoned ten years later because so few ships had been able to get to it from the west, as we had just done, because of the ice. We went ashore for the day. The island was a slick slab of Precambrian granite thrust up through a yellow Cretaceous crust; its shore was little more than a pile of fist-sized rocks, ground smooth by ice and dumped there as though after some huge construction project. God's gravel pit. The sight of so much debris made me uneasy. I preferred the friendly-looking ice waiting for us farther north, out in the open sea; it looked less treacherous. If I had to walk out of here, I thought, if I were Franklin or M'Clintock or M'Clure, I would walk on the flat sea ice, not on this loose gravel. Sea ice seemed perfectly solid compared to the land.

I was terribly mistaken. As Franklin's men must have learned to their horror, sea ice is perpetually moving, splitting up, rafting together, wallowing in its own saliva. I wouldn't have made it a mile before being stopped by an open lead, or swallowed by a snow-covered melt pond, or crushed by a ridge of multi-year ice pushed high into the air by the pack's internal pressure. Sometimes blocks of ice the size of buildings crash back into the pack, continue rotating until they are upright again and then freeze suddenly in delicate, leaning poses, jutting out of the ice like giant broken teeth; these are called tombstones. Perhaps it was the ice's slow-moving, siren-like charm, its illusion of benignity, that drew so many explorers, like Frobisher and Franklin, year after year, until they disappeared into it.

Sometimes sailors in the Arctic, after a four-hour watch of looking at nothing but ice, remain on the bridge or out on deck to look at ice some more. When I wasn't leaning on the rail or watching from the boat deck as the ship's prow shrugged aside huge hunks of glistering crystal streaked with emerald and cobalt, I would lie in my bunk below decks and listen to the ice scrape along the water-line a bare three-quarters of an inch from my ear. Sometimes it sounded light and skittery, like a squirrel running across a ceiling. At other times it was heavy and booming, like someone hitting an oil tank with a padded baseball bat. Whenever the ship stopped to tend a buoy or send an away party onto the ice, the ice kept groaning, grinding, gnashing past the ship's flank like an army on its way to a decisive battle. Never before had I met with such direct evidence of the single-minded power of nature. Forest fires, volcanoes, hurricanes have such power, but theirs has a beginning and an end. Their power can be spent. Ice goes on forever. I tried to think what it must have been like a century, two centuries ago, to be lying in a wooden ship, listening to these same dreadful sounds, floe after floe, night after night, for years on end.

I talked about this with Larry Solar, the ship's Ice Observer, the lucky man whose job it was to watch the ice and tell the captain the best way to get around it or through it. Larry's experience of ice was more intimate than acoustical. He would stand for hours on the bridge, or go off on two-hour helicopter forays along the ship's projected course, then come back with his map and tell the captain, Go here, or here. I would accompany him on these flights and he would show me how to make ice eggs: oval hieroglyphs on maps that encode the ice's age, concentration and thickness. Miles from the ship, he would tell the pilot to set us down on a floe, and we would walk out onto the ice, drill holes through it with huge augers to see how thick it was, break off chunks to determine how hard it was, taste it to find out how salty it was. A big man with long grey hair and beard, Larry would stand with feet spread wide for balance and his laughter would boom across the ice. He looked like God on the first day of Creation, taking stock of the raw materials with which he would soon make the world. It was his twenty-first consecutive summer in the Arctic.

He had joined the Weather Service in 1966 and the next year had been sent north to take charge of the Upper Air Observation Post at Coral Harbour, at the western tip of Hudson Bay. Most people couldn't stand such complete isolation, living in a box the size of a garden shed for months at a time. Even ice observers have had it after three months. Larry stayed on without a break until the spring of 1971, when a pilot on an ice-reconnaisance flight for the Department of the Environment landed at Coral Harbour for repairs. The pilot recruited Larry for the Ice Patrol. "He said they needed someone with supervisory experience who could deal with isolation in the North," Larry told me, "and I said, I've been supervising myself for four years—I'm your man."

Every year for two decades he had found some way to get back to the Arctic. In 1982 he volunteered for the Mould Bay Experiment, a research project on the northeastern coast of Banks Island, the first purely scientific investigation of ice formation ever conducted. No one had ever thought about sea ice as a branch of physics before. Larry worked with ice scientists investigating "frost flowers," the earliest stage in the congelation of water. "We cut a hole in the ice three metres square by one metre deep," he said, "and in the bottom we drilled a four-inch hole straight down to the ocean. When the pool filled up with water, we lowered thermisters into it, set up wind gauges around it, aimed a scatterometer at it, and photographed it every ten minutes." They had no idea what to expect, but they ended up with a sequence of photographs so perfect and beautiful that Larry's eyes watered at the remembrance.

In another experiment, Nirmal Sinha, a glaciologist from the National Research Council in Ottawa, cut a beam of multi-year ice with a chainsaw and subjected it to the same kind of stress and sheer tests that engineers apply to bridge girders; he found the ice to be stronger than steel. Nirmal had held a chunk of the ice up to the sun and looked at it like a jeweller examing a perfect crystal. Larry thought Nirmal had probably meant to say "Eureka," but through some complicated association of emotion and idea that Larry completely understood, it had come out, "Erotica!"

Nirmal still had a piece of Mould Bay super-ice in his laboratory when I visited him at the NRC complex in 1990. His lab was actually a walk-in freezer full of ice from every frozen corner of the world—from glaciers in the Himalayas, ice-caps in Greenland and Alaska, from the North and South Poles, all different colours, some of it thousands of years old. One slice, from a core drilled in central Greenland, had been formed 280,000 years ago. He showed me the Mould Bay chunk, handling it with such reverence, describing its properties with such awe, that I felt as though he were handing me the Holy Grail. I was holding a chalice of ice.

"I love ice," Larry said one night as we were sitting in the *Martha's* officers' lounge, a poshly redecorated room on the starboard side of the ship, two decks down from the bridge but still high enough above the water-line to afford a view of the ice. The lounge had recently been renovated in preparation for a visit from Jeanne Sauvé, the governor-general at the time. Madame Sauvé's favourite colours were garnet and grey. Larry was spread out over a grey sofa, drinking a Diet Pepsi, holding it like medicine—he was on one of his occasional abstention binges. I had a glass of Glenfiddich with a chunk of multi-year ice in it that I'd hacked off an ice floe that afternoon with one of the ship's geology hammers. The chunk had already lasted through several drinks without becoming perceptibly smaller. No one south of 75° north latitude has even seen ice as hard as that. It glowed. The Scotch oozed around it like liquid amber.

We were in twenty-four-hour daylight. Through the garnet-curtained portholes the ice stretched to the horizon like cracked skin under the thin Arctic haze.

"To me," Larry said, "ice represents the last frontier on this planet. In the south we have distance barriers: the Prairies are a long way from the seaports, the grain farms are a long way from the elevators. Or we have feature barriers, mountains and rivers and such, that get between you and where you want to go. But up here we have a substance barrier, which is ice. Whenever we want to do anything—find oil, do science or just go farther than anyone has gone before—we have to deal with ice. Ice becomes an element, like air or fire, an obsession. It is pure form. I know what Nirmal meant when he held his great chunk of ice up to the sun and said, 'Erotica.' He loves ice. He loves ice the way Lewis and Clark loved mountains."

Earlier that afternoon, on a helicopter recon flight that had taken us nearly fifty miles ahead of the ship, Larry had spotted a small island that was not on the map—a not unusual occurrence in the Arctic—and we had flown down to investigate it. It was a low, flat mound of sand and gravel that barely rose above its own high-tide line. We hovered over ancient tent rings, tracks of a million shorebirds—I

imagined sanderlings, ruddy turnstones, semipalmated sandpipers—
and, above the tide line, an association of larger rocks that looked
as though they had once formed a makeshift grave.

"Go down, go down!" Larry shouted over the headset, motioning
the pilot to land.

The site had been much disturbed. No longer a neat pile cover-
ing a human body, the grave was a mere scattering of rocks with
human bones strewn among them, bleached white by the sun, worn
smooth by blowing sand. The skull lay in fragments. While the pilot
kept the helicopter's engines idling, Larry leapt out under the
whirling blades and began repiling the rocks over the bones, frantically restoring the grave to its intended sanctity. He worked with a
kind of possessed fervour, as though he were personally affronted by
the desecrated grave. I jumped out to help him, and together we
undid the damage that had been done by whatever wild force had
come along to desecrate that unnamed adventurer's last resting-place.
Then, without a word, we climbed back into the chopper and
returned to the ship.

Sitting in the grey, twilit lounge, sipping our drinks, I asked Larry
if he thought the grave had been broken up by polar bears trying to
get at the body inside.

"No," he said uneasily, "bears didn't do that."

"What was it, then?" I asked. "Arctic foxes?"

"No," he said. "It was ice. That's the other side of it. Ice can be a
great despoiler of men's dreams."

Jerusalem artichoke grows in waste places and has become one of the most valuable weeds which plague the farmer, who finds it in his corn field.

—*The Vegetable Encyclopedia and Gardener's Guide,* 1943

THE CANADA POTATO

Dorothy Thomson has been selling vegetables and fruit at the Kingston Farmers' Market for the past sixty years. A small, dainty-looking woman with fine white hair and a piercing eye, she started coming into town with her father on a horse-drawn buggy when she was a teenager. They used to deliver eggs on the way in, she says, and remembers the house we live in now as "the old Walton place, owned by an accountant or some such thing, a tall, thin man who never paid a bill on time." She's had the same corner stall since she started at the market, and always sells local produce, never backing her truck up to the National Grocers' terminal the way some at the Farmers' Market do, alongside the refrigerator trucks from A&P and Loblaws. She sniffs at them but won't point them out: "Just look for wax on the turnips" is about as disloyal as she gets.

Today, an unusually warm day in mid-October, she has Northern Spies from her own orchard, carrots with the dirt from her garden still on them, flawless tomatoes and tiny pearls of new potatoes. I almost buy a basket of potatoes for $1.25 when I notice that she also has quart baskets of Jerusalem artichokes for seventy-five cents.

"Did you grow these?" a woman beside me asks Dorothy.

"No, they're Helen's," Dorothy says. "She couldn't come in today because of her chickens, so I'm selling them for her."

"Helen?" asks the woman.

"Yes, Helen. Lives down the Jones Road."

"Oh, you mean Eilleen."

"Eilleen!" says Dorothy, stepping back. "Now, why did I call her Helen?" She shakes her head quickly, as though dismissing a suggestion that she's getting old. "I guess it's because she always calls me Gladys."

The small, hairy Jerusalem artichokes in the basket look like bloated ginger roots. As Irma Rombauer says in *The Joy of Cooking*, the Jersalem artichoke "should get some sort of prize in the misnomer sweepstakes," since they have nothing to do with the Holy Land and are not artichokes. The Jerusalem artichoke (*Helianthus tuberosus*) is in fact a sunflower with an edible tuber like a potato, which explains why it is sometimes called the Indian or Canada potato. "Of all the hitherto unknown foods which a newly discovered America bestowed bountifully upon Europe," writes Waverley Root in *Food*, "the only vegetable of any consequence contributed by North America was the Jerusalem artichoke."

The plant was named in 1605 by Samuel de Champlain, whom Native people presented with home-grown tubers on one of his exploratory expeditions from Port-Royal to Cape Cod, long before these same Native people showed the Puritans how to eat turkey. He correctly noted that it was the root of a wild sunflower, and also thought it tasted like an artichoke. He therefore called it an *artichaut de girasol*, the latter from the Italian word for sunflower (*gira* = turns to, and *sol* = sun).

Upon his return to Port-Royal, he found the plant growing wild and in 1613 shipped a boatload of the tubers to France, where they were sold in farmers' markets under the name *topinambour*. Apparently, a boatload of Topinambour Indians from Brazil had arrived in France at the same time, and were probably sold in the same markets, and the two novel items became one, just as the French thought of Canada and Brazil as the same place. Or perhaps, since the word *topinambour* came to mean "uncultivated," the French regarded anything that came from Canada as uncultivated. In any case, the plant was cultivated in England in 1620, when the OED has it as "artichock of Jerusalem," a literal anglicization of Champlain's designation.

New World plants did not fare well in the Old World. The names were odd, for one thing—Jerusalem artichokes that were not artichokes, breadplants that were not bread, green peppers that were not peppers. No wonder no one wanted to eat these foreign plants masquerading as domestics. Feed them to the cattle, see if they like them first. Most of the New World plants were more nutritious and often tastier than the European varieties whose names they had borrowed; could it be prejudice against the unknown that relegated Jerusalem artichokes to the silo rather than promoting them to the dinner table? Where, I continually wonder, is the pleasure in eating a true artichoke? You peel off half a hundred stringy, bland, chalky leaves, scrape the talcum-like coating off the inner surface with your bottom teeth, and do this over and over until you get to the dramatically named "heart" at the linguistically loaded core (from the French *coeur*), and pretend that this pulpy, tasteless mass of fibre is the *ne plus ultra* of romantic cuisine. I don't get it.

But for reasons of their own, Europeans wouldn't touch Jerusalem artichokes. Root mentions that in 1722, during a food shortage, a French pharmacist named Antoine Parmentier was rewarded by the French government for promoting the potato as a food for people rather than for cattle; he also recommended the Jerusalem artichoke, but that suggestion went unrewarded. Someone suggested that because of its bulbous, disjointed shape, the Jerusalem artichoke probably caused leprosy, and that did it. Smooth, round potatoes became all the rage, while Jerusalem artichokes, oddly shaped, looking deformed and even demented, languished in the barnyard. Even colonists in New France wouldn't touch them unless absolutely forced to. In 1737, La Mère de Sainte-Hélène described a great famine in Quebec during which hundreds of habitants died and the survivors were reduced to eating "Jerusalem artichokes and other things not fit for human consumption."

Farther west, settlers were not so fastidious. John West, a visitor to the starving Red River Colony in 1824, noted that "there is a root which is found in large quantities, and generally called by settlers, the Indian potatoe. It strongly resembles the Jerusalem artichoke, and is eaten by the natives in a raw state; but when boiled it is not badly flavoured." One of its virtues on the frontier must have been that it could be left in the ground over the winter and dug up in the spring for a first-of-season meal.

We now eat a lot of things earlier gardeners wouldn't touch. A neighbour of mine in Toronto once turned his nose up at a patch of zucchinis I was particularly proud of, saying, "In Italy, we call them pig squash." John McPhee, in his *New Yorker* profile of Euell Gibbons (the author of *Stalking the Wild Mushroom*), writes enthusiastically about the Jerusalem artichoke, saying its flesh is "delicate and white. Boiled, it has the consistency of boiled young turnips or summer squash, and the taste suggests the taste of hearts of artichokes," which does not recommend it to me. I like the idea of it because it is a native plant, is entirely free of starch, and has medicinal value: it contains a sugar called inulin that can be used to make bread for people with diabetes, and is often used in diagnosing the disease.

Not everyone in Europe spurned the topinambour. Auguste Escoffier, for example, the French *cuisinier* who opened the Savoy Hotel in London, put several recipes for Jerusalem artichokes in his cookbook, all of which involved quantities of butter. For *Topinambours à l'anglaise*, for instance, he instructs us to "cut the Jerusalem artichokes to the shape of large olives, and gently cook them in butter, without browning. Season them, and combine them with a little thin Béchamel sauce."

Dorothy's recipe was a little less complicated. "Scrub them. Leave the skins on them when you cook them," she told the woman next to me (Escoffier forgot to mention the skins), "they come off better afterwards. Then just mash them up with a little salt and pepper and butter and eat them."

I took mine out to the cabin and made a kind of *mirepoix* with them, cutting them into thin slices, leaving the skins on, and placing them, with sliced carrots and onions, salt, pepper and lemon thyme, under a couple of chicken breasts in a covered frying pan until the chicken was cooked. Then I ate the whole thing. The Jerusalem artichokes were delicious, and they didn't taste like artichokes at all.

Joual Horse. A term used since 1960 in certain intellectual circles to denote *la langue québécoise.*

—*Dictionnaire de la langue québécoise,* Léandre Bergeron

SPEAKING HORSE

Every language has its bizarre mispronunciations that make new words, some of them opposite in meaning to the original. In English, "hussy" is a corruption of housewife, a "gaffer" is a grandfather, "bedlam" came from Bethlehem and "maudlin" used to be Magdalen. In Quebec, the word *joual* is a local pronunciation of the word *cheval,* meaning "horse"; and its now outmoded use as the name for the language spoken in Quebec comes from the French expression *parler cheval,* meaning "to talk gibberish, to jabber." Like "maudlin" and "hussy," it was not intended as a compliment. As in many cultures emerging from colonial submissiveness, however, a term intended to be insulting was adopted as a kind of badge of honour ("Bluenose," for example, or "baaad," which in black America meant "good"). And so Québécoises said they spoke horse. It was a shibboleth: those who understood it could stay, those who couldn't could *sacrer le camp.*

Bergeron was wrong about the date: the term *joual* was first used to describe the Quebec language by the novelist Claude-Henri Grignon in 1939. The French from France, he wrote, "ought to have the good sense and politeness to say that although we speak *joual* and write like cows, we still have enough taste to buy French wine and French books . . . [In fact,] we speak and write the purest French *joual* that one can imagine." André Laurendeau, writing in 1959 in *Le Devoir,* revived the term in describing a kind of bilingualism taking place within Quebec, with the urban working-class *joual* speakers on one hand and the urbane intellectuals pressing for a purer French on the other. The debate was picked up by Jean-Paul Desbiens, author of *Les insolences du Frère Untel* (1960), who obviously supported the latter: "The word *joual* is odious and the thing itself is odious," says Frère Untel. To speak *joual* was "to talk like one might imagine horses would talk if they hadn't already opted for silence and the smile of Fernandel."

This was the view that dominated the period of intellectual and political self-examination in Quebec known as the Quiet Revolution, which began with the defeat of the Union Nationale in 1960. Writers who objected to marginalizing themselves by working in a language that only other Quebeckers would understand began contributing to a magazine that had been founded in 1950 by Gérard Pelletier and Pierre Elliott Trudeau. *Cité libre* scorned cultural nationalism as a sure way of maintaining Quebec as a political backwater, cut off from the rest of Canada and the larger world. Trudeau never spoke *joual*; he spoke flawless English and *français de la France* (*"Mangez de la merde"* is perfectly good Parisian French). His aim, from the first day he entered federal politics until the day he resigned as prime minister, was to undo the intense, ingrown nationalism of the Catholic regime, to drag Quebeckers kicking and screaming onto the world stage—not as pipe-sucking, fiddle-playing, forelock-tugging curiosities but as full and respected participants in the international economic and social community, not as Calibans but as noble Venetians (albeit with himself as Prospero).

Very soon, younger and more rebellious Québécois saw that as sleeping with the enemy. Their own publication was *Parti pris,* a brilliant name that means something like "taking a stand." *De parti pris* means "a thing that is done deliberately," and the word *parti* by itself can mean anything from a political party to a house party to a gang of brigands. Trudeau took the latter meaning; today, *parti pris* might be translated as *In Your Face*. The *Parti pris*ists called for a revolution with a little more blood, a little more guts, and a lot more passion. The child of *Cité libre* was the federal Liberal party; *Parti pris* spawned the Parti Québécois.

Caught in the cross-hairs was the use of *joual* as a written language, a language of literature. To speak *joual* was a political statement; to write it was an act of defiance at least as significant as, say, rejecting the eighteenth-century Classical English poetry of Alexander Pope, who thought the proper English poem was an imitation of a Horatian ode, and writing like William Wordsworth, who championed a poetry "written in the language of the common people." In Quebec, *joual* was the language of the common people, and to write it was to enshrine it. "We refuse to become pretty eunuchs protected from the plague," wrote Gérald Godin in *Parti pris*, in an essay entitled "Le joual politique." "We refuse to be backdoor Frenchmen, a French crown on a *joual* head. We refuse to use beautiful words to disguise the rotten language of our people." To write *joual*, in other words, was to rub the noses of the *Cité libre*ists in the fact that Quebec *was* a backwater, and it was the fault of the English; Québécois should not be sucking up to the rest of Canada or France, they should be defying them. Writing *joual* was the fundamental principle of the new Quebec nationalism, which Trudeau found just as self-defeating as the old one had been.

The most defiant cry came in the form of Jacques Renaud's short novel *Le cassé*, published in 1964 when Renaud was twenty-one years old. It has been translated into English twice: once in 1968 as *Flat, Broke and Beat* by Gérald Robitaille, a Quebec writer living in Paris and working as personal secretary to Henry Miller—he also translated Miller's *Quiet Days at Clichy* into French the same year—and again in 1984 as *Broke City* by Montreal novelist David Homel. *Le cassé* was one of the first works of Quebec literature to be written obstinately in French as it was spoken on the streets and in the brasseries of working-class Montreal, in what Renaud called "a language of submission, revolt, and pain." Like other Quebec writers before him, Renaud had started writing in proper French. "I had written in a story, 'Elle s'en fout,'" he told Malcolm Reid, author of *The Shouting Signpainters: A Literary and Political Account of Quebec Revolutionary Nationalism*. "Then it struck me that no one says that; they say, 'Elle s'en sacre.' The more I thought about it, the more I knew that the first sentence was unreal, taken from a book I'd read, not from the language I'd learned from people. I crossed it out and wrote it the second way." *Elle s'en fout* is fairly tame: "she didn't care;" *elle s'en sacre* is more expressive: "she didn't give a damn."

Le cassé was filled with street-French words and pronunciational spellings (*moé* for *moi*, *crisse* for *Christ*, *pis* for *puis*, etc.). "You have to imagine how it was back then," Godin wrote in a preface to Homel's translation. "Just writing the word *crisse* in the pages of a book was a scandal. Any change was met with resistance. Spoken words, once they were written, were taboo."

The first line of *Le cassé*—"Cette chambre lui a coûté cinq piasses"—stated its allegiances. *Piasse* is the *joual* pronunciation of *piastre*, which is the Quebec word for "dollar." A writer like Gabrielle Roy, to take an extreme example, who was no less sympathetic to the working poor than was Renaud, would have written: "Cette chambre lui a coûté cinq dollars." This novel isn't going to merely depict the rottenness and despair at the core of Québécois society, Renaud was declaring; it was going to roll in it.

"*Broke City* is nihilist," Renaud wrote of his own work,

It's a moment from my life. People have talked a lot about the *joual* part. *Joual* isn't style, it's a way of thinking, a way of existing. *Joual* is more than the language that *Broke City* is written in; it stands for the whole pariah situation. *Joual* is the language of both revolt and submission, of anger and impotence. *Joual* is a non-language. A denunciation.

The novel contains some hilarious head-on collisions between Parisian French and *joual*. The following dialogue between two waitresses, after a "nationalist intellectual" customer has berated one of them for speaking *joual* and then left a fifty-cent tip, gives a flavour of the language in Renaud's hands:

> La serveuse: Cinquante cennes . . . Addition, ça paye . . . Y a du foin, c'gars-là.
> L'autre serveuse: Deux ord' de tosses. Pour qui qu'ça s'prend, c'monde-là? Moé, à ta place j'l'aurais mis à sa place!
> La serveuse: Oui, mais y a tipé, l'gars . . .
> L'autre serveuse: Waingne . . .

You need to know only that *Deux ord' de tosses* is "Two orders of toast" and that *Waingne* is *Oui* to get an idea of the difficulty Renaud encountered when *Le cassé* came out. One reviewer called it not so much a novel as a punch in the face. It wasn't just the characters who were *cassé* (broken or broke); it was the French language. Soon other writers—Michel Tremblay and André Major, for example—snatched up the freedom of expression unleashed by Renaud's lyrical howl of pain. "A solution born of despair, compassion, and love," wrote Lise Gauvin in 1981, "the use of *joual* was, in the sixties, an active form of resistance."

After 1976, however, calling the language spoken in Quebec *joual* began to decline in favour of *la langue québécoise*. It was still a question of nationalism: *joual* did not have the history of the Quebec people behind it. Switching from *joual* to *québécois* was the same as switching, in medieval England, from Anglo-Saxon to English. It was a political statement. One of the first doubts about *joual*'s usefulness to effect change was expressed by one of Quebec's most iconoclastic and nihilistic writers, Victor-Lévy Beaulieu, who felt that *joual* "was not dangerous" enough, because "it existed only at the level of words, not at the level of continuity of thought, which remained French." Consequently, Beaulieu's later novels were written in almost classical French, which produced a satisfying shock wave among his readers.

In the massive *Dictionnaire de la langue québécoise*, published by Beaulieu's publishing company, VLB éditeur, in 1980, Bergeron set out to compile "the most exhaustive and most complete list possible, excluding not a single word no matter how bad, vulgar, raunchy, debauched, etc." Just as Renaud set out to do in his novel. "To pretend to be making a serious and objective survey of the vocabulary of a people," Bergeron continued, "while leaving out certain words because they were fermented in the street, or in the heart, or in a sleeping bag thrown together in the open air, to leave out the *osti de câlice de tabarnac, bizoune, chenolles, foufounes* and *se passer un Dieu-seul-me-voit*, exactly as these words are spoken every day and every night in the country of Quebec, would be to make the work a model of discipline, prudery, narrow and cramped." Would Renaud have argued with that? And yet *joual* is included in the dictionary only as a brief entry, almost disparagingly: "*Joual* n.m.—Horse. A term used since 1960 in certain intellectual circles to denote *la langue québécoise*."

Now *that's* in your face.

Kerosene *Cdn.* A thin oil, a mixture of hydrocarbons, usually produced by distilling petroleum; coal oil.

—*Gage Canadian Dictionary,* 1997

THE MAN WHO PUT THE TIGER IN YOUR TANK

I love used bookshops partly, I think, for their smell. When I was young, I went to a one-room country school, and the school library was a derelict, retrofitted school bus known as the Book-mobile. It rattled into our schoolyard once a week, and we were allowed to take out only three books at a time, three times the number of students in our school district being precisely the number of books on the Bookmobile's Meccano-set shelves. The year I was in Grade 7, I read fifty books. I kept a list: *Pinocchio, Little Women,* all the works of Robert Louis Stevenson, some Jules Verne, no Dickens. For Canadian content, all the Hardy Boys books.

I chose books for the way they felt and smelled. *Pinocchio* was a very soft book, the pages having been turned so often by small, eager fingers that the paper had softened into a kind of thin chamois. The individual letters in the word "Pinocchio" were pressed so deeply into the title page that I could feel them on the other side, like Braille. Most of the books I read that year smelled the same. The corners of *Treasure Island* were worn and frayed, as though by years of exposure to sun and salt wind. The books had been produced long before the era of paper bleaches and chemical smudge-resisters, and so they smelled of the forest they had come from and the homes they had had before ending up in the Bookmobile. They smelled of pulpwood and carbon, and woodsmoke and kerosene.

That is pretty much what our cabin smells like now. When we come out here to read and think, we enter a world that has changed very little since those books were made and first read. No electricity, running water, central heating, humming refrigerator, clacking mail slot, canned laughter. Our few concessions to the twentieth century are a chainsaw, an airtight woodstove, two pairs of binoculars and the blue plastic container we keep the kerosene in (red plastic is for gasoline). The five kerosene lamps we light at night fill the cabin with a soft, yellow light that makes the transition from reading to dreaming almost perfectly undetectable.

The invention of kerosene signalled the beginning of the end of the whaling industry, in some ways the beginning of the end of the nineteenth century. Before kerosene, just about every book in the world that was read at night was read by candle or whale oil; after kerosene, whalers continued to hunt and kill whales, but for increasingly silly things, like perfume and the stays in women's corsets, and whaling became a shameful occupation. And kerosene was invented in Canada. When American poet Billy Collins, in a poem called "Canada" ("I am writing this on a strip of white birch bark / that I cut from a tree with a penknife"), apostrophizes, "O Canada . . . / You are the rapids, the propeller, the kerosene lamp . . ." he is being historically accurate about the kerosene.

Abraham Gesner was born in Cornwallis Dyke, on the Fundy side of Nova Scotia, in 1797, the grandson of a United Empire Loyalist who had settled on land vacated by the Acadians in 1755. Whether or not this bothered Gesner is not known, but he did make his first attempt at earning a living in a decidedly Sam Slick kind of way, as a horse-trader. He bought horses in Nova Scotia and tried to sell them in the West Indies, unsuccessfully as it turned out: his ships kept sinking with his horses still on them. A year after his last ship sank, Gesner married Harriet Webster and her father paid for his training as a doctor in England. While studying at St. Bartholomew's in London, he became intensely interested in science—especially after meeting the future father of English geology, Charles Lyell, in the study of rocks and minerals. Returning to Parrsboro, Nova Scotia, in 1827 to set up medical practice, he spent most of his free time roaming the hills for samples, and in 1836 published *Remarks on the Geology and Mineralogy of Nova Scotia*, a 300-pager with a decided lean towards the more exploitable aspects of the colony's landscape.

Later that year he was appointed New Brunswick's official geologist, and he moved with his family to Saint John, where he lectured, explored, mapped and surveyed, largely, it seems, at his own expense. Trouble with the government over his salary ended with Gesner's return to Nova Scotia, where he resumed his career as a doctor and continued his scientific investigations. "He experimented with the newfound wonders of galvanism, as electricity was then called," writes Tom Carpenter in *Inventors: Profiles in Canadian Genius*, "and he designed a small motor that was a forerunner of the dynamo, a machine capable of converting mechanical energy into electric current." He also invented a machine that insulated electrical wire, and figured out how to compress coal dust into biscuits that burned like charcoal. He dabbled in asphalt and wood preservatives and became interested in distillation. It was this latter preoccupation that resulted, in 1846, in his first attempts to distil oil from coal.

Gesner produced this coal oil in the woodshed behind his Parrsboro infirmary by burning dry coal and condensing the gas given off into a liquid. The distillate was allowed to settle so that the oil and water would separate. He then drew off the oil, mixed it with sulphuric acid, which precipitated out any tars still present, allowed it to settle again, then neutralized it with calcined lime and distilled it again. The distillate this time he named *keroselaine*, which is Greek for "wax oil." He later perfected the process and changed the name to kerosene. For some reason it became better known as coal oil, and its first public use was as a fuel for lighthouses.

New Brunswick might now wish it had not fired Gesner, but it had, rather messily, and so rather than develop his invention in Canada or even show it to Canadian entrepreneurs, he took it to New York. Perhaps his grandfather had instilled in him a sense that New York was where the big money was and so that was also where he should take big ideas. Kerosene was a big idea. Bigger, at the time, than insulated wire, much bigger than wood preservatives. Several wealthy people in New York thought so, anyway, and they bought Gesner's patent from him and in 1854 set up the North American Kerosene Gas Light Company, hiring Gesner as their chief chemist as a sort of gesture of good will. He worked with them in New York for four years, until they fired him in 1858 and sold the patents to J.D. Rockefeller, who owned Standard Oil. This was farsighted of Rockefeller because, as it turned out, Gesner had been working on three grades of kerosene, which he called grades A, B and C. He thought the first two grades were useless, because they were too volatile for lamp oil; when he put a match to them, they were likely to blow up the lamp. But Standard Oil continued to look into the possibilities of these volatile substances. Today, grades A and B kerosene are called gasoline, and Standard Oil is called the Exxon Corporation.

The ghost of Standard Oil lives on in Canada, however. Exxon's Canadian affiliate is Imperial Oil, the largest petroleum company in Canada, with annual losses in excess of $35 million. Imperial started out as a small Canadian oil company in 1880 but was absorbed into the Standard Oil family in 1896. The brand of gasoline sold by Imperial Oil is still called Esso—"S.O." for Standard Oil.

In Canada, kerosene has become a quaint fuel, a hobby fuel. The general store in Delta used to sell it by the gallon when we first moved out to the cabin, then by the litre (I had to tell the clerk how many litres there were in our five-U.S.-gallon blue plastic container: twenty. She had to hand pump it from a large tank out back, and when I went out to help her the smell reminded me of growing up in Dalston and going down to the corner store for a can of kerosene for the living-room stove. We called it coal oil, but it was kerosene, and I'd forgotten all about it. Two years ago the store in Delta closed down. We can still buy kerosene at the hardware store in Lansdowne, but it comes premeasured in ten-litre clear plastic containers that sell for fifteen dollars. Gesner's ghost is about to be laid.

But it is still around in books, and I don't just mean the smell. I see it every time I come across a mention of kerosene, as I do quite often. Jon Krakauer, for example, in his book about death on Mount Everest, *Into Thin Air*, sees Sherpas carrying kerosene into their remote village high in the Himalayas. Linda Spalding, in *The Follow*, travels two days by canoe into central Borneo and finds a Dayak village whose only concession to the nineteenth century is a kerosene lamp. Inman, at the opening of Charles Frazier's novel *Cold Mountain*, lies in darkness in a Civil War hospital because of a shortage of that newfangled lamp oil, kerosene. These are all tributes to Abraham Gesner.

And there are others. It was Gesner who developed the distillation technology that made petroleum refineries possible, and in 1933, Imperial Oil recognized that by erecting a monument in Cornwallis, Gesner's home town in Nova Scotia. The honour is Gesner's: "His treatise on the geology and mineralogy of Nova Scotia," reads the monument, "was one of the earliest works dealing with those subjects in the province. And about 1852," it goes on, "he was the *American* inventor of the process of kerosene oil."

The italics are mine.

Mackinaw A short, rough coat of material much like a grey horse blanket. It is worn by most lumberjacks, explorers, miners and woodsmen north of the great Canadian lakes.

—*The Shagganappi,* Pauline Johnson, 1913

IT'S A LUMBERJACKET AND IT'S OKAY

A friend of mine recently came over wearing a beautiful red-and-black checked woollen jacket. It was quite old, dating perhaps from the 1920s, but in perfect condition. It was lined with blue quilted silk. It had side and chest pockets, all with button-down flaps, and a curious fifth pocket at the back that might have been a kind of glove compartment, or a place to carry the day's bag of small game or a field guide to the rocks and minerals of Quetico National Park. The mind raced. Its collar was so wide that it could be pulled up to form a hood against inclement weather. And yet it was so elegant it could be worn with a shirt and tie to, say, a foreign ministers' conference. I confess I immediately coveted this jacket.

"I like your jacket," I said to him, thinking that if this were Mexico he would take it off and give it to me. This is not Mexico.

"I picked it up for a song at a second-hand clothing store," he said. He allowed me to feel the thickness of the cloth.

"It has," I said lamely, "bone buttons."

"It's a mackinaw," he said.

"If I tell you why it's called a mackinaw," I said, "will you let me wear it?"

"No," he said.

I told him anyway. The mackinaw blanket jacket is the old North

West Company's equivalent to the Hudson's Bay Company blanket coat. The adjective "mackinaw" originally applied to a rough, woollen blanket used as an item of trade at Michilimackinac, a fur-trading post near Sault Ste. Marie. The strait between Lake Huron and Lake Michigan, and the island situated within the strait, were called Michilimackinac (Great Turtle) by the Sioux, and that name was kept by the Jesuits who established the mission of Saint-Ignace on the strait in 1670. La Salle built a fortified post on the south shore in 1679 and called that Michilimackinac also.

The Jesuit explorer and historian Pierre-François-Xavier de Charlevoix stopped for several weeks at the Michilimackinac mission in 1721. He had been charged with determining whether the Great Lakes provided a passage to the western ocean or just petered out into a dead end, and while at Michilimackinac he was told of a great river that led to a large sea. He decided to take the river. Before leaving, however, he noted in his *Journal* that Michilimackinac had once been

> the chief residence of a nation of the same name, whereof they reckon as they say to the number of thirty towns, which were dispersed up and down in the neighbourhood of the island. It is pretended they were destroyed by the Iroquois, but it is not said at what time nor on what occasion; what is certain is, that no vestige of them now remains. I have somewhere read that our ancient missionaries have lately discovered relicks of them.

Charlevoix thought that "the name of Michilimakinac signifies a great quantity of turtles, but I have never heard that more of them are found here at this day than elsewhere." In fact it was the offshore island that was called Great Turtle, "to which animal," artist Paul Kane remarked during his visit there in 1845, "it bears a strong resemblance in form when seen from a certain point." Charlevoix set off on his journey and discovered that the great river was the Mississippi, and the large sea it drained into was the Gulf of Mexico; by the time he returned to Quebec, he had paddled around the entire perimeter of New France.

Fort Michilimackinac, the name of which was shortened by the French to Mackinac, was later the scene of one of the bloodiest massacres in Canadian history. In 1763, Pontiac, who had sided with the French during the French–English war and had apparently not heard that the war had ended with the siege of Quebec in 1759, led an army of four hundred Ojibway warriors to Michilimackinac and captured the fort, which comprised ninety English soldiers and three hundred French traders and voyageurs. Pretending to be chasing a lacrosse ball, the Ojibways entered the fort and killed seventy of the English defenders. One of the survivors, the English trader Alexander Henry, observed the carnage while hiding in the attic of his French neighbour's house: "I beheld, in shapes the foulest and most terrible, the ferocious triumphs of barbarian conquerors. The dead were scalped and mangled; the dying were writhing and shrieking, under the unsatiated knife and tomahawk and, from the bodies of some ripped open, their butchers were drinking the blood scooped up in the hollow of joined hands, and quaffed amid shouts of rage and victory."

After this and a similar attempt on Detroit (the subject of John Richardson's novel *Wacousta*, 1832), Pontiac switched his allegiance to England and Fort Michilimackinac was returned to the British. In 1772, when the trader Peter Pond visited it, it was still called (in Pond's eccentric spelling) "Mishlemackenack." The North West Company, which was formed in 1779 and was headquartered at Grand Portage, at the western end of Lake Superior, established a kind of subsidiary company in 1806, which they called the Michilimackinac

Fur Company. The American businessman John Jacob Astor tried to buy it but was unsuccessful, and in 1809 Astor formed the American Fur Company in order to ensure that furs collected in American territory remained in American hands. He dispatched Wilson Price Hunt, one of his partners, to travel from Montreal to the mouth of the Columbia River by canoe—following Alexander Mackenzie's 1796 route—to squeeze the North West Company off the Pacific Coast by establishing an empire there to be called Astoria. Hunt left Montreal in July 1810, and he had the effrontery to stop and resupply at Michilimackinac, which by then was just starting to be called Mackinac. This was two years before the United States declared war on Canada.

An account of this expedition, written in 1839 by Washington Irving, describes "the famous old French trading post" as "a rallying point for a multifarious and motley population. The inhabitants were amphibious in their habits, most of them being, or having been, voyageurs or canoe-men." The outpost itself, he thought, was

> a mere village, stretching along a small bay, with a fine broad beach in front of its principal row of houses, and dominated by the old fort, which crowned an impending height. The beach was a kind of public promenade, where were displayed all the vagaries of a seaport on the arrival of a fleet from a long cruise. Here voyageurs frolicked away their wages, fiddling and dancing in the booths and cabins, buying all kinds of knick-knacks, dressing themselves out finely and parading up and down, like arrant braggarts and coxcombs. Sometimes they met with rival coxcombs in the young Indians from the opposite shore, who would appear on the beach painted and decorated in fantastic style, and would saunter up and down to be gazed at and admired, perfectly satisfied that they eclipsed their pale-faced competitors.

Fort Michilimackinac had been abandoned by the British army in 1796, when it was assumed that hostilities with the French and the Ojibway were over, and at the commencement of the War of 1812 it was in the hands of the Americans. At first glance it would seem to have been of little interest to the Americans, since the avowed purpose of the war was to secure free trade for American seaports. But John Jacob Astor wanted Michilimackinac for the American Fur Company; the post controlled all the trade routes into Lake Michigan and connected them with Lake Superior, and it was sufficiently distant from the three theatres of war chosen by the American invaders —Montreal, Niagara and Detroit—that the Americans no doubt thought they could simply slip into Mackinaw, as they called it, and no one would notice.

They might have done so, too, had it not been for Captain Charles Roberts of the 10th Royal Veteran Regiment. Since 1811, Roberts had been in command of a small British garrison on St. Joseph Island, at the northern end of Lake Huron forty miles from Michilimackinac. When he learned on July 7, 1812, that war had been declared on June 18, he suddenly realized what all the American activity across the river had been about. He was in command of only forty-six soldiers, all of them veterans, but could rally about two hundred French Canadian fur traders and four hundred Indians who traded with the Canadians. With these, possibly on orders from Sir Isaac Brock but probably not, he crossed the river and laid siege to Mackinaw.

The American fort was held by sixty-one men, and the governor of Michigan, William Hull, had effectively rendered them terrified at the possibility of fighting against Canadian Indians. Hull had issued a warning to American Loyalists living in Upper Canada that if the Indians joined the war on the Canadian side, "the first stroke of the tomahawk, the first attempt with the scalping knife, will be the signal of one indiscriminate scene of desolation." He told his troops, which included the men at Mackinaw, that "no white man found fighting by the side of an Indian will be taken prisoner—instant death will be his lot." The Americans, watching the approach of Roberts and four hundred Ottawa, Chippewa and Sioux warriors, and perhaps recalling the famous lacrosse massacre of 1763, surrendered Mackinaw without a shot fired.

Roberts and his men occupied Mackinaw throughout the winter of 1812. They were extremely poorly equipped; Roberts complained that his men did not even have warm clothing. What they did have was a warehouse full of trade goods, including liquor and blankets. Roberts's men made good use of both. He wrote that his men were "debilitated and worn down by unconquerable drunkenness." To make up for the lack of military greatcoats, he had his men cut up the post's stock of North West Company blankets and sew them into coats. With these and the liquor, his men made it through the winter, and the next year Roberts was recalled to Montreal and quietly praised for his actions. As Pierre Berton noted in his account of the war, *The Invasion of Canada* (1980), Roberts had not known that his conquest of Mackinaw had forced Colonel Hull to surrender Detroit less than a month later; nor could he guess that his Mackinaw blanket coats, "created out of necessity, [were] destined to become fashionable" among Canadian backwoodsmen for the next two hundred years.

Not much changed in Mackinaw itself. When Anna Brownell Jameson visited the outpost in 1836, an account of which is in her *Winter Studies and Summer Rambles in Canada* (1838), she found it "thickly studded with Indian lodges," the harbour filled with "canoes, fishing, or darting hither and thither, light and buoyant as sea-birds; a tall graceful schooner swinging at anchor . . ." She noted that "the dress of the men was very various—the cotton shirt, blue or scarlet leggings, and deerskin moccasins and blanket coat, were most general."

Blanket coats worn by the men were usually bright red; those worn by women were dark blue. Farther west, knee-length blanket coats of this sort were worn by Indians seen by Paul Kane in the 1840s, and David Thompson records that one of his men, who was handy with needle and thread, was asked to make blanket coats by Hearne's Indian guides near Lake Athabaska.

The popularity of the mackinaw jacket soared during the Klondike Gold Rush, when it became the "Klondike coat," a garment made from mackinaw cloth. The T. Eaton Co. mail-order catalogue for spring and summer 1898 offered "Men's Klondike mining coats, made of heavy black Mackinaw cloth, with 6-inch storm collar and capot to pull over the head, strap across the throat." This sounds a lot like my friend's coat, except his was checked. A capot (or capote) was a sort of parka hood, and when drawn up made the wearer look something like a turtle. As though to bring the etymology full circle, Washington Irving wrote of Native people encountered by Hunt that "they wear a capot or surcoat, made of a blanket." This must have been the mackinaw, though still of solid colour. Eaton's also sold "Men's mining coats for Klondike use, heavy Mackinaw, in black shade" and "Men's Klondike shirts, heavy blue and black Mackinaw." Blue and black checked, that is: the true mackinaw was born.

Nowadays just about anyone *but* lumberjacks, explorers, miners and woodsmen wears mackinaw jackets. Teenagers wanting to look cool or tough tie the sleeves of their mackinaw jackets around their waists and wear them like skirts. Writing in *The Globe and Mail* recently, Mark Kingwell recalled that during his university days, Yonge Street was generally "athrong with lumber-jacketed thugs in Greb Kodiaks and Gregg Allman haircuts." Television characters who want to look typically Canadian—Red Green, the Monty Python cast singing "I'm a lumberjack and I'm okay"—wear mackinaw shirts and suspenders.

While I was working at *Harrowsmith* magazine a few years ago, we were bought by the publishing conglomerate Telemedia, and executives from Toronto arrived at our homey offices near Kingston driving brand-new BMWs and wearing brand-new mackinaw jackets they had ordered especially from L.L. Bean, thinking they would thereby endear themselves to those of us who had worked there for years and regarded the takeover as a hostile one, an assimilation into everything the magazine stood against. We all showed up wearing suits and ties, but, as Frank Edwards, another of the editors, later pointed out, "Their cars cost more than our houses, and their clothes cost more than our cars."

At a massive economic conference of Pacific Rim countries held in Vancouver in November 1997, Prime Minister Chrétien made a gift of typical Canadian clothing to the twenty-four APEC leaders in attendance, and at the end of the weekend session they all trooped out of the conference centre for a group photo op, wearing "typically Canadian" light-blue denim cowboy shirts and, on top of these, identical brown leather jackets. I was disappointed. Before the conference Chrétien had said something about giving them all tuques, but cooler heads must have prevailed. But if he had to give them jackets, I wished he had given them mackinaws. They would have been exceptionally good mackinaws, thick and silk-lined, with high capots and buttoned-down pockets and a pouch in the back for a sandwich or a Peterson's guide. And eventually, some of them would undoubtedly have turned up in second-hand clothing stores, to be had for a song.

Muskrat On an individual basis, the muskrat might seem
to be one of nature's more persecuted creatures.
—*The Muskrat,* Ontario Ministry of Natural Resources

THE SHOP GIRL IN HER MUSQUASH

One morning last spring, I watched two muskrats playing in a
shallow swamp in front of our cabin. I had been considering
draining the swamp because of the mosquitoes it bred throughout
the summer, and in the spring the water inched right up to the cabin
door and threatened to come in, but watching the muskrats changed
my mind. It was mid-April, the ice had just gone off the water, and
the muskrats seemed to be celebrating. There was a bright clump of
lily spears at the water's edge, and the male would swim over to it,
pull up a shoot with his webbed forepaws and feed it straight into his
mouth like a pencil into a pencil sharpener, probably the first green
food he had had since freeze-up last fall. His mate would swim up to
him, touch his nose with hers, then turn abruptly and swim off across
the pond, whereupon he would drop the lily shoot and chase off after
her, swimming with his own nose close to the base of her smooth,
round tail. As I watched, they did this three or four times, then at
some point the female stopped to chew on something in shallow water
and the male began vigorously grooming the sleek, wet fur on her
back, standing beside her, raising himself on his hind legs and rum-
maging through her fur as though frantically searching for something
valuable he had dropped. When he had completed messing up her
fur, he smoothed it again. Then he climbed up on her back, padded
around for a few seconds with all four feet, and slid head first down
her back like an otter off a mud bank and swam away.

The muskrat takes its scientific name, *Ondatra zibethicus*, from the Iroquois word for the animal, *ondatra*, and a Greek reference to its two anal glands, which enlarge during the animal's breeding season and secrete a strong odour of musk, especially in the males. The common name for this rodent has a more convoluted history. Because it looks like a rat and smells of musk at certain times of the year, it is assumed that is why it is called the muskrat. But the Powhatan Indians of Virginia called the animal *mussascus*, which is sometimes cited as the source of the English word via New England settlers: John Smith noted in 1623 that "Mussascus is a beast of the forme and nature of our water Rats, but many of them smell exceedingly strongly of Muske."

But *mussascus* has nothing to do with musk. "Musk" comes from the Sanskrit word *muska*, which meant "testicle," and was applied to the scrotum-shaped pouch of the musk deer; it also meant "little mouse," because somebody thought the deer's scrotum looked like a little curled-up mouse. The association between musk and rodent travelled from Sanskrit to Persian to Old French to Old English—none of which, however, was spoken by the Powhatans. They spoke a dialect of Algonquin, and *mussascus* is related to the Abenaki *muskwessu*, and it is this word that came into English via Canadian trappers, first as musquash, then, by folk etymology, as muskrat. *Muskwessu* actually means something like "swamp dweller." Our word "muskeg" similarly comes from the Cree word *muskek*, meaning "swamp." Folk eytmology is also at play in the fields of the musk ox: in 1744 a fur trader named Arthur Dobbs, writing about the area surrounding Hudson Bay, noted that the territory was frequented by "a kind of Ox, called the Musk ox, which smells at some Time in the Year so strong of Musk, that it cannot be eat." It is far more likely that "musk ox" is derived from the northern Cree and meant something like "the ox that lives on the muskeg." In the 1790s the explorer David Thompson referred to all the land between Hudson Bay and Lake Winnipeg, a land of shallow lakes and peat bogs, as "Musk Rat Country."

Seeing muskrats, even frolicking muskrats, in the spring always sets up conflicting emotions in me, because it makes me think both of nature unfettered and of trapping, in the same way that seeing a white-tailed deer in the fall makes me worry about hunters, and a red sunset makes Bill McKibbon, in *The End of Nature*, think of air pollution. It isn't that the experience is ruined for me, just rather more complicated. Muskrats are fur-bearing swamp-dwellers, unfortunately for them. It takes sixty-five of them to make a mid-length muskrat coat. Muskrat became a popular substitute for beaver fur when overtrapping made the latter affordable only to toffs; as Peter Matthiessen puts it, muskrat fur came into its own "in a less glorious age." In E.R. Punshon's 1934 mystery *Death Among the Sun Bathers*, one of his more unsavoury characters, a London furrier, declares that "the really good furs, the mink, the ermine, the true Persian lamb, the blue fox, and so on . . . will always command their price. The charlady may have her ponyskin to keep her warm, the shop girl may go to work in a musquash, but the rich woman will still want her thousand-guinea mink." To supply the off-the-rack garment industry, muskrats were trapped by the millions. It has long been Canada's most important fur export, with annual harvests even now, when Canadian garment fur is at a 400-year nadir of popularity, of more than 8 million animals. Beaver skins might have been more highly valued, but the economic base of early Canada was firmly built on the backs of the lowly musquash.

It took a while for musquash to become muskrat in the garment fur industry, euphemism being the foundation of good marketing. When even musquash hinted too strongly of musk (or squash), muskrat fur was called Hudson seal. John Ciardi notes a marketing parallel in *Good Words to You*: "Early canners found a sales resistance to *horse mackerel* and achieved wide market acceptance only when they renamed their product *tuna*." There are many others. Manufacturers of synthetic leather got away with "leatherette" for a while, but the product didn't really pass for leather in middle-class households until someone dubbed it Naugahyde. And no one in the 1960s wore fake fur coats; they wore Borg.

That the lowly muskrat has long been a more important animal than the aristocratic beaver is reflected in Native mythology. The Innu of Labrador have an *atnukan*, or story, in which Wolverine, the Trickster (a role filled by Coyote in the west), wishes to restore order after "a time of great floods." (I am quoting from Lawrence Millman's recent collection of Innu stories, *Wolverine Creates the World*.) First he sent Otter down to the bottom of the floodwaters to bring up some ground, but Otter came up with nothing. Next he sent Beaver, but Beaver couldn't reach the bottom either. Then Wolverine asked Muskrat, and Muskrat came up with so much ground in him that Wolverine had to put his lips to Muskrat's anus and blow it all out. "This ground is the very ground we walk on today." And incidentally, as Apinam Ashini, the Innu storyteller who related this *atnukan* to Millman, added, "That's why the world is so much shit."

I am not a trapper, but I have a friend who is, and I have spent some time with him in his skinning shed. Donny does all his trapping during the winter, when the skins are prime—thick, grey underhairs, long, sleek, brown guard hairs—and by April the rafters of his shed are hung with hundreds of skins, each one turned carefully inside out and stretched over an oval wooden board, like a sock drying over a wire stretcher, with the darkly marbled skin exposed to the air and a cord looped through the eye holes and slung over a nail. I'm not sure that musk is the right word for the smell in Donny's skinning shed. It isn't exactly a bad smell, but it's a powerful smell.

In 1796, Mrs. Simcoe recorded in her diary that, while visiting a remote Ontario cabin, she "slept well without mosquitoes, but the smell of muskrat skins, which had been drying in the house, was disagreeable." I wouldn't call the smell disagreeable, but it did make me realize how unaware of smells we normally are.

Every spring Donny loads up his truck with the winter's catch and drives up to North Bay, where about half a million muskrat pelts are sold at auction every year. These days a "good winter rat" will sell for about seven dollars, and Donny trucks up about a thousand pelts a year. The auction barn used to be run by the Ontario Trappers Association, but the OTA went bankrupt a few years ago, partly because of the European boycott of Canadian fur but mostly because of internal disputes. Since 1991 the operation has been run by a new group, the Fur Harvesters Auction Inc., the "Inc." standing for the eighteen thousand licensed trappers in Ontario who own shares in the company. The FHA stresses careful wildlife management and sensible harvesting practices. Its goal, wrote vice-president Mark Downey in a recent issue of *The Fur Harvester*, is "to retain, promote and enhance our oldest land-based industry." That is, admittedly, a self-serving philosophy, but it also serves the muskrats. As Donny says, "It's to my advantage to keep the muskrat population on my trapline healthy and sleek and in good breeding condition. A muskrat is like a tree; it's a renewable and sustainable resource." Even though Ontario's muskrat population is depleted by a million or more individuals every year, and its habitat shrinks with every drained or polluted wetland, the species is increasing in numbers. And as Paul Toswell, a fur grader with the FHA in North Bay and a trapper himself, points out, every year the trade in muskrat furs puts millions of dollars into the pockets of rural entrepreneurs like Donny, who are thereby able to continue to live in the country and support their families.

Most of the muskrats trapped each year are males, partly because males far outnumber females, but also because females stay in their dens while the males busy themselves outside, looking for food and getting caught in traps. Donny sets his traps under the ice in swimways, not near den sites, although he knows where the den sites are and marks them with flagged poles that stick up through the snow. Females have on average three litters a year, with anywhere from five to a dozen young per litter; thus a single female muskrat this year potentially becomes thirty muskrats next year, nine hundred the year after that, twenty thousand the year after that, and so on ad infinitum, not allowing for natural attrition, which cuts it down considerably. To Donny, a healthy female muskrat means about $20,000 over five years. There seems to be a six- to ten-year boom-and-crash cycle for muskrat populations, but even so, without trapping and other more natural limitations, it wouldn't take long for muskrats to replace water in most of Canada's wetlands.

And, unlike beavers, muskrats are content to live in swamps. Beavers are always trying to downgrade a swamp into a lake—to change box turtle and frog and muskrat habitat, in other words, into playgrounds for power boats and Sea-Doos. I'd rather live by a swamp than a lake. In fact, our cabin is situated exactly between a swamp and a lake, and I find myself watching the swamp more often. Loons and ospreys and even a Caspian tern are busy over on the lake, but this spring a pair of wood ducks have taken up their quiet residence in the swamp, and a red-shouldered hawk occasionally swoops low over the brackish water and lands in a tree beside the wood pile, listening for mice. A swamp is stiller than a lake, and I go to the cabin to seek stillness.

Muskrats apparently agree with me. They are perfectly at home negotiating around lily-covered hummocks and fallen logs. In larger swamps the females sometimes build lodges, but more often they dig burrows into the mud surrounding the swamp, starting about six inches below the water-line and progressing sometimes forty feet inland, gradually rising so that the actual living area is high and dry and connected to air by a narrow ventilation shaft. Burrows are safer than lodges: predators such as foxes, coyotes and raccoons can dig through the roof of a lodge, but only mink can swim into a muskrat burrow, and there aren't that many mink around any more.

There are, however, a lot of mink coats, and at one time there were more beaver hats in England than live beavers in Canada— which brings me back to my original conflict over trapping. Donny and I have talked about the fact that he kills animals for a living, and through him I have discovered that there is a tolerance (although limited) within me for things like trapping and hunting and logging, particularly when it comes to killing things for my benefit. It isn't all or nothing with me. I wear leather boots, I eat game—with Donny, I have eaten beaver stew and roasted Canada goose—our cabin is made from pine logs, my books are arranged on pine shelves and I am writing this on an antique cherrywood table. I do not like what might be called convenience trapping—taking a family of beavers out of your pond because you want to swim in it, for example—or hunting for purposes not connected to survival, or clear-cutting a biodiversified forest for fibre and replacing it with monocultural aspen for plywood. But, like World Wildlife Fund president Monte Hummel, I have no quarrel with subsistence trapping by people who know what they are about.

I suppose, being Canadians, we want it both ways. We don't think humans have an inalienable right to kill animals or cut down trees, but we don't object to the trapping or logging of populous species. The natural population density for muskrat is about two dozen per acre of swamp, and Donny carefully keeps it at that so there are not fifty or sixty this year and none two years from now. I find it amusing that a large Greek garment firm recently bought twenty-eight thousand raccoon pelts at the North Bay auction, had them clipped short and dyed blue-black, made coats from them and sold the coats in Russia as blue fox. There are more raccoons killed on our highways each year than are sold by trappers, and the true blue fox (a winter phase of the coastal Arctic fox) is relatively rare. And I like the fact that Inuit communities can once again live proudly and independently by selling seal pelts rather than using welfare money to buy gasoline, or endlessly carving stone narwhals for tourists.

Thoreau approved of hunting, at least of the kind of hunting known as "still hunting," in which the hunter and the hunted enter into a kind of natural duet that sharpens and defines both as a species. Not the kind of hunting I see every fall around the cabin: bands of city men in orange vests leaning against their trucks, bottles of Canadian Club in their hands and expensive .303 rifles in the crooks of their arms, waiting for their dogs to chase a deer across the road. Paul Toswell tells me that the most expensive fur coat on the market today is one made from bobcat belly fur. I think there is an essential difference between trapping a healthy species like muskrat and killing a threatened species like bobcat for its belly fur, and I do not think that tolerating the one necessarily means inviting the other. If you open your front door to a friend, you do not by definition have to let a thief run in. The world is not *that* much shit.

Newfoundland dog Attempting to evaluate a dog
without first formulating a fixed image of an ideal in your mind
is synonymous to driving a car without a steering wheel. It soon
ends in tragedy.

—*This Is the Newfoundland,*
The Newfoundland Club of America

TO MAKE A MONGREL

There are many theories about the origin of the Newfoundland
dog, but the one I find most intriguing has Leif Ericson coming to Vinland in AD 1000 with a pack of the famous Viking "bear
dogs," which were purported to be descended from Tibetan mas-
tiffs. Leif's own dog was called Oolum. When the Vikings left Vinland, they abandoned some of their cattle and dogs, probably because
the animals had increased during their stay and there was no room
for them all on the boats. They also left Oolum, though, which is
harder to explain. The dogs seem to have survived: an anonymous
British naturalist writing in 1732 noted that "the Bear dog is of very
large size, commonly sluggish in his Looks, but he is very watchful.
He comes from Newfoundland." And modern science confirms the
Viking saga accounts: researchers have found Tibetan mastiff DNA in
the Newfoundland dog.

That would seem to clinch the Newfoundland's Norse roots. Bear
dogs must not have been all that friendly; if they had been, then the
Beothuks would have known about them, and they apparently did not.
Even George Cartwright, who named the Newfoundland dog in 1775,
corroborated his brother John's report that "providence has even
denied [the Beothuk] the pleasing services and companionship of the

faithful dog." The northern Innu had dogs, but they were of a breed that was later called Eskimo dogs (later still shortened to "Husky" dogs), not Newfoundland dogs. Oolum and his descendants must have gone feral in the five hundred years that separated Leif Ericson from John Cabot; friendliness was something they got later on.

The modern Newfoundland is likely to be a mixture of bear dog and several hardy breeds brought to the island by fishermen after Cabot's rediscovery of the island in 1497. This was the contention of Harold Macpherson, president of Royal Stores in St. John's in the 1950s and a long-time breeder of Newfoundland dogs. In 1937, Macpherson speculated:

> Basque fishermen, reported to have visited Newfoundland as early as 1506, would naturally bring as ships' dogs their white or cream-coloured Pyrenean sheep-dogs . . . The English, being a sporting people, would naturally take water spaniels, bird-dogs and mastiffs; likewise, the French, Spanish and Portuguese would bring their large dogs on salt trips from Cadiz . . . [and here] has evolved and developed a new type of dog named the Newfoundland.

E.J. Pratt knew what he was about, then, when he wrote his tribute to Carlo, the Newfoundland dog that saved ninety people from drowning after a shipwreck off Bonne Bay (now a part of Gros Morne National Park) in 1919:

> I see no use in not confessing—
> To trace your breed would keep me guessing;
> It would indeed an expert puzzle
> To match such legs with jet-black muzzle.
> To make a mongrel, as you know,
> It takes some fifty types or so . . .

The breed was described by Sir Joseph Banks when the famous biologist visited Newfoundland in 1766. Banks first described the run-of-the-mill dogs he met with as "mostly curs with a cross of the Mastiff in them." But he also mentioned a man living at Trepassy, on the South Shore, "who had a distinct breed which he called an original Newfoundland dog." The man may also have been known to George Cartwright, who supplied Banks with biological specimens. Banks eventually examined this breed, became fond of it, brought it back to Europe, and presented pups to such celebrated figures of the day as George III, Captain Cook, Lord Byron, Napoleon Bonaparte and Sir Walter Scott. The Newfoundland's fame was secured.

Pratt's poem pays tribute to the breed's best-known characteristics: its fierce loyalty and indomitable determination. Accounts of lives saved by Newfoundlands fill several volumes of marine history—the Newfoundland was, after all, bred to dive for objects, including people, that fell overboard from fishermen's boats—and the breed is known as "the dog that changed history." When the exiled Napoleon was secretly being conveyed from Elba one dark night, he reportedly fell into the water and was feared drowned; but his dog, the Newfoundland that had been given him by Sir Joseph Banks, dove in and dragged the emperor back to the ship.

The Newfoundland is also a powerful sled and pack dog. Lewis and Clark took one along on their overland expedition to the Rockies in 1802, and Elisha Kent Kane took ten Newfoundlands to pull his komatik when he set out in search of Sir John Franklin or the Open Polar Sea (he found neither) in 1853: "Six of them made a powerful traveling team," he wrote, "and four of them could carry me and my instruments for short journeys with ease."

For most of the nineteenth century the Newfoundland was extremely popular in England. In 1823 a black-and-white Newfoundland dog named Bob turned up in London and took to roaming up and down the banks of the Thames saving children from drowning. He saved twenty-three children in fourteen years, and his portrait, by Sir Edwin Landseer, the most celebrated portrait artist of the day, was called "A Distinguished Member of the Humane Society" and was exhibited at the Royal Academy in 1838. Landseer's painting created a fashion for the Newfoundland among the aristocracy—the black-and-white variety is still called a Landseer—that spilled over into the lower classes in the form of Landseer cups, plates, bowls, miniatures, porcelain figurines and other collectible gewgaws. (The modern equivalent would no doubt be the Dalmatian; you can buy Dalmatian hand puppets, Dalmatian-spotted boots, even Dalmatian umbrellas. If there had been movies in the 1840s, one would certainly have been called *101 Newfoundlands*.)

The Newfoundland's popularity spread to the United States, where it was also associated with loyalty and reliability—witness this passage in Herman Melville's novella *Benito Cereno*, published in 1852, in which Melville's narrator, the American Captain Delano, recalls a small boat he had owned as a child: "That boat, Rover by name, brought to his threshold for repairs, had familiarly lain there, as a Newfoundland dog." In the States, however, it was the black variety that predominated, as witness another passage from Melville's novella: "Like most men of good, blithe heart, Captain Delano took to negroes, not philanthropically, but genially, as other men to Newfoundland dogs."

The Newfoundland's reputation peaked in 1858, when several were sent to Switzerland to be bred with the failing St. Bernards, a breed that was succumbing to a genetic disorder to which the Newfoundlands were immune. Since then, the fashion for Newfoundlands seems to have declined. There are more Labrador retrievers around now than Newfoundlands, from which the black Lab was bred. And although there was a brief flurry of renewed interest in the early 1990s, when young women of alternative culture took to walking city streets behind enormous black dogs on taut leashes, the fad seemed to favour the more ferocious sort of dog, the Dobermann pinschers and the Rottweilers, rather than the even-tempered Newf. In general, though, the post-Victorian trend to smaller families, hence smaller houses, hence smaller pets, has done for all large breeds. As one American writer put it as early as 1885, "Newfoundland dogs are good to save children from drowning, but you must have a pond of water handy and a child," and both are in increasingly short supply.

In E.J. Pratt's other, longer and sadder elegiac poem about a Newfoundland, "A Reverie on a Dog," written in 1932, the poet's lifelong companion, which once would "jump from the bow-sprit to the sea or take / A two-mile morning swim across a lake," is now old and dying. Gone are the humorous feminine rhymes and the vaudevillian tum-te-tum rhythm of the earlier poem; grief has reduced the poet almost to plain speech:

> So here you are, your head upon my knees;
> Your joints are stiff, your blood is running cold;
> How strange it is, in all these fantasies,
> I had forgotten that you had grown old.

We have a heavy bronze statuette, a collectible gewgaw, that dates from the period of the Newfoundland's prime, inherited from an uncle of my wife's who died of cancer. It is cast in the shape of a Newfoundland dog, weighs about ten pounds, and stands on its own bronze base, looking like Carlo poised on the headland near Woody Point, ready to dive into Bonne Bay. Its articulated tail is inwardly connected to its lower jaw; when you lift the tail, the jaw drops. You insert a nut into the dog's mouth, press down on the tail and the nut is very efficiently cracked. Over the years it has saved many children from drowning in a sea of boredom during the Christmas holidays, and for the rest of the year it lies familiarly on the dining-room floor doing yeoman's duty as a doorstop.

Pablum Literally, *pablum* and *pap* mean baby food; figuratively, these words describe something lacking intellectual substance or artistic quality.

—*The Oxford Guide to Canadian English Usage,*
1997, Margery Fee and Janice McAlpine

FODDER AND CHILD REUNION

The box of baby cereal on my desk has the words "Pablum: The Original Infant Cereal" in bold letters across the top, and most of the rest of the box front is a close-up photograph of a bright-eyed, fair-skinned, intelligent-looking baby, the kind of baby I like to think I was in 1949, when I was a year old. His baby-blue eyes are wide open, his lips glisten wetly as though fresh from the nipple, and there is a hint of two bottom teeth poking up below a tongue that seems poised on the brink of articulating its first "Dada." According to my mother, I was a Pablum baby: bottle-fed, then weaned on a thin gruel of Pablum mixed with formula, first in the bottle, then gradually from a bowl, until I was living totally on cereal and an array of vitamin supplements, especially cod-liver oil (which my mother's family had produced in Newfoundland) and a thick, treacly substance called Virol that I reportedly licked enthusiastically from a spoon. Old Dr. Lansbury also told my mother to give me boiled eggs, which she mashed up and mixed in with the Pablum. It must have been all right, because when I was one year old I came first in the annual Windsor, Ontario, baby contest, sponsored in part by the Mead Johnson Company, which made Pablum. That's why it could be my picture there on the box on my desk.

Pablum is made and marketed only in Canada. On the back of

the box, a little text summarizes its history: "In the 1920's," it begins (unpromisingly, because of that unnecessary apostrophe), "children didn't have the nutritious diets that they do today" (well, they did, but no one gave it to them). "Research was undertaken to develop a nutritious baby food which would help provide some of the essential nutrients required for normal growth and development. In 1931," the text continues, "after much research and testing, the first batch of infant cereal fortified with vitamins and minerals was made. It was called 'Pablum', which comes from the Latin *Pabulum*, meaning food."

The word "pabulum," as it was used in English, actually meant something like fodder, grist for the lower organisms, plants and cells and such. The OED quotes an early anatomical textbook to the effect that "the blood is the immediate pabulum of the tissues," and notes that the word was used "rarely in reference to higher animals." English novelists, however, took it in its metaphorical sense, more as food for thought; thus Tristram Shandy boasts that his modern story "affords more pabulum to the brain than all the Frusts and Crusts and Rusts of antiquity."

Pablum, whether as fodder or in its more cerebral sense, was the brainchild of a group of Toronto doctors who were trying to find a cure for rickets. In January 1930, Alan Brown, director of the Nutritional Research Laboratories at the Hospital for Sick Children and a professor of pediatrics at the University of Toronto, presented a paper at a meeting of the Academy of Medicine in Toronto. Brown's was the last name associated with the authorship of the paper; the first was Frederick F. Tisdall, a doctor at the Hospital for Sick Children, and the other two were researchers Theo Drake and Pearl Summerfeldt. The paper, published the next month in the *Journal of the Canadian Medical Association*, was called "A New Whole Wheat Irradiated Biscuit Containing Vitamins and Mineral Elements," and was the result of nearly a decade of advances in what were then the new fields of vitamin therapy and preventive medicine.

Tisdall too worked in the Nutritional Research Lab. Described as "a clever businessman," a "wheeler-dealer" and even as "a publicity hound" in Max Braithwaite's history of the Hospital for Sick Children, Tisdall became interested in preventive medicine through his work on rickets. At the turn of the century, rickets was one of the most prevalent of childhood diseases, particularly, for reasons not then understood, in Canada. Characterized by fever, loss of muscle tone, swelling in the neck and chest, and eventually gross bone deformities in the limbs—knock knees and bow legs—rickets sent children into hospitals in droves until about 1920, when it was discovered that the disease was caused by extreme vitamin D deficiency.

Vitamin D is produced in the body by sunlight. The breakthrough in rickets treatment came in 1922, when researchers in Germany, the United States and Canada discovered that short-wavelength ultraviolet rays from the sun, striking the human body, transform fatty or oily substances in the skin into pure vitamin D. Two years later, Brown determined what vitamin D did that was so useful: it helped the body distribute calcium and phosphorus in the bloodstream to the tips of the bones. Tisdall and Brown even isolated the precise wavelength of the sun's uv rays—313 millimicrons—that was most effective in producing natural vitamin D. Brown then instituted a regimen at Sick Kids hospital that included direct-sunlight treatments for rickets patients. Tisdall exposed various foodstuffs to artificial low-wavelength uv rays, and found that natural oils in grains and milk were also transformed into vitamin D, and in enormous concentrations. The oils in human skin were called cholesterol, and the oils in grains and other foods were called ergosterol.

"One of the most striking discoveries of medical science made during the past five years,"Tisdall wrote in 1929, "is the observation that a substance known as ergosterol can be so changed or acti-vated by exposure to ultra-violet rays that when fed to an individ-ual it will prevent or cure rickets." Tisdall calculated that "one ounce of activated ergosterol has the same antirachitic [anti-rickets] effect as 2 to 6 tons of good cod liver oil." It didn't take Tisdall and his colleagues long to figure out that adding a small amount of irradi-ated ergosterol to a child's daily diet would be a good thing. "We are just beginning to realize the importance of the various vitamins on the different phases of the body metabolism," Tisdall wrote. But it was obvious that increasing the vitamin D intake of the average person, especially children, would go a long way to preventing a whole raft of bone-related ailments, from rickets to osteomalacia (softening of the bone), osteoporosis (caused by calcium deficiency) and even tooth decay.

The problem with vitamin D in Canada is one of geography and climate. Because the sun is low on the horizon during winter, it passes through more of the Earth's atmosphere; the atmosphere acts as a filter and shuts out most of the low-wavelength UV rays that we need to make vitamin D. That, plus shorter day length and our ten-dency to cover our bodies with clothing, means that from October to April we don't get nearly enough sunlight to produce natural vit-amin D. If we don't take large doses of artificial vitamin D, in the form of fish oils (halibut and cod livers are best, but there are no more cod, and any fatty fish will do) and egg yolk, then we get poor bone development and repair. Dark or tanned skin is also a poorer producer of vitamin D than fair or untanned skin.

A few years ago I flew up the west coast of Hudson Bay with a bush pilot who was taking supplies from Churchill, Manitoba, to such communities as Eskimo Point, Pond Inlet and Baker Lake; most of the supplies consisted of boxes of cookies and cans of soft drinks. My only fellow passenger was a dentist from Winnipeg, who told me that because Inuit diets in these communities consisted almost entirely of sugar, tooth decay was a major problem. It seemed ironic to her that the plane contained several tons of sugar and a dentist, but it occurs to me now that the real problem may not have been too many cookies and Cokes, but too little vitamin D: Inuit families spend six months of the year without sunlight, and are told not to eat fish because of pesticides in the ocean. Perhaps as well as dentists they should be getting massive shipments of irradiated ergosterol or, as my mother's family would say, shiploads of halibut-liver oil.

In 1930, Tisdall and his associates announced their new biscuit. Their paper began with a brief survey of what was known about vitamins at the time. "A lack of vitamin A results in deficient growth and the development of xerophthalmia," a dryness in the eyes associated with conjunctivitis, and one of the four main causes of blindness. Vitamin B1 deficiency "causes peripheral neuritis and poor growth"; B2 prevents "pellagra and certain skin conditions"; vitamin C prevents scurvy; vitamin D "is necessary for the growth and repair of bone and other tissues"; vitamin E is "essential for reproduction, and possibly other body changes at the age of puberty." A diet low in vitamins, they wrote, "results in a lowered resistance to infection" and can cause "arthritis, hypertension, and other degenerative diseases."

Their biscuit, which they hoped would replace white bread (the frusts and crusts and rusts in the diet of the "wage-earning classes"), was made of "whole wheat flour, irradiated wheat germ, milk, bone meal and iron." The wheat germ was irradiated, i.e. "exposed to the rays from a mercury quartz lamp," in order to multiply its vitamin D content. The biscuit also contained powdered milk, butter and yeast. They added cream of tartar instead of alkaline salt, since salt "readily destroys vitamin B1 and B2 during cooking," and the biscuit was baked at a temperature not exceeding 300°F (148°C), because higher temperatures were found to destroy vitamin D.

The biscuit was not exactly a magic pill, and was not intended to supply all the vitamin requirements of a daily diet. But the doctors believed that it would "assist in the repair and growth of cells and the maintenance of resistance against disease." And they arranged with a biscuit company—McCormick Manufacturing—to produce an item called McCormick's Sun Wheat Biscuit. The patent remained with the Hospital for Sick Children, and royalties from the sale of the biscuit went to the hospital's Nutritional Research Lab.

But McCormick's Sun Wheat Biscuit did not seem to catch on with the masses. The blue-collar set hadn't gone in much for zwieback and rusks in the first place, and Sun Wheat Biscuits were probably poor substitutes for bread in the sandwiches in a worker's lunch pail. Tisdall admitted as much in a paper published in 1931 entitled "The Incorporation of Vitamins in Bread," in which he informed the medical association that "bread is consumed in large amounts by the wage-earning class." He quoted a survey which found that, although "about one-eighth of a loaf per person per day was consumed in well-to-do families," as much as a whole loaf per person per day was eaten in the poorer sections of the city. "The reason for this," he speculated, "is that bread is the cheapest form of food." And white bread was the cheapest form of bread; 85 percent of the bread consumed in Canada in 1931 was white. Tisdall advocated adding vitamin D to white bread, in the form of irradiated yeast and wheat germ, as an even better way of delivering wholesome food to adults. As for infants, he recognized the recent shift from breast-feeding to bottle and spoon feeding (a shift he disapproved of but had the sense to acknowledge), so he decided to invent a new kind of infant cereal. The result was Pablum.

The original formula for Pablum reflected Tisdall's findings in the vitamin-therapy field: wheatmeal (or farina), oatmeal, wheat germ, cornmeal, powdered beef bone ("specially prepared for human use"), sodium chloride, powdered alfalfa leaf, powdered yeast and iron. To reduce cooking time to almost nothing, the ingredients were pre-cooked and mixed with powdered milk, which made it one of the first just-add-water-and-stir food products on the market. Tisdall, the publicity hound, thought McCormick's was too small to get Pablum into the mouths of enough babies, and so he contacted the Mead Johnson Company in Chicago, which ended up making and selling Pablum from its plant in Belleville, Ontario. The deal gave Mead Johnson the formula and the doctors' endorsement in exchange for a portion of the proceeds going to the Hospital for Sick Children for twenty-five years.

Mead Johnson is now owned by Heinz, the ketchup people, and although the twenty-five-year royalty period is long over, the box on my desk notes that Pablum is still helping Sick Kids hospital: "Parents are invited to send the upc codes from any Pablum cereal to the Hospital for Sick Children Foundation, Agincourt Civitan Club, Suite 76, 180 Station St., Ajax, Ontario." For each label received, Heinz donates ten cents to medical research through its Labels for Life programme. Since 1991, Heinz has donated $1.3 million to children's hospitals across Canada, and in 1997 the Toronto Sick Kids hospital received just under $38,000 from the programme. Being a staunch supporter of royalty agreements, I'm going to tear off the code on my box and send it in.

But a check of the new Pablum's ingredients reveals a significant change since Drs. Tisdall, Drake, Summerfeldt and Brown put their heads together seventy years ago. Today's Pablum is not what it was; in fact it differs very little from its chief competitor, which is also made by Heinz. The side panel of my box of Pablum Sobee Cereal lists "soya flour, corn flour, sugar [!], dibasic calcium phosphate, soya lecithin, reduced iron, niacinamide, riboflavin and thiamine mononitrate." I cooked some up the other day and had a taste, or rather tried to have a taste. There *was* no taste.

No wonder "pablum" (without a capital, although editors seem to want one) has come to mean anything that lacks intellectual rigour—the exact opposite, in fact, of food for the brain. In Bill Deverell's book *Fatal Cruise*, a nonfiction account of a notorious murder trial in Victoria, Deverell writes that "a jury of lay persons, fed a diet of TV lawyer Pablum, might easily believe the defence had some obligation to actually *prove* something." And Sarah Hampson, writing about middle-aged, middle-class Canadians in *Toronto Life*, sighs: "So here we are: ageless, sexless, as benign as Pablum." In everyday Canadian speech, "pablum" has come to mean what "white bread" connotes in the United States: boring, bland and tasteless. Is it not ironic, given that Pablum was intended to replace white bread, that the two terms have come to mean almost exactly the same thing—that, in fact, pablum has replaced white bread only in the Canadian idiom?

Come to think of it, that photo of the ideal baby on the box front doesn't look like me at all.

Peking Man An intriguing tale with an unhappy ending.
—*Missing Links: The Hunt for*
Earliest Man, 1981, John Reader

SKULDUGGERY ON CHICKEN BONE HILL

The drive from Beijing to Zhoukoudian was, like so many things about China, a disconcerting blend of delight and torture. We left the Institute of Vertebrate Paleontology and Paleoanthropology (IVPP) at 8 a.m., when the streets of Beijing were already thick with human traffic, eerily silent except for the incessant whirr of cicadas and bicycle wheels, and travelled south along a highway so new that the shoulders were still being tamped into place by thousands of workers, kilometres of workers, using the backs of shovels, the bottoms of rock-filled baskets, boards nailed to broken tree branches.

It was the first of August, my birthday, the hottest day of the hottest year on record. Dust clogged the air, scummed the still rivers. The sky was a fierce gun-metal grey, but inside the clattering yellow van, windows rolled tight against the dust, the air was sodden with humidity, so heavy we could scarcely breathe. And yet the countryside through which we slowly passed—undulating hills, tranquil valleys, breeze-rippled rice paddies, farm compounds walled and wing-roofed like temples—seemed ancient and undisturbed, as though we had somehow entered one of the paintings we had been shown in the Forbidden City.

There were four of us in the van: me, two Canadian paleontologists—Don Brinkman and Dave Eberth, from the Royal Tyrrell Museum in Drumheller, Alberta—and our driver, a tense, fortyish man with black-framed glasses and white cotton gloves who worked for the IVPP. We had spent the past two months in the Gobi Desert, part of the Dinosaur Project, an expedition of fifty Canadian and Chinese paleontologists working the rock formations at Iren Dabasu, Bayan Manduhu and Erenhot, in Inner Mongolia, hunting for dinosaurs. The others had been coming to the Gobi for the past five summers, and dozens of plaster-packed skulls and ribs, colossal vertebrae, whole dinosaurs, some known and some entirely new to science, had been carefully crated and labelled and trucked to the IVPP warehouse in Beijing for safe storage. It was now the year after Tiananmen Square, and everything was still in a state of anxious confusion. Some of the crates had gone missing. The IVPP had a second warehouse in Zhoukoudian: perhaps the missing crates were there. And so, when the rest of the Canadians returned to Canada, three of us stayed behind to look.

We didn't mind. Don and Dave were old China hands and loved the kind of ambiguous beauty that pervaded the country. I was content just to keep moving. And I wanted to see Zhoukoudian for my own reasons. Zhoukoudian in an earlier transliteration was called Chou K'ou Tien, known in English as Chicken Bone Hill. Seventy years before, another Canadian had travelled along this route from the capital to the Western Hills. Davidson Black, like me, had been part of a team of scientists that had come to China to look for fossils; in fact, Black had founded the institute that had become the IVPP. And he too had found bones: at Chicken Bone Hill one of his team had discovered two fossilized hominid teeth, and Black had written the paper that alerted the scientific world to the discovery. He called the proto-humans who had owned the teeth *Sinanthropus pekinensis*: Chinese man from Peking, better known as Peking Man.

* * *

Davidson Black was born in Toronto in 1884. He graduated from the University of Toronto School of Medicine, and researched and taught for two years in Amsterdam and then Cleveland. When the United States entered the First World War in April 1917, Black returned to Canada and enlisted in the Canadian Army Medical Corps. When the war ended, he was offered the post of professor of neurology and embryology at Peking Union Medical College, established the year before by the Rockefeller Foundation and already one of the most advanced medical schools in the world.

Black was excited about his appointment, not only for the chance to teach medicine but also because he had become extremely interested in paleontology. In 1915 he had read *Climate and Evolution* by W.R. Matthew, a Canadian anthropologist working at the American Museum of Natural History. Matthew's book argued that prehistoric climate changes had caused the dispersal of the world's mammals, including human beings. After reading it, Black became convinced of the then contentious theory that Asia was the place of origin of *Homo sapiens*. Although the Rockefeller Foundation was sending Black to Peking to teach anatomy, it also placed Black in charge of a major survey of Chinese ancient and modern anthropology. In other words, Black's real mission was to look for evidence to support the Sinocentric theory of human evolution.

Asia as the birthplace of early hominids was the pet theory of Henry Fairfield Osborn, director of the American Museum of Natural History. In 1915, the year Matthew wrote about mammal dispersal from a central originating point, Osborn (Matthew's boss) also wrote a paper in which he expressed alarm at increasing evidence that the central originating point might have been in Africa. A race of early humans, it was known, had migrated north out of Africa into Europe twenty-five thousand years ago, where they clashed and presumably interbred with the humans already there to become

Neanderthals. "This does not mean," Osborn wrote, "that . . . these Lower Paleolithic races were of negroid or Ethiopian affinity, because the Neanderthals show absolutely no negroid characteristics."

Osborn was clearly worried that white Europeans, and therefore white Americans, might be descended from black Africans. The possibility was disturbing at a time when blacks and whites were regarded, even in scientific circles, as members of two different species. Osborn decided that the best way to refute the African genesis theory was to find fossil hominids somewhere else that were older than those turning up in Africa. Matthew's work inclined him to think that such fossils might be found in Asia.

There was other evidence. In 1892, Eugene Dubois, a Dutch paleontologist working in Java, had discovered fragments of an early hominid he named *Pithecanthropus erectus* ("upright ape-man," also known as Java Man), presenting this as the Missing Link between apes and human beings. But Dubois's claim was based on scanty evidence—a bit of skullcap, two teeth and a femur—and was widely disbelieved. Osborn wanted more fossils from Asia.

It is almost certain that Osborn persuaded the Rockefeller Foundation to send someone knowledgeable in paleontology and anthropology to the Peking Union Medical College. The museum was endowed by the Foundation, and it supplied the college in Peking with a large collection of duplicates of paleontological material, the purpose of which could only have been to form the basis of an even larger collection of original material to be collected by Black. And it was the Rockefeller Foundation that gave Black the $80,000 he needed to set up the Cenozoic Research Lab in Peking, which later became the IVPP.

As a paleontologist, Black was far from alone in China. The Swedish government had a long-standing relationship with the Chinese, and had more or less set up the Chinese Geological Survey in exchange for exclusive paleontological rights in southern China, where the hominid fossils were believed to be. Gunnar Andersson was in Peking, and his assistant Otto Zdansky. Then there were the French Jesuits, including Teilhard de Chardin, the paleontological priest who believed that the sole purpose of evolution was to produce human beings in the image of God. And, in 1921, there was Roy Chapman Andrews, the pistol-packing paleontologist from the American Museum of Natural History, sent by Osborn to lead the largest scientific expedition in history (before ours) into the Gobi Desert. Andrews invited Black to go along, but Black preferred to work with the Swedes. Human fossils were in the south, he believed, not in the Gobi, where all the exposures were far too old to contain hominids.

And he was right. Zdansky found two hominid teeth at Chicken Bone Hill in 1921, although he didn't tell anyone about them until 1926. That year Black wrote his description of the find for *Nature* magazine, naming the new species *Sinanthropus pekinensis*, perhaps over-hastily, since there was not enough evidence to support his contention that Peking Man was a new species. In fact, as more fossil material was collected from Chicken Bone Hill—early humans had occupied two caves in the hill from 500,000 years ago until about 200,000 years ago—it became clear that Peking Man was identical to Java Man, and both hominids were joined into one species now known as *Homo erectus*, the direct precursors to *Homo sapiens*. The Peking Man material, it turned out, was much more recent than the fossils turning up in Africa—in 1924, Raymond Dart had found a human skull in Africa that was more than two million years older than Peking Man—but the Chicken Bone Hill material appeared to become older as the digging went deeper, and Black continued to work the quarries until his death in 1934, still hoping to unearth evidence that the earliest humans had radiated out of Asia before colonizing Africa.

By the time he died, Black had amassed a huge hoard of Peking Man material: more teeth, entire skulls, leg bones and mandibles representing some forty individuals, as well as early stone tools. Although he never found anything as old as the African fossils, what he did find represents the full 300,000-year sequence of *Homo erectus*. They were the only hominid fossils to show that human beings before us controlled fire, dwelt in permanent shelters, and lived in family units—in other words, that they entertained thought. Harvard University paleontologist Bjorn Kurtén has written that the skulls from Chicken Bone Hill "show that the base was broken up and the brain extracted before the heads were brought into the cave. The brain was evidently eaten." On this evidence, some scholars have declared Peking Man to have been a cannibal. Kurtén takes the notion a step farther: "This is the earliest evidence of anything that could possibly be a religious ritual," he writes. "It may suggest that *Homo erectus* was concerned with the problem of life and death."

* * *

After the seventy-million-year-old sandstone exposures we had been working on in the Gobi, the tree-covered ridge at Zhoukoudian seemed more like a park to us than a paleontological site. It was cool under the trees and even cooler in the caves. Their limestone walls ran with moisture, and the sound of hollow dripping, like clocks ticking in another room, made us conscious of time: people, humans, had lived here only 200,000 years ago. See, here is where they threw their bones, here is where they walked to scoop water out of that pool. Perhaps someone slept in this small indentation in the cave floor, or a child played with this ball-shaped rock. It all seemed so real after months of trying to imagine the life of dinosaurs. We followed chip-strewn paths into clefts in the hard limestone. These people were our ancestors, we thought, their spirit still inhabits this place. There, is that a fire pit? That bit of rock, could it be bone?

After twenty years of digging, Black had plenty of material on which to base some comparisons between Peking Man and modern humans. He calculated Peking Man's brain size to be roughly 1,200 cc, smaller than ours (1,350 cc) and much smaller than the Neanderthalers' (1,500 cc). He thought this meant Peking Man was more ape-like than human. He kept the fossils in his safe at the Cenozoic Research Lab, and after his death, just before the outbreak of the Second World War, they were taken out, crated and sent to the United States for safekeeping. They never made it. The ship they were on—a U.S. Navy vessel—was captured by the Japanese, and the fossils simply disappeared.

Before being taken to the IVPP warehouse to look for our own lost fossils, we were invited to drink green tea with the site's director. During the formal conversation I found myself staring through a dusty window, through quivering heatwaves rising from the pavement, to a tree in the centre of the parking lot. An aluminum ladder had been leaned against the tree; a second, wooden ladder attached to the top of the first disappeared high into the tree's foliage. For some reason I found this ominous. I knew we were not going to find our boxes, that the warehouse was going to contain a hopeless jumble of unmarked crates from dozens of expeditions, like the left-luggage department for a railway station as big as all of China. The certainty of it became confused in my mind with an encounter I had had in Beijing the previous day. Our hotel, the Da Du, was owned and operated by the People's Liberation Army; during the months following Tiananmen Square the hotel had served as temporary Army headquarters. We were among the first foreigners allowed to stay in it since the riots. I had been expecting a message from my wife, a letter or a birthday card, and I had asked at the front desk if any mail had come for me while we were away in the desert. The woman behind the desk had looked vacantly at me, shaking her head.

"No letter has arrived for me?" I asked.

"No," she said.

How did she know without looking, I wondered. "Well, when it comes, will you hold it for me?"

Again she shook her head. "No."

"No what?" I asked, taken aback.

"No," she repeated. "It won't come."

"What do you mean?"

She said it again, slowly. "It will not come."

"Never?"

"No, never. I'm sorry."

I left the hotel in a daze. Outside, Dale Russell, the senior paleontologist of our expedition, was standing in the parking lot, watching a small group of workers digging a trench for a new sewer line from the hotel to an adjacent building. Mounds of red earth were piled up along the trench, and Dale was idly bending over the debris, picking up bits of rock being thrown up by the workers' shovels, examining them closely and then tossing them back down.

"Interesting," he said. He handed me a flat piece that I thought was part of a broken drainage tile. I brushed the dirt off it and realized with a start that it was bone.

"Human," he said. "Skull fragment."

"Old?" I asked.

"Oh, no," he said quietly. "Very recent, I'd say." He took the piece from my hand and placed it deliberately back on the mound. "Probably less than a year." Then he turned and walked back into the hotel.

I continued to watch the men digging the trench, and thought about who might have owned the skull: most certainly, Peking Man.

Pogey Money or forms of relief given by the government to unemployed persons, especially in times of extreme economic depression; dole.

—*Gage Canadian Dictionary,* 1997

HARD TIMES IN THE
HOUSE OF INDUSTRY

In Canada, "pogey" now usually refers to what used to be called Unemployment Insurance benefits, as in, "I got my pogey cheque last week" or "I guess I'll go on pogey if I don't find a job." It has always had a pejorative sense; recipients of payments from the Unemployment Insurance Commission would rather say they were "collecting uic" than that they were "on pogey." It's better to be collecting something than to be on something. In *The Oxford Guide to English Canadian Usage* the word "pogey" appears between "podium" and "poison," and is equated with welfare as well as with ui. In the Gage dictionary cited above, "pogey" appears between "poetry" and "pogo stick."

The connection with welfare derives from the fact that the word "pogey" existed long before there was Unemployment Insurance (in fact, before there was much unemployment to insure). It originally referred to a charitable organization, such as a workhouse, a hospital or even a prison, that catered to the needs of migrant workers. Hugh Garner, in his novel *Cabbagetown*, notes that an establishment in Toronto in the 1920s, called the House of Industry, "had long been used by the city to house indigents, and was known to its patrons by the tramp's colloquialism for hospital, 'pogey.'" This is corroborated in a contemporary account by G.H. Westbury, a British immigrant who tramped across Canada in 1928 and wrote a book about his experiences, *Misadventures of a Working Hobo in Canada*, published in England in 1930. While in Toronto, Westbury treated himself to a fine dinner at the Royal York Hotel, and after leaving the hotel "passed the 'pogy,' or House of Industry, as it is called sarcastically, where down-and-outs get cheap food." According to Garner, "before the Depression was over, this word would also be used as a synonym for city relief and public welfare." That is, when migrant workers became indigent nonworkers.

"Pogey" probably comes from "pokey," a term that appeared in the United States in the 1920s to designate a hand-out, such as tramps would ask for. A "pokey stiff," according to Eric Partridge's *Dictionary of Slang*, was "a vagrant who lived entirely on food from householders, and was looked down upon by hoboes who always offered to work for their bread." This may account for the current ambiguity of pogey in Canada: even though it is technically a payback on an insurance premium, it is looked upon by those who receive it (as well as by those who give it) as a hand-out. "Pokey" may have come from "poke," an Old English term for a bag or small sack (don't buy a pig in a poke without first poking it to make sure it's a pig) such as hoboes are popularly supposed to have carried at the end of sticks. A poke was also a purse (cognate with the French *poche*, "pocket"), and in the United States a pickpocket was known as poke-outer.

"Pogey" took on its current sense in Canada, and only in Canada, after the Second World War. *Maclean's* magazine noted on April 2, 1954, that "unemployment insurance payments are often referred to as pogey." In England, the term is "dole." The British novel *Love on the Dole* would have to be retitled *Love on Pogey* if it were published here. In England, not even socialists would vote for a political candidate named Bob Dole.

The Unemployment Insurance Act, which hands out pogey

cheques (i.e. pays insurance premiums to those who are legitimately entitled to make claims on their policies), went into effect on July 1, 1941. At that time 2.1 million workers earning $2,000 a year or less began making compulsory insurance payments based on a percentage of their wages; contributions ranged from 12 to 27 cents a week, with employers contributing 21 to 27 cents a week and the government kicking in one-fifth of the total employee–employer contributions for an estimated grand total in 1941 of $50 million. In return, insured workers who found themselves unemployed for any of a limited number of specified reasons would be eligible to collect from $4.08 to $14.40 per week if they had made at least 30 weekly or 180 daily contributions within the previous two years (the amount collectable was calculated by multiplying the employee's weekly contribution by thirty-four). It was almost as hard to get on Unemployment Insurance in 1941 as it is to get off it today.

UI benefits did not come in without criticism. P.M. Richards, writing in *Saturday Night* in June 1941, outlined three of the strongest objections to the system. First, it was limited to workers in relatively stable sectors of the workforce. The list of "excepted employments"—jobs that were not eligible for UI benefits—included agriculture, horticulture, forestry, fishing, lumbering and logging, hunting and trapping, transportation by air or water, stevedoring, domestic service, nursing, teaching, the armed forces, police work, and commission sales. In other words, said Richards, "the application of the Act is, broadly speaking, limited to workers who, because of the relative stability of their employment, tend to have the least prospect of needing and benefiting from unemployment insurance."

A second objection was that the cost of administering the programme was borne by the government. In 1941 that cost was $4.7 million, and was paid from taxes collected by the government from taxpayers, "many of whom," Richards pointed out, "are in the excepted occupations." In other words, people who were ineligible to collect it were paying for people who didn't need it.

The third objection was that there was no "Unemployment Insurance fund." Instead of putting the contributions from all sources into a separate fund and setting that fund aside for future pay-outs, all the money collected for unemployment insurance went directly into general revenues. When, eventually, employees began making claims on the system, they would be paid out of current expenditures. The problem with that, of course, was that most claims on the system would be made during periods of high unemployment, and therefore when expenditures would be at their highest and revenues at their lowest. We would end up having an embarrassment of riches when we didn't need it and a dearth of dollars when we needed it most.

Quite obviously, the Unemployment Insurance Act had been introduced in order to raise capital for the war effort; it was, in effect, a war tax, and could easily have been called that. Canada had been at war since September 10, 1939, and Mackenzie King had always maintained that Canada's chief contribution to the war would be economic, not participatory. In 1939 there were 529,000 unemployed workers in Canada; many of those enlisted in the First Canadian Division. But after the war, when unemployment would again be high, where would the money come from to pay unemployment insurance benefits?

Today, all workers in Canada (except the self-employed) contribute to EI—"Employment Insurance," which since 1996 has been the new, politically correct term for Unemployment Insurance. It is a ridiculous euphemism. If you buy fire insurance, you are insuring yourself against fire; if you buy employment insurance, are you insuring yourself against employment? At any rate, EI contributions are deducted at source from regular paycheques, and the company that pays them contributes an equal amount to the EI Commission. The only workers not eligible to receive EI benefits are those who work for themselves, like farmers and writers (who actually work for everyone *but* themselves). The government excused itself from contributing to the fund with the passing of Bill C-21 in 1990. To qualify for EI benefits, which now amount to 55 percent of insurable earnings up to a maximum of $425 per week, a worker must have worked at least ten of the previous fifty-two weeks—an arrangement known as the "10/42 package."

In December 1992 the government introduced Bill C-105, which created a furore by announcing that the insurance fund had plummeted from a $200-million surplus to a $7.2-billion deficit in the previous two years. Critics claimed that the deficit was the result of the Conservative government's disastrous economic policies, which had caused high unemployment and decreased contributions—exactly as Richards had predicted in 1941. And in his 1998 budget speech, the first one in two decades to contain relatively good news about the Canadian economy, the finance minister announced that the EI fund had an $18-billion surplus, also a fulfilment of Richards's prediction. The surplus was so great that in the years 1999 and 2000, employees between the ages of 18 and 24 will not be required to make EI contributions. Thus, if they ever do have to collect Employment Insurance, and the odds are good that they will, the cheques they receive truly will be hand-outs and can legitimately be called pogey.

It is perhaps not surprising that the term "pogey," except when it is used by the Ontario government to refer to grants given to writers, is most commonly used today in the Maritime provinces, where unemployment is perennially high. Newfoundland fishermen used to receive stamps for each week worked, and needed to accumulate ten stamps in order to collect pogey. In extreme cases, fishermen would work in fish plants for stamps in lieu of wages. A few years ago, before the collapse of the cod fishery, when offshore fishermen spent only part of the year not fishing, I went bakeapple picking with a friend from the Bonne Bay area on Newfoundland's west coast. He was wearing a pair of black rubber boots that went up to mid-calf; he called them his "pogey boots," because, he said, "fishermen only wears them when they're not fishing."

In Newfoundland, where people have a tendency to drag new things alongside for a while before hauling them aboard, the word "pogey" has also retained its original meaning as a charitable institution, hospital or prison. In Bernice Morgan's 1994 novel *Waiting for Time*, one of the characters, Mark, is arrested for breaking into a Department of Fisheries and Oceans office. He had written a DFO report claiming that the cod fishery was as dead as a doornail, and Wayne, one of his colleagues, had altered it to say that the cod fishery was alive and well and the DFO should "increase harvesting operations to the maximum levels." Only then did Wayne send the report on to Ottawa.

"Never you mind, dear old mudder," Wayne tells Mark's mother after her son is jailed. "I got a lawyer all lined up—the poor lad'll be outta pogey soon as Minister and media takes off for Ottawa."

Polygraph (*psy*) An apparatus for recording, simultaneously, a number of physiological processes: the lie detector.
—*1968, The Gulf Dictionary of Business and Science*

WHERE THE TRUTH LIES

In Thomas Malory's *Morte d'Arthur*, there is a scene I always think
of when I think of lying. Arthur is removing his court to Tintagel,
travelling slowly through dark woods. He suspects that his wife,
Guinevere, is having an affair with his favourite knight, Sir Lancelot,
as indeed she is. In order to be near Guinevere, Lancelot has disguised himself as a monk and is part of Arthur's entourage. When
they come to a raging stream, Guinevere is afraid to ford it, and
Lancelot (in his monk's robe and cowl) offers to carry her across.
That evening Arthur, unable to contain his suspicions about his wife's
conduct, asks her point-blank if she has been unfaithful to him. Guinevere hesitates, then with queenly sang-froid replies: "The only other
man who has held me in his arms except you, my lord, is that monk
who carried me across the river this afternoon." Arthur is satisfied.
So would a polygraph have been.

The polygraph, or lie detector, was invented by John Augustus
Larson in the 1920s. Larson (who was born on December 11, 1892,
in Shelburne, Nova Scotia) had graduated from Boston University
in 1914 and received a Ph.D. in psychiatry from the University of
California in 1920. In the years between then and his appointment
in 1928 as medical director of criminology at Rush Medical College, he perfected a machine that he believed would catch people
who told lies.

The word "polygraph" had been around for a long time. It simply means "multiple writings," and was first applied to an invention patented in France in 1763 that made mechanical copies of handwritten letters. The writer wrote a letter using a pen attached to a system of jointed rods, and a second pen, attached to the other end of the rods, moved exactly as the first pen. Later developments involved various liquids and viscous plates; the Gestetner machine is a polygraph, as is the Xerox machine and its clones. In fact, clones are polygraphs, because the word came by extension to refer not only to the machine but also to the copy made by the machine, and hence to any person who copies or apes another, or is himself a copy of an original. Sir Lancelot, in his hooded robe, was a polygraph of a monk.

In his 1925 satire *Heart of a Dog*, the Russian writer Mikhail Bulgakov creates a Frankenstein-like doctor who specializes in "rejuvenation operations," usually of a sexual nature. The doctor transplants a man's pituitary gland and testicles onto a dog, and the dog thus becomes intellectually and sexually human (he is the narrator of the story) while remaining physically a dog—a dog who is a human copy and makes copies of humans. Bulgakov names him Poligraf Poligrafovich, after the famous Moscow publishing house Mospoligraf. A 1996 stage version of *Heart of a Dog*, by Canadian playwright Robert Astle, keeps the hero's name, Polygraph Polygraphovich, but since a polygraph is now better known as a lie detector than as a publishing company (thank goodness), Astle might have made Bulgakov's original point better had he changed the named to Xerox Xeroxovich.

The connection between Bulgakov and Larson's lie detector is hidden in the word "duplicity." A lie detector detects duplicity by duplicating a subject's inner reactions on a scroll of paper. Larson's polygraph produces "multiple graphs," each one recording a particular aspect of the subject's reaction to certain yes–no questions. In looking for a foolproof way of determining whether or not a person was being duplicitous, Larson reasoned that lying took more effort than telling the truth, because the lying subject had to remember two things—the truth and the lie—whereas an honest subject only had to remember the truth. This effort, he believed, could be measured. Larson also knew that fear (in this case, of being found out) triggers adrenalin surges that produce detectable changes in heart and respiratory rates, blood pressure and perspiration. Attach sensors to the right spots on a subject's body, monitor the four functions simultaneously, compare what happens when the subject is asked a series of questions—some straightforward and some loaded —and you have an exact duplicate of the inner state of the subject's innocence or guilt.

Maybe. Polygraph tests are still not admissible in court. Many people—including members of the Society for Psychophysiological Research and Fellows of the American Psychological Association, when they were surveyed by the *Journal of American Psychology* in 1995—believe that "polygraphic lie detection is not theoretically sound." Polygraphs cannot provide reliable proof of innocence or guilt, they say, because some people behave guiltily when asked innocent questions, while others remain perfectly unperturbed when grilled on the most gruesome crimes. In other words, while honest people have only to remember the truth, there are dishonest or deluded people who remember their lie, or who, like Guinevere, so phrase the lie that they believe it to be the truth. For them, a polygraph is little better than a stack of Bibles.

Polygraphs are used by police, but only to weed out unlikely suspects, and then with sometimes ambiguous results. O.J. Simpson failed two polygraph tests a few days after being arrested for the murder of Nicole Simpson, for example, and yet was acquitted by a jury of his peers. Did the polygraph lie? General Jean Boyle, former Chief of Defence Staff, passed a polygraph test concerning his role in tampering with documents relating to the conduct of the First Airborne Division in Somalia, but later admitted that he had violated "the spirit" of the Access to Information Act by telling a CBC reporter that certain documents no longer existed when in fact they existed under a new name. Perhaps General Boyle had read *Le Morte d'Arthur*. Or he may have read Douglas Williams's best-selling book *How to Sting the Polygraph*, which proclaims on the jacket: "If you are scheduled to take a polygraph, relax! It can be beaten rather easily."

The Canadian Bar Association agrees that polygraph tests cannot be relied upon. "The polygraph is not sufficiently sophisticated," says Sheldon Pinx, chair of the CBA's National Criminal Justice Sector. "The machine does not, at the end of the day, say whether you're being truthful or dishonest. It simply provides certain information to a polygraphist, who then has to interpret those readings and come up with an opinion. It's really opinion justice."

Not so, according to RCMP polygraphist Robert Russell. In 1996, Russell was called in to polygraphically test Al McLean, Speaker of the Ontario Legislative Assembly, who had been accused by his assistant, Sandi Thompson, and two other female employees of sexual harassment in the workplace. The tests cleared McLean. Russell says polygraph tests are "95 percent reliable in the hands of experts." But 95 percent reliable still means that one out of every twenty people in prison might be there because they break out into a cold sweat whenever anyone asks them their name, and one out of twenty criminals are at large because they can coolly deny any knowledge of how their landlady got into a dumpster.

Outside the courtroom, polygraphs are being used more and more for ordinary industrial security and routine surveillance. For $500, a company like Paragon Investigations and Polygraph Services Ltd. will come to your home or office and tell you if your partner is having it off with your favourite knight, or whether your trusted employee is selling preliminary lab results to your competitor. Some people find this an invasion of privacy: with enforced polygraph testing, the whole notion of presumed innocence flies out the window.

In the end, as the author of *Morte d'Arthur* knew, the best lie detector is one's own conscience, and a polygraph cannot distinguish among subjects who are cold-blooded, or unconvinced they have committed a crime, or merely innocent. Which was Guinevere? Such ambiguity lies behind Quebec filmmaker Robert Lepage's 1996 movie *Le polygraphe*, in which François, a waiter in Quebec City, is suspected of having murdered his girlfriend, Lucille. While the police are investigating, François's friend decides to make a film based on the case and asks François to play the part of (i.e. to duplicate) the murderer. The film's title refers to a surrealist twist in which François's confessor is not a priest but one of Larson's little machines. The film, like a good polygraphist, poses some disturbing questions about the nature of guilt and innocence, lies and equivocations—and, like a good confessor, leaves it to us to puzzle the answers out for ourselves.

Potlatch During the winter months all the Pacific Coast
tribes held festivals, or potlatches, at which every visitor
received a present more or less in accordance with his rank.
—*The Indians of Canada,* 1932, Diamond Jenness

THE GRAND GIVE-AWAY

In December 1995, the Fraser Institute, an influential right-wing
think-tank in Vancouver, reported on what it thought about Native
land claims in British Columbia. Given, the report stated, that there
were forty-eight tribal groups representing 86,978 Native people
claiming 1,048,744 square kilometres of British Columbia (111 percent of the total land mass of the province), the only sensible thing
the B.C. government could do was divide the province into small
parcels and give one parcel to each resident of British Columbia,
just as the federal government had done in the 1860s. "The treaty
process," the report stated, "will neither succeed nor fail, but just
continue." Giving the province away would be, in the words of Owen
Lippert, the institute's senior policy analyst, "the potlatch of the mil-
lennium."

"Potlatch" is Chinook jargon for "gift," and was incorrectly applied
in English to a festive northwest coast Native ceremony at which gifts
were lavished on each guest by a wealthy host. The word comes
from the Nootka verb *Pa-chitle,* which means "to give." According to
George Clutesi (*Potlatch,* 1969), the early Tse-shaht people of Vancouver Island held four different kinds of feasts: *He-nim-tsu,* a small
feast for clan members; *Tlee-dtsoo,* held for the whole village; *Hutch-
yahk,* in which the host travelled to another village and held the feast
there; and *Tloo-qwah,* to which guests from all over were invited.

Clutesi believes that it was this last feast that the early Europeans called a potlatch, because it is the only one that they were likely to be invited to. At a *Tloo-qwah*, the European guests, who did not speak the Nootka language, would have heard the word *Pa-chuck* ("gift," the noun that is related to the verb of *Pa-chitle*) often, and could easily have mistaken it for the name of the festival. It would be as though aliens, after observing a wedding reception in Mississauga, went back to their planet thinking our word for wedding was "toaster-oven."

Whatever the whites thought the ceremonies were called, it was clear they did not approve of them, nor of any other religious practices of First Nations people, for the federal Potlatch Law, passed in 1884, banned all traditional rituals and confiscated their accoutrements, such as masks, costumes, drums, pipes and so on. Some of these artifacts were placed in the Museum of Civilization, and some have since been returned to descendants of their original owners, but many have been lost forever. In 1996, for example, there was the interesting case of the beautiful Echo mask belonging to the Bella Coola people. Carved in 1860 for use in potlatches, it had flared nostrils, bulging cheeks, and six different interchangeable mouthpieces, and had been preserved intact by the family of a Nuxalt woman who, in 1995, sold it to a Victoria art dealer for $60,000. That same year the art dealer offered the mask to a Chicago commodities trader for $300,000. The Nuxalt (a band of the Bella Coola people) sought a court injunction to stop the sale, claiming that the mask had not belonged to the woman but to all Nuxalt people, and therefore could not be sold by her nor by the art dealer. The B.C. Supreme Court has placed the mask in the Royal British Columbia Museum in Victoria until the fracas is settled, which does not appear likely to be soon: the art dealer has generously offered to sell the mask back to its putative owners for "less than $250,000," but as

Nuxalt chief Archie Pootlass has observed with impeccable logic, if the mask cannot be sold, then it cannot be purchased either.

The Potlatch Law suppressed traditional Native ceremonies in an effort to suppress traditional Native peoples, but pretended it was banning potlatches for the Native peoples' own good. At a potlatch, a wealthy chief would demonstrate his power and authority by literally giving away everything he owned to his guests, each of whom would have to reciprocate with a potlatch of his own. As George Bowering observes in his history of British Columbia, *Bowering's B.C.*, "a man who had just attained the position of chief had to hold a potlatch to proclaim his name. Later his daughter might reach puberty or his son might earn a noble position. The father was obliged to hold a potlatch." Although the potlatch tradition shouldn't have seemed all that different from the European concept of dowry—I have known several Canadian families to go seriously into debt to pay for a daughter's wedding—the idea of giving something away for nothing was anathema to the Scottish traders who gradually took over the management of the coastal people. Potlatch was the opposite of thrift.

The geologist and surveyor George Dawson put his finger squarely on the potlatch problem in a curious government publication, *Report on the Queen Charlotte Islands, 1878*. "The distribution of property, or potlatch, as it is called in the Chinook jargon, implying, as it appears at first sight, such entire self-abnegation and disregard of the value of slowly accumulated wealth, requires some explanation." Dawson recognized the importance of the potlatch as "a means of combining labour for an industrial 'bee'" and "a method of acquiring influence with the tribe and of attaining even to the chieftancy." The potlatch, he said, was even a safe way of expressing rage and grief, and a vehicle for revenge. "At Masset, lately," Dawson reported, "it became known to a father that a young man had made improper advances to his daughter. The father, in great anger, tore up twenty blankets, which not only served as an outlet for his feelings, but placed the young man under the necessity of destroying a similar number of blankets or living in lasting disgrace."

Dawson's attempt to understand the importance of potlatches to Native cultural and even psychological life, however, was no match for the formidable might of the missionaries who lobbied hard for an end to such heathen outbursts. Merchants and traders sided with the missionaries, and the end of northwest coast culture followed hard upon. Stories like the following appeared often in the press, depicting potlatches as wild, drunken ceremonies in which naïve Native people, in thrall to ancient debilitating traditions, gave away all their worldly possessions and thus placed themselves at the mercy of the government. This story was told by a B.C. salmon canner to the Reverend Herbert H. Gowan, who reported it in the *Canadian Magazine* in 1894:

Last year I had an Indian working for me who earned $1,400. He drew the whole of this in a lump sum, and laid it out in eight muskets, a dozen boxes of crackers, and the balance—about $1,200—in blankets. Then the noble redman called all the Indians within reach together, and announced his intention of giving a grand potlatch.

The blankets were spread out in a two-acre field, with the crackers on the outside for his friends to lunch on, and the muskets in the centre. When the appointed time arrived to begin the ceremonies, the Indian waded through the sea of blankets to where the muskets lay. Here he climbed on a box and began a long oration, which lasted over an hour, at the end of which time he picked up the muskets one by one and smashed them over the box, signifying that all enmity between the tribes present was forever ended. Then he gave the signal that the potlatch had commenced, and the Indian women sailed in and packed away not only one pair of blankets but as many as they could carry, and in a few minutes there was not even a single blanket left for the use of the generous contributor. This grand give-away, of course, made the Siwash very popular, and a few days after he was elected sub-chief of his tribe. A few weeks later this same Indian came to me dead-broke, and got a sack of flour on credit.

One of those whose job it was to enforce the Law was the poet Duncan Campbell Scott, who was a senior bureaucrat with the Department of Indian Affairs at the turn of the century. There are many letters from Scott to provincial administrators, advising them that Native dances, feasts and especially potlatches were to be discouraged. I would have thought that the author of "The Wood-Spring to the Poet," for example, a poem about the nature of art and generosity—

Give, Poet, give!
Thus only shalt thou live.
Give! for 'tis thy joyous doom
To charm, to comfort, to illume

—would be sympathetic to a culture that had the selfless sharing of material goods at its core. But Scott evidently believed that Native traditions were dangerous to European interests. In 1906, in an article in *Scribners' Magazine*, he described "the Indian nature" at the time of European settlement as being "ready to break out at any moment in savage dances, in wild and desperate orgies in which ancient superstitions were involved with European ideas but dimly understood and intensified by cunning imaginations inflamed with rum." He decried the old treaties "that seemed to be founded on debauchery and licence" as "puerile negotiations . . . based on a childish system of presents."

No wonder he deplored potlatches. He preferred the kind of treaty he negotiated in 1905 with the Native peoples of northern Ontario on behalf of the Canadian Pacific Railway. In exchange for 90,000 square miles of "unregarded" territory, which contained "much arable land, many million feet of pulpwood, untold wealth of minerals, and unharnessed water-powers sufficient to do the work of half the continent," Scott agreed to pay "eight dollars once to every man, woman and child; and, forever afterward, . . . four dollars each; and reserves of one square mile to every family of five or in like proportion, and schools for their children; and a flag for the chief." Scott also noted with satisfaction that the feasts at Moose Factory and New Post seemed not like barbaric potlatches at all, but rather "like primitive tea-meetings."

The Potlatch Law was revoked by the Indian Act of 1951, and since then the word has come back into general use, even as far away as New England. The American writer Paul Theroux, in a short story called "Yard Sale," uses the word aptly when he has one of his characters turn a yard sale "into a potlatch ceremony by bestowing his power tools on his next-door neighbour and clowning among his junk with the word 'freebie.'" Curiously enough, among whites in British Columbia, "potlatch" seems to have become confused with "pot luck": some friends of mine recently mentioned they had been invited to a potlatch dinner, at which they each had to bring a salad or casserole. The odd thing about this is that "pot luck" originally meant the same thing as potlatch: being invited to a pot luck dinner meant taking your chances on eating whatever the host happened to be cooking that day. Now it means bringing your own food so that the host doesn't have to give anything away at all, the exact opposite of a traditional potlatch.

Since the passing of the Indian Act, many confiscated artifacts have been returned to their rightful owners and are on display at places like the Kwagiulth Museum and Cultural Centre on Quadra Island, one of the Queen Charlottes. And potlatch ceremonies—never very far underground in remote Native communities—became legal, though they returned with a twist. When the landmark South Moresby Agreement was signed in July 1987, ending fifteen years of intense and bitter negotiations over the protection of the South Moresby Archipelago (formerly the Queen Charlotte Islands, later called Haida Gwaii, now called Gwaii Haanas) from intensive logging, the event was marked in Skidegate by a huge potlatch, attended by Native leaders as well as by representatives of the B.C. and federal governments.

The ceremony was a true potlatch because, as it subsequently turned out, all the giving was being done by the Native peoples, and all the taking by their white guests.

Puck A hard, black rubber disk used in hockey.

—*1997, Gage Canadian Dictionary*

THE PUCK STARTS HERE

Paul Quarrington's dog Jessie spent much of her life creating hockey pucks. In *Hometown Heroes* (1988), his book about Canada's national hockey team, Quarrington speculated on the origin of the puck and reported the theory that a McGill student named W.F. Robertson made the first puck in 1879 by cutting "an overly bouncy rubber ball in half," which led Quarrington to remark that if that is so, then Jessie makes dozens of pucks every year. He goes on to theorize "that the hockey puck was probably invented by some turn-of-the-century mastiff, who chewed and slobbered on a ball until it was rendered into a flat and mushy thing that promptly froze hard as a rock out in the wintry air."

That's as good a theory as anyone else has come up with. W.F. "Robbie" Robertson, an Applied Science student at McGill in the 1870s, was credited with inventing the game of ice hockey, using field-hockey sticks made on the Caughnawaga Indian Reserve outside Montreal and a rubber lacrosse ball with its top and bottom sliced off to make it flat on both sides. But he didn't call the mutilated lacrosse ball a puck. The word "puck" made its first appearance in the American magazine *Field* on April 7, 1891, in an article describing a Canadian game: "The ball (or 'puck' as it is called) is a flat piece of india-rubber, circular in shape, about two inches thick, and with a diameter of about four inches." Since that time the puck, unlike the baseball, hasn't changed much. Its first recorded use in Canada was in the Rat Portage (now Kenora, Ontario) *News*, on

January 11, 1895: "The puck is about the size of a blacking box, made of rubber." Apparently, shoe-polish tins haven't changed much either.

No one seems to know for sure why a puck is called a puck. It has never yet been suggested that it is named after the troublesome *diablotin* in *A Midsummer Night's Dream*, although there may be something in that: is there not a reference to the slap-shot in Puck's farewell?

I go, I go, look how I go,
Swifter than arrow from the Tartar's bow.

But Shakespeare's Puck took his name from the Old English word for devil: *puca*. The OED suggests that the hockey puck may have derived from the verb "to puck," which in turn comes from "to poke," meaning "to hit or strike at a ball," as in the Irish game of hurling (in which it is usually opposing players who are hit or struck). The earliest such use the OED could find for the verb "puck" was 1900, however, long after pucks were being dropped in Canada. (The "face-off," by the way, at which the referee puts the game in motion by dropping the puck between two opposing centres, was originally called the "puck-off," but was changed when women began attending hockey games. This suggests a measure of how times have changed. Guy Lawson records a new use of the word "puck" in a recent essay on Junior "A" hockey, published in *Harper's* magazine. In Flin Flon, a small hockey town that straddles the Manitoba-Saskatchewan border, Lawson writes that young women who date members of the Flin Flon Bombers are known as "Pucks" because, he says, "they get passed around a lot.") There is a survival of the puck–poke connection in the "poke check," the manoeuvre by which a player takes the puck from an opponent without making body contact. A poke check is a puck check; the verbal switch could easily have suggested itself.

At any rate, it is certain that Canadians were playing hockey in more or less its present form long before someone thought to note down the name of the black rubber thing. The long-standing feud among Halifax, Montreal and Kingston for the distinction of having hosted the first organized hockey game in Canada is never going to be settled; the Hockey Hall of Fame and Museum in Toronto, in true Canadian fashion, refuses to referee the dispute, giving equal credence to all three claimants (probably because none of them is Toronto). But whichever city it was, it has no relevance to the word "puck," since accounts of all three "first games" state that they were played outdoors using a lacrosse ball, not a puck.

The first indoor hockey game, however, was played on March 3, 1875, in the arena of the Victoria Skating Club in Montreal, and one version has it that it was this game, or rather the game played immediately after this game, that gave the world its first hockey puck. The Victoria Skating Club rink was a large, enclosed arena with a high ceiling and lots of windows, and the story goes that the wildly bounceable lacrosse ball used in the first game broke several hundred dollars' worth of glass. The next day the Club's manager called the players (one of whom was not Robbie Robertson, who skated at the rival Crystal Skating Rink) into his office to discuss the damage, and when the players showed him their offending lacrosse ball, he took it from them, sliced off the top and bottom leaving a one-inch slab in the middle, and gave it back to them, telling them to use it next time or else find another rink.

If this story is true, then it discredits the claim made by the International Hockey Hall of Fame and Museum in Kingston, which sells what it calls replicas of the original puck used in the "first Hockey Game" between Queen's University and Royal Military College in 1886. That puck is not a round disk, but rather a square one with slightly rounded corners, measuring two and a half inches on each side and an inch thick. If games in Kingston in 1886 were played with this primitive square puck, then it's hard to believe games in Montreal in 1875 were played with a more highly evolved round one. I've fooled around with one of the squared replicas in a rink in Kingston, and it makes for some pretty erratic shots, even more unpredictable than my shots with a round puck. And forget about rebounds off the boards. The Queen's–RMC game was played outdoors, of course (on Kingston Harbour, behind the Tête-du-Pont Barracks), so there wouldn't have been any rebounds off boards because there weren't any boards; a lot of square pucks must have gone missing over the snowbanks. Maybe divers should look for them—not that that would settle the dispute.

In French, a puck is *une rondelle*, which at first suggests roundness, but, according to Sylva Clapin's *Dictionnaire canadien-français* (1894), *un rond* in Quebec was a hippodrome, or horse-racing track, and *un rond à patiner* was a skating rink, which was essentially a rectangle with rounded corners, like the Kingston puck. Could the squared puck used in Kingston have been designed to resemble the shape of a skating rink? In English, the term "rink" was borrowed from curling, and a curling rink is anything but round. The word originally comes from the Old English *renc*, which meant "a jousting arena"—a long corridor down which knights wearing armoured protection and carrying long sticks charged at one another from opposite ends with intent to injure, just as hockey players do today.

Pucks are still an inch thick and just under three inches in diameter, and are made (by the Viceroy Reliable Group in Toronto at the rate of 2.5 million per year) from a mixture of natural and synthetic rubber (so they don't snap in half when they freeze), sulfur, antioxidants and a filler such as coal dust. This is extruded into long, soft bars that are then sliced into puck slugs, or "preforms," and baked for twenty-two minutes at 150°C. They come in plain black or emblazoned with any number of logos, including those of all the National Hockey League teams, local amateur hockey associations, charitable organizations, even gasoline companies that give them away with tankfuls of gasoline. There probably isn't a house in Canada that doesn't have two or three of the things lying around somewhere, but that wouldn't account for 2.5 million a year. Where do old pucks go? Maybe we should ask Paul Quarrington's dog.

Pullman Hamilton was the birthplace of the first sleeping cars known to the world. The plan was rendered by Samuel Sharp, first master mechanic of the Great Western, and Pullman copied the design.

—*Canadian Railway Development from Earliest Times,* 1933, Norman Thompson

SHARP CARS

I was recently in a coffee shop in Toronto, one of those new ones in which the word "coffee" is murmured with the kind of hushed reverence once reserved for single-malt Scotch and Sobranie tobacco. On a blackboard beside the cash register was written, "Today's Trivia Quiz—winner gets a free cuppa." The quiz question was: "Who invented the first railway sleeping car?" The question threw me into one of those familiar moral quandaries in which you know that the truth will not serve you well. I knew the correct answer—the sleeping car was invented by a Canadian engineer named Samuel Sharp— but I also knew that the answer most likely to be rewarded in the temple of coffee would be the one wrongly accepted by history: George M. Pullman. After all, it's called the Pullman, isn't it? Well, yes, but it should be called the Sharp. How badly did I want a free cup of coffee?

A Pullman is a railway car that operates as a coach or parlour car during the day and a sleeping car at night, and is so named because it is presumed to have been invented by George Pullman, a Chicago industrialist. Pullman did indeed build a dual-purpose railway car in 1859; it cost him $20,000 and he named it the Pioneer. It became so successful that he changed its name to the Pullman Palace Sleeping and Drawing-Room Car and set up a factory outside Chicago to produce hundreds like it. Pullman was the first industrialist to hire blacks; they worked as porters on his Pullman cars, and for decades all black railway porters were called George, after George Pullman. The first transcontinental train, which pulled out of Boston in May 1870, carried 129 passengers in eight cars, two of which were Pullman Palace Sleeping and Drawing-Room Cars (they were named the Palmyra and the Marquette); the others were a baggage car, a smoking car, two "hotel" cars (which were fitted with offices and a wine-room), and two commissary or dining cars. Fifty thousand people toured the train before it left the station.

The area on the Far Southeast Side of Chicago was called Pullman, Illinois, when it was founded in 1880 because it was originally the company town for Pullman's workers, all of whom did nothing all day but build Pullman cars. It was a nice suburb; my friend David Homel, who is from Chicago, says it is still a nice suburb, though a little run-down. From the beginning, however, the workers were paid low wages and charged high rents, and they were obliged to do their shopping at Pullman's company stores. There was much labour unrest and therefore a strong police force. Pullman is distinguished by having brought about the first occasion on which federal troops were sent to dispel a workers' strike: only a year after it was built, in 1881, George Pullman decided that the town should show a 6-percent profit, so he lowered workers' wages without reducing their rent. The workers went out on strike, and President Grover Cleveland called in the army.

However, Pullman's "invention" was in fact an idea originally conceived by Samuel Sharp, the master mechanic of the Great Western Railway in Hamilton, Ontario. In 1857, in preparation for a visit to Canada by the Prince of Wales in 1860, Sharp designed a railway coach that the Prince could use both day and night, the seats being fitted with springs and mattresses which, when flipped and surrounded by heavy curtains, became private sleeping compartments at night.

The Prince was delighted with the convenience and comfort, and said so. When he left Canada, the general population was so keen to travel in a railway car designed for royalty that the GWR began manufacturing them, and charged fifty cents extra per night for the privilege of being able to sleep horizontally on long overland trips without the bother of having to move to separate sleeping cars. The new conveyances caught on so quickly that, when the Englishman J.J. Hargrave travelled from Toronto to Sarnia on the Great Western line in 1861, he described the journey thus:

> Travelling during the night, we exchanged our regular day carriages for others, the interior furnishings of which were so constructed that, with wonderfully little trouble, the series of seats could be turned into rows of sofas or cushioned benches, serving the purposes of beds. Curtains, blankets and pillows, which during the day had been stowed away in their boxes, were brought out and so utilized that considerable comfort and privacy were obtainable. These carriages, commonly called "sleeping cars," are of great service in the course of long journeys, continued by day and night sometimes for nearly a week. The result of the ingenuity with which every piece is dove-tailed into its neighbour, so that the ordinary car of the day becomes the dormitory of its occupants during the night, must be seen to be adequately appreciated. The same number of passengers can, I believe, be accommodated in each carriage under the night arrangements as under those of the day. Sufficient attendance is provided to secure passengers, who desire to be roused at any spot during the night, against the risk of being carried past their destination.

In fact, "sleeping cars" were railway cars that contained sleeping compartments only, which were not convertible into coach seats during the day. These had been in existence since the first one did an overnight run from Harrisburg to Chambersburg, Pennsylvania, in 1836. What Hargrave was describing was one of Sharp's cars.

But it was Pullman's invention that revolutionized overnight travel in North America, not because it was the first of its kind, but because Pullman was smart enough to organize, advertise and commercialize its construction. For some reason, the Great Western Railway did not capitalize on Sharp's invention. In fact, it stopped production of Sharp's luxury cars and ordered Pullman's Palace Sleeping and Drawing-Room Cars instead, because it could buy them more cheaply than Sharp could build them—an early instance of the current government's "lowest bid" policy, by which any capital purchase has to go out to public tender and the government is obliged by law to accept the lowest bid, regardless of where it comes from. The result—taking Canadian taxpayers' money and shipping it out of the country in trainloads instead of investing it in Canadian companies—is called free trade. Thus, during John Cabot Days festivities in Newfoundland, for example, when Canadians travelled to St. John's to celebrate the five hundredth anniversary of Cabot's sighting of the New Found Land, the federal government handed out thousands of Canadian flags that had been made in the United States.

In 1886, Pullman built the first railway car to be intended exclusively as a dining car. These were elaborately appointed rolling restaurants (the first dining car was named the Delmonico, after an expensive New York establishment) with starched white tablecloths, and silver sugar bowls and cream pitchers heavy enough to stay put when the train rounded a curve. As American poet and lexicographer John Ciardi notes, "retired dining cars began to appear on sidings by railroad stations as cheap, quick eating places." They soon became known as "diners," and eventually moved off the tracks and into downtown small-town America, where diners still have the rounded windows and general shape of what Ciardi calls "railroad" cars. The equivalent spin-off in Canada would have to be the Chinese restaurant, hundreds of which sprang up along the original CPR route as Chinese workers were shunted off the CPR gravy train and established themselves in small towns from Ontario to British Columbia.

Attentive readers will have noted that I have been trying to distinguish between "railroad" and "railway." In the United States it is always railroad, in Canada it is railway. Gordon Lightfoot's famous song about the building of the CPR is called "The Canadian Railroad Trilogy;" it ought to be called "The Canadian Railway Trilogy:" CPR stands for Canadian Pacific Railway. And the question chalked up beside the cash register in the Bean Machine—"Who invented the first railway sleeping car?"—suggested to me a typically Canadian compromise solution to my moral dilemma.

"George Pullman invented the first rail*road* sleeping car," I told the guy at the cash, "but it was Samuel Sharp who built the first rail*way* sleeping car."

I got the coffee.

Sasquatch   The strange people of whom there are but few
now—rarely seen and seldom met—are known by the name
of Sasquatch, or "the hairy mountain men."

—J.W. Burns in *Maclean's magazine*, 1929

WILD MEN OF THE WOODS

"We are now entering the defiles of the Rocky Mountains by
the Athabasca River," David Thompson wrote in his journal
on January 5, 1811. "The woods of pine are stunted, full of branches
to the ground, and the aspen, willow, &c., not much better. Strange
to say, here is a strong belief that the haunt of the mammoth is about
this defile. I questioned several; none could positively say they had
seen him, but their belief I found firm and not to be shaken."

The hairy giants living in the mountains were a universal bogey,
being known as far east as Manitoba, but Thompson's Native companions were probably recounting something they had heard from
the coastal tribes rather than seen themselves. We don't know what
name they gave it; there are more than twenty Pacific Coast Native
words for these giants, most of which translate as "wild men of the
woods." The descriptions are quite uniform: they were nine feet tall,
weighed up to four hundred pounds, were covered with brownish-
black hair (except for the face and nipples, which were black), with
flat noses, no necks and abnormally long arms. Thompson evidently
thought his Native informants were mistaken, guessing they were
describing legends of the woolly mammoth. That species of elephant
(*Elephas primigenius*) had been found frozen into the Siberian permafrost—so fresh that its meat could be eaten and its stomach con-
tents analysed—and was not then known to have been extinct for

the past ten thousand years. The word "mammoth," from the Siberian *mammanta*, had been in use in English since 1690, and the most recent mammoth excavation had taken place in 1806, only five years before Thompson's journal entry.

Two days later, Thompson's hope of finding the world's first living woolly mammoth were dashed when his party

> came on the track of a large animal, the snow about six inches deep on the ice. I measured it: four large toes each of four inches in length, to each a short claw; the ball of the foot sunk three inches lower than the toes, the hinder part of the foot did not mark well; the length fourteen inches by eight inches in breadth, walking from north to south, and had passed by about six hours. We were in no hurry to follow him.

Although "the men and Indians would have it to be a young Mammoth," this was obviously not the track of anything elephant-like. Thompson was a rationalist: "I held it to be the track of a large old grizzled bear."

Thompson was whistling in the dark. Even he knew he was not looking at grizzly tracks: "The shortness of the nails, the ball of the foot, and its great size was not that of a bear, [unless it was] that of a very large old bear, his claws worn away." Claws worn away and one toe missing, he should have said, because grizzlies have five toes, not four, and their claws can be up to three and a half inches long. Thompson's measurements are all wrong for grizzlies. Grizzly tracks are 6 inches long by 5 inches wide for the front foot, and 9 inches long by 5 inches wide for the hind foot, when the heel pad is registering—well shy of Thompson's 14 inches long by 8 inches wide. Whatever made that mammoth track, it had big feet. The Alaskan brown bear, a large subspecies of the grizzly, makes tracks that measure up to 16 inches long and 8 inches wide, but it has never been recorded down where Thompson was, which was near present-day Jasper, Alberta.

Thompson's interpretation of the wild-man legend as referring to a mammoth persisted long after anyone could possibly attribute the evidence to an elephant, or even an elephant man. The town of Mammoth, Wyoming, now surrounded by Yellowstone National Park, was not named after some woolly pachyderm found frozen in a crevasse; it was named after these hairy ape-men. Maybe they went there for the hot springs (this is not as entirely facetious as it sounds).

It is now believed that Thompson was the first European to see the footprints of a Sasquatch. Since that time there have been hundreds of reports of Sasquatch footprints, Sasquatch howls, even Sasquatch scat, as well as encounters with Sasquatch (called Bigfoot in the United States) him- or herself. One of the first was written by Theodore Roosevelt, who, in his book *The Wilderness Hunter* (1893), told of an encounter between a Sasquatch and a trapper named Baumann in the American Rockies. In the April 1, 1929, issue of *Maclean's* magazine (note the date), J.W. Burns, an Indian agent at the Chehalis Indian Reserve in British Columbia, wrote the article quoted at the outset. Called "Introducing B.C.'s Hairy Giants," it described the legendary wild man and named the creature Sasquatch, from *Saskehavas*, one of the Coastal Salish names for it. (This was rather insulting to the Chehalis, since they had their own name for it: *Syakwa*, meaning "Stick Man." No doubt Burns thought his readers would not be impressed by tales of hordes of Stick Men descending on hapless West Coast pioneers.) The article was reprinted in 1940 in the American *World Wide Magazine* (touched up by someone named C.V. Tench), and again in *Liberty* the following year, by which time there were almost as many sightings of the article as there were of the Sasquatch.

The Chehalis Reserve is just upriver from Harrison Hot Springs, and in the 1950s the Harrison Hot Springs Hotel began promoting the Sasquatch legend as a way of promoting the hotel. In 1957 the hotel began sponsoring something called "Sasquatch Days," inviting anyone who had spotted or encountered a Sasquatch to send in their stories. There were more than three hundred submissions, many of them from the Harrison area—there are hot springs there, remember. The avalanche of raw material prompted John Green, then editor of the nearby *Agassiz-Harrison Advance*, to take a long look at the evidence. Green soon became the world's foremost promoter of the Sasquatch legend, and has since published five books presenting and analysing the scientific evidence for its anecdotal reality (a clear case of essence preceding existence).

There have been more than 1,500 "well-documented" reports of Sasquatch and Bigfoot sightings, including some dubious 8-mm film footage shot near Eureka, California (Eureka, of course, means "I found it!"), taken by an ex-rodeo-cowboy named Roger Patterson in 1969 while he and a partner were riding up in the area around Bluff Creek. The film has since been examined by experts and declared authentic, i.e. undoctored, and apparently of a live creature and not of Patterson's partner dressed up in a gorilla suit. It looks at least as convincing to me as any of the UFO videos we've been subjected to on the Space Channel.

Reports of Sasquatch and UFO sightings have much in common: muddy photos, amateur videos, conspiracy theories, abduction reports. There is even an account of a Sasquatch capture, one of the earliest of all Sasquatch anecdotes. It appeared in the Victoria *Colonist* on July 4, 1884, and tells how a railway crew from Lytton, B.C., captured "a creature which may truly be called half man and half beast." The railwaymen found it lying beside the tracks, having apparently fallen from the top of a rock cut during the night. They called it Jacko, and described it as "something of the gorilla type standing about four feet seven inches in height and weighing 127 pounds." Not exactly a giant, but the rest of the description fits:

> He has long, black, strong hair and resembles a human being with one exception, his entire body, excepting his hands (or paws) and feet are covered with glossy hair about one inch long. His forearm is much longer than a man's forearm, and he possesses extraordinary strength, as he will take hold of a stick and break it by wrenching it or twisting it, which no man living could break in the same way.

Sounds to me like an escapee from some Wild West Show. In fact, the creature was shipped east with the intention of exhibiting it somewhere, but apparently it died on the way. Maybe John Green should find out what happened to Jacko's body. Green thinks someone has to kill a Sasquatch in order to provide physical evidence of its existence; his talk at the first conference on Humanoid Monsters: Sasquatch and Other Phenomena, held in 1978 at the University of British Columbia, was entitled "To Shoot or Not To Shoot," and Green said, "Shoot!"

John Green's frustration is understandable. Despite all the reports of sightings and soundings, no one has ever come up with any real reason to believe that the creature exists—no bones, no den sites, no middens, nothing that couldn't have been imagined or faked. After two hundred years, no one really knows what a Sasquatch is. There have been a few theories, of course. I'm going to start with what seem to me to be the most plausible among them, and work through to some that require certain adjustments to our definition of sanity.

The best guesses so far are those that provide a sort of zoological explanation for Sasquatch, like Thompson attributing the footprints to a huge, four-toed, clawless grizzly bear. Myra Shackley, a

British ethnographer, thinks that Sasquatches are a tribe of lost hominids, possibly "closely related through descent to the extinct great ape *Gigantopithecus.*" According to her theory, a pod of these creatures wandered into North America from northern Asia across the Beringian land-bridge just before the last Ice Age, 1.8 million years ago. These giant apes, says Shackley, would "have evolved considerably *in situ* since that time," which explains why their descriptions don't match what we know of *Gigantopithecus* from fossil remains in Asia.

They would also have multiplied. Consider that all the moose in Newfoundland are descended from three females and two males that were introduced to the island in 1906, and then figure out how many descendants there might be from even a single *Gigantopithecus* family after 1.8 million years. And yet John Bindernagel, a zoologist from Courtenay, B.C., and author of *North America's Great Ape* (1988), who proposes that Sasquatch is really an isolated subspecies of the great ape, places the current population at fewer than three thousand individuals. Both Bindernagel's and Shackley's theories have Sasquatch related to us by a common ancestor, and one that was not, so far as we know, nine feet tall and covered with chocolate-brown hair. But they are interesting theories—and 1.8 million years ago, by the way, is about exactly when the first waves of mammoths crossed over into North America via the Bering Strait. I like it when unrelated things dovetail like that.

William O. Pruitt, a wildlife biologist from Alaska, thinks Sasquatch might be a huge subspecies of wolverine. "An interesting comparison can be drawn," he writes in *Alive in the Wild*, "between the wolverine tracks in the snow and the published tracks attributed to the Yeti, or Abominable Snowman, in the Himalayas. The similarity of the tracks plus the wolverine's penchant for venturing into the permanent snow and ice zone has led me to conclude that the

Yeti is a large, perhaps undescribed, species of wolverine." Support for this idea might come from the facts that Sasquatches, like wolverines, are solitary, nocturnal, extremely shy of humans, very powerful, appear to like water, and roam over vast territories. But it would have to be an almost incredibly large wolverine: the largest known wolverine tracks to date measure only 4 inches long by 2 inches wide, and the average weight of a wolverine is about 40 pounds, a long way even from the 127 pounds given for the Sasquatch/wolverine man captured in 1884.

Pruitt's explanation would find no favour at the North American Scientific Institute (NASI), an Oregon-based organization whose goal is to establish the reality of Sasquatch or Bigfoot as a viable species unto itself, not as something else already known but yet to be identified, such as a great ape or a Neanderthal. "Bigfoot is likely the closest relative human beings have," NASI research director Tod Deery said during the Fifth Annual International Sasquatch Symposium, held in June 1997 in Vancouver. "Confirmation of its existence," he added, "would be the most significant find of this century." That's placing Sasquatch right up there with life on Mars and a cure for AIDS. Some of the people at the symposium were genuine Sasquatch seers. Betty Unger and her grandson Dallas Yellowfly, for example, while driving home from a skiing weekend in 1989, saw a powerful figure with short, chocolate-brown hair and a hairless face climb down from a snow bank and approach their car. "His eyes were clear and brilliant and seemed to be intelligent," said Unger. Although the creature was under six feet in height, she added, it probably weighed more than two hundred pounds. This hardly makes the creature a giant—they think he might have been a juvenile—but what makes me think they really saw something was the interesting way young Dallas described the experience. "It was kind of like a Kokanee commercial," he told a reporter from *British Columbia Report*. (Kokanee beer has been using Sasquatch images in its commercials lately, the way other Canadian beers are using cougars, wolves, grizzlies and polar bears.) He couldn't have been making that up.

At the low end of the credibility scale, at least for me, is the theory proposed by Jack Lapseritis, author of *The Psychic Sasquatch: The UFO Connection*. According to Lapseritis, Sasquatches are aliens who were brought to Earth by "star people"; none have ever been found, he says, because they are "shape-shifters" who can change themselves into deer or mice whenever they want to avoid capture. He also says two Sasquatches "soul-travelled" into his apartment in Milwaukee in 1980—the first of 350 encounters he has had with Sasquatches "on the astral level"—to beg him to deliver their message to mankind. We are, they wanted him to tell us, destroying our environment. We have, they told him, "divorced ourselves from nature." They are, I think, right about that, although they didn't have to travel all the way from Glaukon II to tell us. And I do wonder what message these shape-shifters might have had for the Coastal Salish, to whom they showed themselves first.

The UFO–Sasquatch connection is interesting on a deeper level, however. According to the Center for UFO Studies in Illinois, there are more reports of extraterrestrial beings and unidentified flying objects in Canada than anywhere else, and more from western Canada than from the east. Think about all those crop circles. A poll conducted by *Weekend* magazine in 1978, when I was working there, found that 41 percent of Canadians believed that Sasquatches definitely or possibly existed, and 73 percent believed the same about flying saucers. We didn't break the numbers down geographically, but we did relate the results to "the view of some social commentators that people are moving away from rational thinking."

Carole Henderson Carpenter, a cultural anthropologist at York University who became interested in Sasquatch stories years before

it was groovy to do so, notes that Canadians are not prone to bor-
rowing evil characters from Native legends. She views Sasquatch
stories, when told by non-Native people, as "vestiges of the retreat-
ing wilderness," connecting them with "the persistence of the garrison mentality, which, according to many scholars, was engrained in
Canada's early settlers. This mentality results from the isolation of
pockets of civilization amidst the wilderness and the zealous protection of these pockets, or garrisons, from the dangerous, fright-
ening wilderness." Sasquatch legends intrigued Europeans because
they confirmed their worst fears about the demonic powers of
nature: "The monsters in Canada . . . represent the antithesis of the
culture the British sought to foster here—the beasts are negative;
civilization is positive."

I don't know about that. Carpenter herself points out that no
one has ever reported being harmed by a Sasquatch; in most cases
the thing is seen running away, and even John Green, who wants us
to go out and shoot one in the name of science, says it is "not a
fearful monster, but a remarkably inoffensive animal." If it does
shape-shift (ahem), it transforms itself into a deer or a mouse, not
a mountain lion or a grizzly. Surely, if we were trying to frighten
ourselves, we would have come up with something more terrifying
than a large, solitary, apelike creature that seems hell-bent on keeping out of our way. The coastal Indians, from whom we borrowed
(or stole) the Sasquatch, had far more fearsome creatures than the
timid Sasquatch with which we could have fed our fear of the wild—
if we had a fear of the wild. There is, for example, the Kwakiutl
deity D'Sonoqua, described as a female giant twice the size of
humans, with huge ears, eyes set in cavernous sockets, and a black
body. Also called the Basket Ogress, she lured children into the
woods and carried them off for her dinner. It seems to me that, if
we were afraid of nature, we would have passed these stories around

the campfires at night. The Basket Ogress could even have replaced the old witch in "Hansel and Gretel," but she didn't. Instead, there is a wonderful chapter in Emily Carr's *Klee Wyck* (1941) in which Carr writes of meeting D'Sonoqua in a remote abandoned village on the Queen Charlottes. Rather than a monstrous, cannibalistic child-stealer, Carr discovers a being that is "graciously feminine," a hauntingly beautiful spirit that "summed up the depth and charm of the forest, driving away its menace."

Our attitude towards nature is often mentioned as a way of distinguishing Canadian from American culture: we fear nature and cower from it in garrisons, Americans arm themselves with weapons and go out to kill it. But it is interesting to note that, whereas Bigfoot reports in the United States are almost always of footprints, most of the Sasquatch stories in Canada are of actual Sasquatch sightings. We seem to want, or at least to want to see, the real thing.

Shinny A violent early form of field hockey played with
curved sticks and a ball.

—*A Second Browser's Dictionary*, 1983, John Ciardi

CHOOSING UP

Every Thursday afternoon during the winter, I go down to the local
hockey rink with about twenty other 40-plussers, put on a raggle-
taggle set of hockey equipment—some of it left over from my youth,
some of it acquired more recently to protect a portlier frame—then,
fully armoured, step out onto the magical surface of freshly Zambonied
ice. Ah, the smell of ice. There is a wonderful passage in one of W.P.
Kinsella's baseball books in which baseball players lift their noses to
the smell of grass in the outfield, "like ponies smelling water." A similar thing happens when old hockey players smell ice. We skate around
in circles for a few minutes, a herd thing we call "warming up." Then,
for the next hour or so, we play what we like to refer to as hockey,
but which in fact is the game of shinny. Shinny is an older, simpler
form of hockey; it is to hockey what rounders is to baseball. And shinny
is transitional in another way: when I was kid, I played shinny, then I
played hockey; now I'm playing shinny again.

People were playing shinny in Canada long before they played
hockey. The first hockey game in Canada was played either in Halifax or Montreal or Kingston, depending on how you define "hockey,"
but it was definitely not played until the 1880s. Ralph Connor, whose
real name was Charles William Gordon, recalled playing shinny in
Glengarry County, in what is now southeastern Ontario, in the 1870s.
"Shinty or shinny, as we called it," he wrote in his autobiography,
Postscript to Adventure,

was an importation from Scotland and was usually played on the hard-beaten snow of the schoolyard. There were few rules. The game was played with a hard rubber ball and homemade sticks. We would cut from the bush a good elm or hickory cudgel with a natural crook. It was a savage game which often gave rise to fights. For we went in for no such frills as umpires or referees.

Except for the savagery, that is still pretty much how shinny is played today, except we use a puck and play on an outdoor hockey rink or, if we get organized about it, in a real hockey arena. One year, when I nearly broke my arm during a game of shinny early in the season, I borrowed a striped shirt and a whistle and played as a referee until my arm healed. But it wasn't the same, and I was glad to give it up when my arm sort of felt better.

A form of shinny, called bandy, was played on ice in England in the 1830s. It was field hockey—curved sticks, rubber or wooden ball, large teams, bruised shins—that continued into the snowy months. A game of bandy was apparently played in Montreal in 1837. Each team had eight players and the game continued until one team had scored three goals or else until four o'clock in the afternoon, whichever came first. This sounds like shinny to me. The game soon spread to Kingston. The diary of a soldier in the Kingston garrison during the winter of 1846–47 mentions that, although figure skating was popular with the troops, "shinny was their great delight." Games were played on the frozen surface of Lake Ontario between City Hall and Fort Henry, "and fifty or more players on each side would be in the game." This sounds like hell on ice.

The word "shinny" apparently comes from the cry "Shin ye!"—a kind of terrifying war-whoop let out preparatory to the violence mentioned by Connor, which makes it sound like an English form of the Irish game of hurling. But as played in Canada it owes more to lacrosse, a game that had been played here between Native villages from Quebec to British Columbia long before European contact, than to any other imported game. Canada's official national sport is still lacrosse. Again, Ralph Connor provides the link.

In his autobiographical novel *Glengarry School Days*, Connor devotes a lot of time to the game of shinny. Shinny, he believed, helped to teach a person to harness the more primitive, violent emotions and aided in the evolution of aggressive tendencies into positively directed social skills. I've noticed this myself about shinny. Connor's school on the twentieth concession is in a state of perpetual shinny challenge from a school at the Front—"front" being the term for the property contained in the first concession. The smaller boys of the Twentieth invariably lost to the larger louts from the Front until the arrival of the Twentieth's new schoolmaster, John Craven. Craven introduced two innovations to the game of shinny: he put his players on skates and had them play on a frozen pond instead of on the tramped snow of the schoolyard; and, having once captained the champion Quebec lacrosse team when he lived in Montreal, he organized the players according to the strict rules of lacrosse. The boys from the Twentieth, newly skilful at playing positions, passing the ball, setting up plays, back-checking and stick-handling, easily beat the gang of ruffians from the Front—and in the process learned valuable lessons about social behaviour and civilized restraint. Since Connor was born in 1860 and was in about the seventh grade when this momentous transition took place, we may take it that shinny was born into its present guise in the early 1870s. Hockey came well after that, but, contrary to the accepted law of evolution, is far less civilized than shinny.

Most Canadians, even when they think they are playing hockey, are playing shinny. The violence has leached out of shinny and settled into hockey. Hockey is now the type specimen of violent sport, having superseded even professional wrestling, which is not violent at all. The American poet John Ciardi, quoted at the outset, believes that "any form of hockey will equate to violence (I went to a fight, and a hockey game broke out)." The American novelist Russell Banks, whose father was Canadian, has written about playing what he calls hockey as a child growing up in Canada: "hockey, especially as played by Canadian schoolboys, is a violent game." But the game Banks describes in his short story "The Defenceman" is not hockey, it is shinny. Banks and Ciardi understand hockey, but they do not understand shinny.

There were few rules in bandy (no swinging at the ball in the air, no bandy stick can be wider than two inches), and in Connor's day there were even fewer rules for shinny, but in the game I play there are dozens of them, albeit unwritten, and chief among them is no violence. No slap-shots, no body-checking, no roughing it up against the boards, no desperate hacking after pucks in corners. That's how the louts from the Front played, and they lost. In shinny, we eschew violence. Whenever violence is involved, you have to care who wins; in shinny, you do not.

In shinny, teams are seldom fixed; they are made up after everyone is assembled and dressed and on the ice ready to play. The usual method is for every player to place his or her hockey stick in a pile at centre ice, and someone stands in the middle and blindly tosses one stick one way and the next stick the other way, until all the sticks are divided into two equal piles. Then the players find their own sticks, exchange sweaters so that one team is wearing light and the other dark, and the game commences. There is no face-off; everyone just starts to play.

This method of selecting teams, called choosing up, is perfectly democratic, which is to say it has the appearance of being random and therefore unbiased but in fact is usually rigged. The difference between hockey and shinny lies in this: in hockey, the idea is to stack a team so that one is more powerful than the other, whereas in shinny the idea is to make the two teams as even as possible. That's because the idea in shinny is not to dominate a weaker opponent, but to be as good as an equal. The ideal game of shinny ends in a tie. When it does, you remember who played on which team, and rig the selection process next time so that the balance is maintained. You do this by memorizing who owns which stick.

During the game, the two basic etiquettes are simple and often difficult to remember: no slap-shots and no body contact. Sometimes a player will forget himself and wind up for a slap-shot as though out of habit (if he is pretending that he once played semi-pro hockey, for example, or if he has had a frustrating day at the office). When this happens, no one says anything about it, everyone just skates around for a few moments, looking disappointed, and it usually doesn't happen again. Sometimes two players will collide and one will fall down in a way that has more to do with goal-prevention than it does with gravity. When that happens, play stops, and the player who did not fall down helps the player who did to his feet, apologizes to him, helps him wipe the snow off his sweater, and then the player who fell down asks the player who did not fall down whether he is all right. When one player is obviously tripped by another player, it is always accidentally, and the tripped player merely gets up and apologizes for stepping on the other player's stick. And play resumes.

When I say that the ideal game of shinny ends in a tie, I do not mean to imply that anyone actually keeps score. It sometimes happens that someone, usually a new player, counts goals and announces a score at the end of the game, but no one pays much attention unless it's to tell him he's mistaken. The closest any seasoned shinny player comes to keeping score is to say at the end of a game that the teams seemed to have been evenly matched, which is good. If one team absolutely and incontrovertibly dominates another team, scoring a dozen goals to the other team's one, for example, very little mention is made of it because the score reflects badly on one of the goalies and the imbalance is an implied criticism of the person who chose the sides. If mention is made of it, it is not the winning side that makes it; it is the losing side that apologizes for playing badly. "I think you were up a couple of goals," a player on the losing side might say to a player on the winning side, to which the second player replies, "Maybe one," and the person who chose the sides makes a renewed study of everyone's stick.

These shinny etiquettes are so ingrained, so obvious, so sensible, that there is never any need to explain them to new players except by example and implication. Any Canadian who has ever played a single game of shinny knows everything about it, as if it has been part of our national consciousness all along. As indeed it has. Perhaps the best writing about shinny I have read was written by someone who played the game only once or twice, in his distant youth: Robert Hilles, a Calgary poet, wrote a tribute to his father, who had died of cancer, called *Kissing the Smoke*, and in it he included a chapter on shinny, which he called "Hockey." As though by osmosis, Hilles perfectly captures the essence of the game. He knows it is not our lost youth that we are trying to recapture in shinny, it is more an acceptance of aging, a testing of the limitations imposed by time: my knees now will bend only this far, my lungs will hold only this much air. Hilles's book is a celebration of the continued possibility of grace in our lives. "The grace of the game transforms them," he writes of his brother and father playing shinny on a frozen pond. "Through the complicated twists and turns a player finds in his body the skeleton of an angel."

Yes.

Ski-Doo A type of snowmobile.

—*Gage Canadian Dictionary,* 1997

THE MONSTER

First of all, a Ski-Doo is not a type of snowmobile. Everyone just says "snowmobile" when they don't want to refer to the Ski-Doo by its brand name, like saying you went for a "soft drink" because you don't want to say Coke or Pepsi. But these two snow machines could not be mistaken for each other, not even in a blindfold test. A snowmobile is a large, boxed-in, heavy-duty vehicle with round portholes and revolving treads like those on a tank, and is steered by means of two short skis at the front that steer like wheels. Snow-mobiles have been around since the 1920s. Robert Moon, in his book *This Is Saskatchewan* (1953), records that the first person to manufacture snowmobiles as a business was Bob Fudge, of Moosomin, Saskatchewan, who began a production line in 1930, in the depth of the Depression. The business was short-lived, not for lack of finances but because "a rural municipal convention passed a resolution branding snowmobiles a 'menace' to horse-drawn vehicles."

At about the same time, Joseph-Armand Bombardier, a native of Valcourt, Quebec, began experimenting with more idiosyncratic ways of travelling over snow. In 1922, when he was fifteen years old, he mounted an automobile engine on a wooden sleigh, hooked an airplane propeller to the drive shaft, tied ropes to the front runners, started up the engine and careened down the main street of Valcourt, snow flying out behind and citizens fleeing from in front. After that he spent three years studying to be an automobile mechanic in Montreal, then returned to Valcourt determined to bring

Henry Ford's automobile revolution to northern Quebec. And since northern Quebec is under snow for the greater part of the year, Bombardier set about inventing an automobile that would travel over snow. He took a standard Model T Ford, added a second rear axle to it and, leaving the four rubber tires in place, ran treads around them. The front wheels he replaced with skis that he could steer from inside the car, and *voilà*. He called his contraption an *auto-neige*, or "snow car," which was as close to calling it a snowmobile as he could get. It looked amazingly like the kind of snowmobile that Bob Fudge was experimenting with in Saskatchewan.

Bombardier wasn't the only person tinkering with snow machines at this time. In Baddeck, Cape Breton Island, for example, there was Doctor C. Lamont "Monty" MacMillan, who designed and built something he called a snowmobile (and which his wife called "That monster!") for getting out to his patients during the winter. "It consisted of all sorts of extra parts added to my own car," he recalled in his autobiography, *Memoirs of a Cape Breton Doctor* (1978), "to provide traction in the snow: there were skis mounted in front under the radiator, six wheels in the back, three on each side, and great big tractor belts around them. The rear tires had special lugs that fitted into the little openings in the belts." He débuted the thing on December 23, 1931. He had to gear the machine up so that the speedometer read seventy miles an hour when he was really going only twenty-five, which meant he got fewer than six miles to a gallon of gasoline. "It cost me more to run than I made from the visits," he wrote. It also broke down a lot. He scrapped it in 1934.

Bombardier did not scrap his auto-neige. By 1930 he had built a dozen of them, selling them to local hotel owners and ski-lodge operators. Like MacMillan's machine, they were ill-suited to cross-country travel: they would break through the ice on lakes and sink into snow banks. They could go from the train station to a hotel in fairly rough weather, but so could a horse and sleigh. So far, Bombardier's invention was little more than a curiosity.

Still, curiosities sell. Bombardier's new company, l'Auto-Neige Bombardier, sold so many of his snow cars that he was able to close down his automobile garage and dedicate himself solely to selling and improving his auto-neige. By the late 1930s he had steamlined the Model-T-inspired cab design to look like an oversized vw Beetle, patented a rubber-and-steel rear tread, and was making snow cars, snow trucks and snow schoolbuses at the rate of about a hundred a year. During the war he made snow armoured-troop-carriers for the Canadian army. After the war he made sand cars for the French Foreign Legion and something called the Muskeg Tractor for summer travel on the northern tundra, which proved so versatile that in 1957 Sir Vivien Fuchs travelled in one to the South Pole.

Bombardier was astute enough to realize that the South Pole was about as far as he could go with these large, industrial-size, all-terrain snow machines. Just as he had recognized the transportation revolution represented by the automobile in the 1920s, he realized early on that after the war people would have the money and leisure to devote to more individual pastimes. In 1950 he began working on an inexpensive, one-person auto-neige, which would take a person just about anywhere there was snow—a kind of snow motorcycle. He says he had people like trappers, hunters and missionaries in mind when he designed his first "Ski-Dog" in 1952—he called it a Ski-Dog because he thought it would replace the dogsled in the North— but from the moment the prototype Ski-Dog #1 was introduced to the public in 1959, it was seen primarily as a recreational vehicle. The logo he painted on the hood—a Superman-style triangle with the word "Bombardier" across the top and "Ski-Dog" stretched out in a delta beneath it—made the final letter "g" so small that everyone thought it was an "o" and called it a Ski-Doo. The name stuck.

The design, under the new name, was patented in 1959, and collectors of curiosities now know it as the 1960–61 Ski-Doo.

L'Auto-Neige Bombardier began turning out the hand-built snow-dogs at an ever increasing pace. According to Tom Carpenter's *Inventors: Profiles in Canadian Genius*, Ski-Doo sales doubled every year until by 1964, the year Bombardier died, the company was producing fifteen thousand of them annually. Today, Bombardier Inc. has forty-one thousand employees worldwide and revenues of $8 billion a year. In 1996, sales of Ski-Doos and their summer aquatic equivalent, called Sea-Doos, accounted for 22 percent of the corporation's total revenues.

Since then the demand for both Ski- and Sea-Doos has declined, but as usual the company anticipated the downturn and had already expanded into a number of other, more lucrative markets, notably the manufacture of airplanes and subway cars. Bombardier supplied the cars for the Montreal subway system in 1974 (for $118 million), and the spiffy, rubber-tired cars were so popular that New York City ordered $1-billion worth of them. In 1986, Bombardier bought Canadair from the Canadian government, and in 1992 it bought de Havilland Aircraft for $590 million (the Toronto *Globe and Mail*, announcing the purchase, did not once mention the word Ski-Doo). It now makes Learjets, Dash-8s and Regional Jets, and controls a considerable share of the world aerospace market. In the past five years Bombardier has sold 259 Canadair Regional Jets; at $27 million a pop, Bombardier can afford a slight downturn in the recreational vehicle market.

If the Ski-Doo's amazingly sudden success indicated a postwar occupation with individual pleasures, a kind of Romantic interlude, does its decline suggest we are returning to a more community-minded society? There are cultural indications that this might be so. Our lack of interest in poetry in favour of the novel might be one of them; the subsequent decline of the novel in favour of nonfiction might be another. The drop in Ski-Doo sales may just be the result of a lack of snow thanks to global warming, but it may also be something else. Consider the failure of Bombardier's most recent machine, the Sea-Doo—a summer version of the Ski-Doo that can go on water—to imitate the early success of the Ski-Doo. In August 1997, Bombardier cut production of the Sea-Doo and laid off 1,260 workers because, it said, reckless driving and accidents had turned the public against the product. But it wasn't just that; it was the product itself. Even when used thoughtfully, a single Sea-Doo makes an annoying whine that cuts through the peaceful calm of a summer lake like a toothache. Cottage communities don't like them.

The problem with both Ski-Doos and Sea-Doos, according to dozens of cottagers' associations across Canada, is the absence of legislation controlling the use of them. The machines, they say, are noisy and polluting; there are no emission controls on them, for example. Canadians tend to want the government to do something about the things they don't like. There are good, historical reasons for this. Encoding community standards into laws and then enforcing those laws may be said to be what a government is elected to do. It might just be that Ski-Doos and Sea-Doos transgress community standards. They redefine our notion of wilderness, and we don't want our notion of wilderness redefined, thank you very much. That is how the community-standards argument goes.

Snowmobile clubs reply that their members stick to public roads or have landowners' permission to go on private property, but not every public road is out of community earshot, not all snowmobilers belong to clubs, and not all club members respect No Trespassing signs. A friend of mine who lives near an abandoned railway track in central Ontario told me that during the previous winter he counted seven hundred Ski-Doos a week roaring within a hundred yards of his house. "And they go from ten o'clock at night until three or four in the morning," he said. "I've complained to the OPP, but there's nothing they can do about it."

His situation was exactly that of George Wilson, the main character in Max Braithwaite's 1978 novel *Lusty Winter*. Wilson retires to a cabin on a remote lake in northern Ontario and has his idyll invaded by a group of "snowmobilers," much as, in another era, he might have been invaded by a pack of Hell's Angels: "Oh Lord, there it is. That rotten roar. Down on the lake a row of snowmobiles. They're headed this way and it's going to be a confrontation." We've all heard the rotten roar of the auto-neige (there are now half a dozen brands, each, to the attuned ear, with its own particular rotten roar), and we've all wondered how we could stop it. Just as, I hazard a guess, when we hear the Sea-Doo's horrible intermittent whine on a lake in the summer, a vision of piano wire comes unbidden to mind.

In the North, the Ski-Doo is not a toy but a working machine, a valuable tool of trappers, hunters, doctors and even Arctic explorers, and it has replaced the dogsled and helped to improve living conditions. Ralph Plaisted, the first human being to make it overland to the North Pole (as far as anyone knows), got there by Ski-Doo (in 1968, the year before the first human being made it to the moon). In Churchill, Manitoba, in 1982, there was only one working dogsled team left, and dozens of Ski-Doos parked in front of the town centre, like bicycles scattered outside a corner store down south. Everyone called them Ski-Doos, even though some of them were Arctic Cats or Polarises. As Bombardier predicted, the Ski-Doo has rendered the ordinary, flesh-and-gristle husky all but obsolete. In 1963 the *Imperial Oil Review* underscored the situation nicely: "Many Mounties," it reported, "particularly around Churchill, now use the Ski-Doo for another ironic task: rounding up for destruction stray dogs put out of work by their successor, the mighty little Ski-Doo."

Superman I teach you the superman. Man is something to be surpassed.

—*Thus Spake Zarathustra,* 1885, Friedrich Nietzsche

LOOK, UP IN THE SKY

When Mordecai Richler was a St. Urbain Street kid in Montreal, he used to steal dimes from his father's pants pockets and sneak off to buy comic books. "Oh, the smell of those new comic books!" he wrote in "The Great Comic Book Heroes," an essay that first appeared in *Encounter* in 1965.

I remember that smell too. By the time I caught the comic-book bug, a new comic cost twelve cents and the smell probably came from a potentially toxic combination of cover-stock coating and newsprint bleach, but I loved it anyway. I lived in a farming community near Barrie, Ontario, and every Saturday my friend Terry and I would ride our bikes on opposite shoulders of Highway 93 or along the back concession roads, our eyes sifting through the weeds in the ditches for beer and pop bottles. I can still spot the glint of sunlight off glass from twenty feet. When we got the bottles home, we'd rinse them in the ditch beside my lane and get my father to drive us to Barrie, where we (or rather he) would cash them in at the Dominion store for two cents each. Then we'd go along to the end of the strip mall to buy comic books.

My father must have hated Saturdays, lugging dirty boxes full of dirty bottles into the nice, clean supermarket and watching the clerk count out the sixty-four cents. He must have hated even more taking eleven beer bottles, all different brands, into the Brewers' Retail and waiting while the clerk made a show of trying to find two dimes and two pennies in the till. My father would have loved us to sneak into his bedroom at night and steal a quarter or even a dollar from his pants pocket, but we never did. It was too much fun cruising the back roads, taking a lunch and maybe a fishing rod, remembering where the wild apple trees were, coming home with our bike baskets filled with clinking Fanta and Coke bottles, and then staying up late at night with a flashlight, or a handful of fireflies in a Mason jar if we were camping in the cedar bush behind Terry's house, reading the comics we had worked so hard to earn.

Long before there were books about the Tao of *Peanuts* or the Zen of *Pogo*, we knew that something big was going on beneath the surface of *Superman* and *Batman* and *Wonder Woman* comics. Superman was created in 1938, at a time when Americans, sensing the approach of the Second World War (or, as they call it in the United States, World War II), needed a hero to lead them into it (or get them out of it). All powers need heroes, and superpowers need superheroes. But for us, in Canada in the late 1950s, it wasn't that, and I'm not all that sure it was that for Joe Shuster either.

Shuster, the artist who drew *Superman*, was born in Toronto in 1914 (he was a cousin of comedian Frank Shuster). He worked as a paperboy for the Toronto *Star* in 1922, and although his family moved to Cleveland, Ohio, in 1924, where Shuster eventually teamed up with writer Jerry Siegel, many of the details of the early *Superman* comic stories were influenced by Shuster's memories of Toronto. The first *Superman* stories had Clark Kent and Lois Lane working for a newspaper called the *Daily Star*. "I still remember drawing one of the earliest panels that showed a newspaper building," Shuster recalled in an article in the Toronto *Star* in 1992. "We needed a name, and I spontaneously remembered the Toronto *Star*. So that's the way I lettered it. I decided to do it that way on the spur of the moment, because the *Star* was such an influence on my life."

Shuster also remembered reading comic strips from the 1920s in the *Star*, especially one called *Little Nemo*, drawn by Winsor McCay, featuring a child who could fly on his bed to futuristic cities and distant planets. (Little Nemo no doubt took his name from Jules Verne's Captain Nemo, commander of the *Nautilus* in *Twenty-Thousand Leagues Under the Sea*. As Verne, at least, knew, *nemo* is Latin for "everyman," and so Little Nemo would be the exact opposite of Superman.) Shuster also spent many hours in a downtown Toronto cinema, where his uncle, Frank Shuster's father, was the projectionist. The movies influenced Shuster's *Superman* strips as much as other comics did. Clark Kent, for example, was drawn to resemble Douglas Fairbanks Sr., and Superman's human name, Clark Kent, was an amalgamation of Clark Gable and Kent Taylor.

It might have been a nascent appreciation of irony that drew us to Superman. His name is neither Canadian nor American, but German: Superman is Nietzsche's *Übermensch*, a concept of human perfection developed in *Also sprach Zarathustra* in 1885 (but not translated into English until 1933) and adopted by the Nazis as the ideal gene-pool specimen for the master Aryan race. Shuster and Siegel thus created a comic strip with a Canadian setting and gave its hero a name fraught with Nazi overtones; this is American war propaganda? It reminds me of the old *Beyond the Fringe* skit of the Second World War in which, over Beethoven's "Pathétique," we hear the words: "The music we are listening to, Jeremy, is German music, and we are at war with the Germans; that is something you're going to have to work out for yourself, later on."

George Bernard Shaw appropriated Nietzsche's *Übermensch* even before Hitler did, and for much the same reasons. In 1903 he wrote the play *Man and Superman*, in which he vaunted Superman as the ideal socialist hero. "What kind of person is this Superman to be?" Shaw asks at the end of the play. "Some sort of good-looking philosopher-athlete, with a handsome healthy woman for his mate, perhaps?" Shuster must have known Shaw's play, because it's hard to find a better description of his Man of Steel.

It wasn't television, either, that made us like Superman. We already knew that Superman was faster than a speeding bullet—he was faster than the speed of light! More powerful than a locomotive? Able to leap over tall buildings in a single bound! Leap??! Who were these guys? We didn't need Marshall McLuhan to tell us that TV was an idiot box. With Superman, television exposed itself as a colossal disappointment. In the comics, Superman could do things he was never actually depicted doing, things we hadn't thought of yet; on TV, anyone could see that his costume was man-made, probably rayon, that his hair could be cut with ordinary scissors, that the flying scenes were faked. We didn't care all that much; we figured the TV guys were doing the best they could with a severely restrictive medium. But Superman on TV never caught our imaginations the way *Superman* comics did. By the 1950s, Americans were already moving into a television culture; Canada maintained a predominantly literary culture.

Mordecai Richler says he liked Superman not because he was so all-American, but because he was so damned Canadian. Clark Kent, he writes, "is the archetypal middle-class Canadian WASP, superficially nice, self-effacing, but within whom there burns a hate-ball, a would-be avenger with superhuman powers . . ." Well, maybe. It certainly was no coincidence that *Superman* comics usually had an ad on the inside back cover that showed the puny, ninety-pound weakling (Canadian WASP) getting revenge on the bully who kicked sand in his face, thanks to a body-building course from Charles Atlas (Superman). But that doesn't explain why Richler liked him. Maybe it wasn't only prepubescent Canadian WASPs who walked around with hate-balls burning in their guts. Or hoping some good-looking girl, maybe some knockout with her own car, would see the real man vibrating under the Banlon sweater. Or wishing that the eyes behind the tortoiseshell glasses could see through her knitted twin-set. Such lascivious thoughts must certainly have crossed Duddy Kravitz's mind from time to time. And isn't there something comic-bookish, something Jimmy-Olsen-like, in everyone's awe of the muscular goon in *St. Urbain's Horseman* they call "the Boy Wonder"?

Richler noted in 1965 that Lois was slated to marry the mad scientist Lex Luther later that year, and that, according to the Toronto *Star*, Joe Shuster was fifty years old, blind and living on Long Island. He and Siegel had sold DC Comics the rights to *Superman* in 1938 for $130 (U.S.), sued to get them back in 1947, lost, and were fired. The *Superman* comics we read were drawn by someone else. Shuster lived on this and that until 1978, when Warner Publications bought the movie rights from DC and voluntarily gave both Shuster and Siegel an annual stipend of $20,000 each. By 1990, Lois was on track to marry Superman himself (as we all knew she would) and, according to a second *Star* feature, Joe Shuster was living in California. He died in 1992. The Toronto *Star* published a nice obit, pointing out for the third time Shuster's debt to the *Star*, but there was hardly a notice of his passing in the American press. In 1995, DC killed Superman off in its March issue and there was a public outcry, mourning in the streets, fist-shaking grief. DC brought him back to life in November.

This is something that has always intrigued me, this resurrection theme in American culture. I think it has to do with television cartoon characters. Americans seem to have taken the Christian tenet that death is a temporary interruption absolutely bone literally: put a stick of dynamite in Bugs Bunny's hand, light the fuse, watch it explode, and there is Bugs Bunny still standing there, a little blackened by gunpowder but otherwise unharmed, maybe even stronger than he was before. Or drop a 100-ton weight on the Road Runner, wait for the dust to settle, lift off the weight and, *Mbeep-mbeep*, watch him go. Change the formula for Coca-Cola, and if the crowds don't like it, bring it back as Coke Classic. Kill Superman in March, raise him from the sepulchre in November. In how many sequels of *Alien* will Sigourney Weaver be resurrected? How many people believe that Walt Disney's body lies frozen in a California cryobiology clinic waiting to be thawed out when scientists discover a cure for death?

"Canada," writes cultural anthropologist Carole Henderson Carpenter in her essay on the role of monsters in Canadian culture, "is not a cultural milieu conducive to heroes, since the majority of Canadians have long denigrated hero-worship." She's right, I suppose, if we're talking about worship. I can't imagine worshipping, say, a politician as Americans worshipped John F. Kennedy, or the way Joe McGinniss describes Robert Kennedy (JFK resurrected) being mobbed at the Philadelphia airport in 1967 by "hero-hungry kids who cared nothing for issues, who wanted only to touch and see and scream and to feel close to something they knew was special." Or the way Martin Luther King, Jr. was idolized by millions of American blacks. Did Trudeau incite such reverence? I think not. He was liked, maybe even loved, but despite talk of Trudeaumania we always knew he was human and fallible. Certainly, when Trudeau faded from power, we did not, as McGinniss (in his 1976 book *Heroes*) says America did when its heroes were all departed and gone, collapse into despair, retreat into alcohol and divorce, and turn on our heroes and shoot them and then try to bring them back to life. We simply shrugged. In an essay about an earlier prime minister, Sir John A. Macdonald, Hugh MacLennan wrote that "Canada is dismally like the Scotland from which so many of our ancestors came. There is no group of people anywhere on the earth's surface that think more highly of their collective selves than the Scotch do, nor any other in which the great native individual is reduced by public opinion to a mere Lilliputian size."

America shares with Germany a sense that ordinary human beings are "something that must be surpassed," as Nietzsche said of his superman. American culture encourages individuals, with the hero as simply an ideal individual. Canada has a collective culture, in which the individual has value only as a member of the community. The fact that we have no heroes in the American sense does not mean that we don't think anyone in Canada is good enough to be a hero. As MacLennan knew, it is not an inferiority complex that makes us diffident towards the individual. It is quite the opposite. We look upon someone who has done something amazingly out of the ordinary and we say, you are good, but you are no better than the rest of us.

So let it be with Superman. We liked him all right. He seemed like a nice guy, not too cocky. He could tell us what Lois Lane had on under her blouse, but he probably wouldn't. And he could definitely hit a softball farther than we could. But we wouldn't worship him for that; we'd just try to get him on our team.

Tourtière A type of pie made with ground meat, generally pork.

> —A Taste of History: The Origins of Québec's Gastronomy,
> 1989, Marc Lafrance and Yvon Desloges

The destiny of nations is determined by how they eat.

> —Physiologie du goût, 1825, Anthelme Brillat-Savarin

PIGEON POT PIE

Modern recipes for *tourtière*, the traditional meat pie of Quebec, call for a basic meat filling of ground beef and ground pork mixed with mashed potatoes and spices. Sondra Gotlieb's recipe, in her book *The Gourmet's Canada* (1972), calls for three-quarters of a pound of each meat, plus three sliced onions, a teaspoon each of garlic, ginger and cinnamon, a quarter-pound of salt pork cut into cubes, three cooked potatoes, also cubed, and a controversial can of tomatoes—controversial because she got the recipe from one of those American Time-Life cookbooks and used it despite protests from her Québécoise friends, who termed the addition of tomatoes "ignorance."

Forget tomatoes. The real fight ought to have been over the meat. *Tourtière* was never meant to be made with beef or pork, but with passenger pigeon, which in New France was called *une tourte*. In France, *tourte* meant "pie" and a *tourtière* was the dish that a *tourte* was baked in. The *Grand Robert*, France's equivalent of the OED, gives three meanings for *tourte*: a round loaf of bread; a round pie containing meat, usually fish; and an imbecile. For *tourtière* it gives only one meaning: "kitchen utensil for making *tourtes*." As the authors of

A Taste of History point out, "the extension of the term [*tourtière*] to mean the prepared dish itself is not specifically Canadian." They note that in Limousin a *tourtière* was made with veal, pigeon, turkey and hare. In Quebec, the poor passenger pigeon (*Ectopistes migratorius*) was probably called a *tourte* as a short form of tourterelle (turtledove). In any case, *tourtière* was made with passenger pigeons, not with ground beef and pork.

Passenger pigeons were eaten in New France and elsewhere in huge quantities. Peter Kalm, a Dutch naturalist travelling through Quebec in 1749, remarked that the birds "flew in the woods in numbers beyond conception," and that "their flesh is the most palatable of any bird's flesh I have ever tasted." And no less an authority than Robert-Lionel Séguin, in his monumental *La civilisation traditionnelle de l'habitant aux XVIIe et XVIIIe siècles* (1967), writes that, although it was true that wild pigeons so ravaged farmers' fields that the Annual Report for 1703 included fervent prayers for the removal of these undesirable pests, "it is also true that pigeon meat was not entirely unwelcome in the succulent *tourtières* that graced the tables of the colony's gourmets from the first half of the seventeenth century."

On New Year's Day, 1646, for instance, a group of Jesuit priests and Ursuline nuns in Quebec City presented the intendant with "many beautiful gifts of candles, rosaries, crucifixes, &c., & at dinner, two beautiful *tourtières*" made with the meat from sixteen passenger pigeons. From then on, reports Le Beau, writing in 1738, the citizens of the colony "avidly sought out the pigeons and took much pleasure in the killing of them: I myself killed forty-four with a single shot." Many habitants, continues Séguin, "resorted to pigeon meat after the crop failures in the dark days of 1760 [this was after the fall of Québec; for crop failures, read crop burnings], and Philippe Aubert de Gaspé relates that 'Every habitant with whom I have spoken agrees that passenger pigeons, which they killed with sticks, were the manna from Heaven that preserved them from certain starvation.'"

Peter Matthiessen, in *Wildlife in America*, states that the passenger pigeon was "the most numerous bird ever to exist on earth," and there are nineteenth-century accounts of great flocks of them flying over Ontario, so thick that they blocked out the sun from horizon to horizon for as long as fourteen hours at a stretch. Alexander Wilson, describing a migrating flock of passenger pigeons in Indiana Territory in 1810, estimated their number at 2,230,272,000—which must make him the fastest counter ever to exist on Earth. In *The Canadian Naturalist* (1840), P.H. Gosse quotes Wilson's figure and remarks that "the mind is lost in endeavouring to form an idea commensurate with these vast numbers; and this small and apparently insignificant bird may justly be considered one of the wonders of this western world."

Pigeon rookeries, some of them more than a hundred square miles in area, were invaded by commercial hunters and the birds were slaughtered by the thousands. John James Audubon witnessed one of these frenzies in which the killing proceeded all night amidst an uproar that could be heard three miles away; in the morning, carts were loaded with dead pigeons "until each had as many as he could possibly dispose of, when the hogs were let loose to feed on the remainder." Passenger pigeons were used for target practice in gun clubs; skeet shooters still call the clay dishes they blast out of the air with shotguns "pigeons" because they originally *were* pigeons—passenger pigeons with cayenne pepper rubbed into their skin to make them fly faster.

The passenger pigeon, once a symbol of nature's inexhaustible bounty in North America, was extinct by the end of the nineteenth century. P.A. Taverner, in *Birds of Eastern Canada* (1922), notes that the last great flock left Canada in 1878, "but failed to return in any commercial number the following spring." The last wild passenger pigeon was shot by hunters in Ohio in 1900, and the last captive member of the species died in the Cincinnati Zoo in 1914.

Since the disappearance of the passenger pigeon, *tourtière* has been made with ground pork and beef. I like to think that the pork is added to remind us of the animal that, in Audubon's report, fed on the slaughtered pigeons themselves, but that's probably too fanciful. The meat is cooked with onion, garlic, sage and cloves, then mixed with mashed potatoes (not tomatoes) and baked in a pie shell. In Quebec it is still the traditional Christmas Eve meal, prepared in advance and eaten when the family comes home from midnight mass. On the Gaspé peninsula the ground pork is mixed with chicken instead of beef, and that, I am sure, is in remembrance of an earlier, tastier and wilder fowl.

Truck System Paying employees wholly or in part in goods and tokens valid only at a tommy shop connected with their employers.

—*Brewer's Dictionary of Phrase and Fable*

WHAT YOU GET

The word "truck" literally means "goods bartered or traded"; in a truck system, workers exchange their work for food and clothing rather than bothering with the intermediate and temporary inconvenience of cash. At first glance it seems like a good idea. The truck system in Canada was a version of the Shetland Truck System in England, whereby tokens given to workers instead of cash wages were redeemable at "tommy shops" (tommy was sailors' slang for soft bread, used to distinguish it from hard biscuit). The tommy shops were owned by the same company that doled out the tokens. That was the problem. With the company determining the workers' wages *and* the price of goods in the tommy shops, the whole system was controlled by one side. Guess who suffered? In the southern United States, the truck system replaced slavery after the Civil War; instead of being provided with food and clothing in exchange for menial labour, black workers were paid for doing menial labour with credit at stores owned by the plantation owners. They didn't see much difference. Tennessee Ernie Ford's song "Sixteen Tons" is about the truck system:

Saint Peter don't you call me 'cause I can't go;
I owe my soul to the company store.

In England the truck system was abolished by a series of Acts of Parliament in 1831, 1881 and 1896, requiring that workers be paid in coin of the realm. In the United States it was abolished in the 1880s. But the practice continued in Canada well into this century.

In Newfoundland, the general store in a fishing outport was often owned by the same company that owned the fishing fleet. Food and equipment were supplied in advance to the fisherman, and to the fisherman's family while he was out fishing or sealing, and the fisherman was required to sell his catch to the company to repay the debt at the store, getting in cash only what was left over after the year's debt at the store was paid. In boom years the system worked tolerably well; in bust years both the fisherman and the store got another year older and deeper in debt. By the 1840s this system had, as historian St. John Chadwick points out in *Newfoundland: Island into Province* (1967), re-created in Newfoundland "the quasi-feudal economic system from which the earlier settlers had originally escaped" by leaving England. The fisherman, dependent on the price the merchant fixed for a quintal of fish or a barrel of flour, as well as on the unpredictable habits of the cod itself, was caught in a familiar vise. To use the truck system, writes Chadwick, "was to keep worker in thrall to capitalist, stamp the thinking and actions of rival political parties, retard economic development, place the burden of the cost of living where it could least well be sustained, and nurture the grievances of the underprivileged." Chadwick also quotes Sir William Grenfell, who described the economics of Newfoundland as "subtle because it impoverishes and enslaves the victims, and then makes them love their chains." Another Newfoundland historian, D.W. Prowse, writing in 1895, castigated the truck system as "dishonest . . . demoralizing to the people and disastrous to the merchant . . . there could be no genuine prosperity while [it] existed."

My own family can attest to the truth of the latter statement—that the truck system was as disastrous to the merchant as it was demor-alizing to the people. My great-grandfather and great-great-grandfather owned Alan Goodridge & Sons, a trading company based in Renews with offices and an entire block of wharves in St. John's. At one time the company operated four trading vessels of its own, and held shares in nearly four hundred fishing boats, and the company store in Renews did a booming business. But by the time my grandfather took over the company, he controlled neither the price of fish nor the cost of flour, and when bad fishing combined with high import costs, the whole outport suffered. I have the company's 1908 ledger that tells the story: the left side of each page in the ledger shows the yearly debits for each family in Renews, and the right side shows the credits. Some-times the two sides balanced. The ledger for one family, for example, lists "2 yds Dungary, 60 cents; 3 yds Shirt Stuff, 80 cents; 1 Bucket Lye, 30 cents," and so on for a total debit of $60.55. The credit side listed four deliveries of cod totalling fifteen and a quarter quintals, worth exactly $60.55. That family was lucky; many others weren't. Too often the last entry on the credit side was Bad Debts: "James Edmond, $9.02; Edward Fairweather, $686.69; Paul Coach, $2,482.93." By the time of my first visit to Renews in 1956, Alan Goodridge & Sons had become the Tors Cove Trading Company. The old company store was nothing grander than the local corner store where, after splitting kindling for my grandfather in the morning, I would go and fill a paper bag with penny goods before walking out onto the wharf to catch sculpins. The store and the grand house next to it are both gone now.

Although Newfoundland's truck system was officially halted in 1911, it continued to exist at least in the outports into the 1930s. Elsewhere in Atlantic Canada it was used in logging and fishing com-munities, particularly in Acadia and the Gaspé, where abuses by absentee owners were rampant. In 1849, Sir James Alexander wrote in *L'Acadie or Seven Years Explorations in British America*, that "some of those men who work saw mills 'grind the faces of the poor' by the truck system of payment, and by the two hundred and three hundred percent profit they demand for necessaries." The system continued there until the 1920s. John Clarke writes in *L'Île Percée* (1923):

> Long years ago, the chief cause of incarceration was violation of the fishing contract. Those were the days when the 'truck,' or credit system was still in full plumage, and it was the practice for the fishing proprietors to make annual contracts with the fishermen in which the master agreed to furnish boat and gear and the fisherman to serve so and so many days, spring and fall, with a *degrat* in summer, if necessary, for farming purposes, etc., he to receive a definite price for his fish, either by the draft green or the quintal dried. Violation of this agreement on the part of the fisherman was no venial sin, for it tended to demoralize the business of the coast and was likely to be visited with severe penalty.

Clarke, an American geologist, saw only that the truck system was disastrous to the merchants. "Our fishermen," he continues, meaning *our* fishermen,

> are not so lazy as some, but lazy enough, God knows, and they have all sorts of well-cherished superstitions about wind, weather and bait, to help keep them so. The proprietor who had bound himself to keep these men going with store credit in advance of fish, often found himself near the edge of the cliff if the contract was broken, and so these procrastinators were very much in the way of being jailed for their sins of omission, which were, after all, but gentle bendings of the law.

Outside Newfoundland, the major challenge to the truck system came in the 1920s, in the coal-mining town of Glace Bay, Nova Scotia, where the British Empire Steel Company (BESCO), then the largest industrial consortium in Canada, owned the coalmines and the company stores, called "pluck-me" stores, and paid the miners with credit—after, of course, setting the miners' wages and the price of goods in the pluck-me's. When coal prices dropped in 1925, BESCO laid off workers and cancelled credit in its stores, creating famine in a town that was already mired in poverty: four years earlier, when the national infant mortality rate was 88.1 per 1,000 births, in Glace Bay it had been 305.9. When miners protested the lay-offs and demanded a 10 percent wage increase, BESCO responded with a 10 percent wage *cut*.

On March 6, 1925, twelve thousand miners struck and two thousand soldiers were brought in to keep the peace. As the *Financial Post* observed, "the situation in the district is not even one of armed neutrality. It is that of a conquered territory held down by the sword." In the ensuing riots, almost the first targets were the pluck-me stores; the miners looted the stores and burned their credit records. The strike lasted until August—that is, until William Davis, a miner, was killed by a BESCO policeman—by which time 1,478,700 man-days of work had been lost, accounting for 84 percent of the total for Canada that year.

When the chastened miners went back to work, the pluck-me stores reopened, and for a time it was business as usual. The last time I was in Glace Bay, all the mines but one were closed and unemployment was the highest in Canada. The pluck-me stores were a thing of the past, replaced by what seemed to be their opposite: stores in which you couldn't get credit if your life depended on it. When I went into a convenience store to buy a newspaper, a sign beside the cash register caught my eye: "No cheques. No credit."

Another store tried to make the same point more lightly: "No cash? No carry!" I'd seen such signs before, of course, but these in Glace Bay seemed to me more significant, even chilling. They represented a kind of defiant defeat. What they said to the out-of-work miners was not Pluck-me, but Pluck You!

Tuque Cotton cap. Fifty years ago, English Canadians called French Canadians, "Blue-tuques."

—*Glossaire franco-canadien,* 1880, Oscar Dunn

DON'T GET YOUR TUQUE IN A KNOT

When Prime Minister Jean Chrétien returned from a trade delegation to Japan a few years ago, he told reporters that he had been presented with a Japanese kimono as a parting gift. As the negotiations were scheduled to continue the following year in Vancouver, the reporters asked the prime minister what traditional Canadian article of clothing he would give to his foreign guests. He thought about it for a couple of seconds and then said, "We'll give them tuques."

He was right, of course. The tuque, like the colourful *ceinture flèchée,* may have started out as a quintessentially Québécois piece of clothing, but unlike the herring-bone belt of the coureurs-de-bois, the tuque is now ubiquitous across Canada: Vancouver hockey fans wear tuques at Canucks games, Prairies kids wear Oilers or Jets tuques to school. In the rest of the world, thanks to ambassadors like Bob and Doug Mackenzie, the tuque rivals the Mountie hat as the universal symbol of Canadian headwear.

And it is tuque, please note, not "toque." The knitted, stocking-like cap that originated in New France in the seventeenth century is often misspelled in English. In 1925, American nature writer Donald Culrose Peattie, in his gentle book *Bounty of Earth,* lamented at Easter that "pokes and toques and sailors and tailors and picture hats there are new all over the world, but none for Narcissa." But in French a *toque* is a chef's cap, or a judge's hat, or a professor's cloth cap, and in Quebec a *toque* is either a burdock or a ball of snow dipped in maple syrup, and Narcissa, Peattie's wife, would have looked odd walking down Fifth Avenue sporting either of those.

The misspelling derives from a misunderstanding of the tuque's origins. Bill Casselman, in his *Casselman's Canadian Words*, states that the cap is called a tuque from the verb *toquer*, "to knock," because the long, tasselled end kept knocking against the wearer's shoulder. This would be a better explanation if tuque were spelled toque. You can *toque* your head on a doorpost or against a wall, and to be *toqué* is to be either stubborn (headstrong) or angry (off your head). *Se toquer* means to become thoughtful (use your head) or insane (off your head), even to the point of falling in love (lose your head). None of these has to do with the cap that covers the head (although there is the expression *avoir la tuque drette*, which means "to be angry"; *Ne porte pas ta tuque drette* would translate into something like "Don't get your tuque in a knot"). There is a pulp-and-paper town in northern Quebec named La Tuque; it is called that because the shape of a rock beside the river reminded someone of a tuque, and the rock looks nothing like a chef's or even a professor's pork pie hat.

The origin of the word "tuque" is the old Languedoc dialect word *tuc*, or summit, the head of a mountain, capped and tasselled with snow. The French writer Jean-Baptiste d'Aleyrac, visiting New France in 1755, noted in his *Mémoires* that

> there is no *patois* spoken in this country. All Canadians speak French exactly like we do, except for a few words peculiar to them—borrowed, usually, from the language of sailors—such as *amarer* for *attacher* [to attach], *hâler* for *tirer* [to pull, obviously from the English verb "to haul"], not only on a rope but on anything. They have forged a few new words, such as *tuque* or *fourole*, a hat of red wool (which they wear often) . . .

The tuque was always a tuque, never a toque. The *fourole* seems to have gone the way of the nightcap.

D'Aleyrac suggests that the tuque is a refinement of the French sailor's cap, which is also a woollen stocking-like affair. The latter, however, is worn tight to the head and has no dangling ends to get caught in windlasses or anchor chains, whereas tuques were originally quite long, with tassels at the end that hung down beside the head. They were made by knitting a long tube, closed at both ends like a sausage, one end being tucked into the other to form a cup (or a cap) and the two ends tied together by the tassel. In 1657, Montreal's first notary, Jean de Saint-Père, willed to his two children "six bonnets of red wool," which is the earliest extant reference to anything that might be described as a tuque.

Jean de Saint-Père's death, which had occasioned the probate of his will, is described in a letter of Marguerite Bourgeoys, and is an excellent illustration of the expression *se toquer*, "to lose one's head." Saint-Père and his brother-in-law Nicolas Godé and a servant, Jacques Noël, were building a house on October 25, 1657, when they were visited by a group of Iroquois, who had been at peace with the French for some time. The three men greeted the Indians courteously, gave them some food, and then climbed back up on the roof to continue work. The Indians shot at them with their arquebuses and "brought them down like sparrows," after which they scalped Godé and Noël, and cut off Saint-Père's head and took it with them. As they headed off through the bush, however, the severed head began to speak to them in Iroquoian, a language that Saint-Père had not known while alive. "You kill us, you inflict endless cruelties on us, you want to annihilate the French," the talking head told them, "but you will not succeed: the French will one day be your masters and you will obey them." The frightened Iroquois lost their heads, scalped Saint-Père's head and threw the rest away. But the scalp, although it too had lost its head, continued to speak to them for quite some time.

In the end, the prime minister did not give tuques to the Asian delegates at the conference, which was held in Vancouver; he gave them leather jackets and denim shirts. Maybe he thought tuques would be too closely identified with Quebec. Or maybe he thought they would be too closely associated with Canada.

Zipper From zip, which represents the sound of cloth rip-
ping, or an insect or a bullet in flight. The zipper moves quickly,
but is supposed to prevent the rip.
—*Dictionary of Word Origins*, 1945, Joseph T. Shipley

ON CLOSING

I don't often notice the flies on men's trousers when I'm watching
television, but there is one scene in a recent movie—*The Quick
and the Dead*, starring Sharon Stone and Gene Hackman, which is
supposed to take place in the American Wild West—in which focus-
ing on a man's clothed crotch is unavoidable because it fills the entire
screen. One of the movie's many unsavoury characters emerges from
a bedroom above the town saloon doing up his pants. First he pulls
up the zipper on his fly, then he does up his belt, then he buckles
on his holster, then Sharon Stone shoots him. Since "to zip" means
"to be quick," this must be the scene that gives the movie its title.

Stone should have shot the costume researcher. Zippers weren't
used in men's clothing until 1917, when the U.S. Navy put them in
flight suits and the U.S. Army used them to close men's trouser pockets. After the First World War, when military-style clothing came
into fashion, British designers incorporated Ready Fasteners in men's
sports suits, and in 1930, Paris designer Mme Schiaparelli put zippers in women's dresses. But a man couldn't come out of a bedroom zipping up his fly until 1935.

On August 28, 1893, an American inventor named Whitcomb L.
Judson was awarded a U.S. patent for something described as "a
clasp locker or unlocker for shoes." This was obviously not a zipper,
but it must have been something like a zipper, because now Judson

is generally credited with its invention. Whatever it looked like, however, it was not called a zipper; he called it an automatic hook-and-eye fastener. When Judson demonstrated his invention at the Chicago Exhibition, a certain Colonel Lewis Walker was so impressed by it that he bought the patent and formed the Automatic Hook and Eye Company of Meadville, Pennsylvania. Judson, now working for Walker, fiddled with his invention for a few years, and in 1896 came up with something described in patent number 557,207 as "two metal chains which can be fastened together by movement of a slider," which sounds a lot like a zipper. Judson fiddled for a few more years, and in 1902 Walker began manufacturing a zipper-like fastener under the trade name C-Curity.

Enter Gideon Sundback and a fair amount of patented confusion. Sundback, a Swedish-born inventor working for Westinghouse Electric in Pittsburgh, was hired away by Walker and Judson in 1906 to improve on the C-Curity fastener, which apparently wasn't as C-Cure as had been hoped. The chains fastened together all right, but the slider kept coming off, the chains would pop open and military contracts would fall out of the pockets. Sundback came up with something he patented in 1913 as "separable fasteners." This didn't impress the military, which already knew that the fasteners were separable—that was the problem. Walker and Judson went back to the drawing board, and in 1917 the Automatic Hook and Eye Company of Meadville, now called the Hookless Fastener Company, patented the Talon Slide Fastener, which looked an awful lot like Sundback's separable fastener. Sundback wasn't pleased.

In 1925, Sundback became president of the Lightning Fastener Company of St. Catharines, Ontario, and applied for and was granted the Canadian patent for his separable fasteners, which of course he now called lightning fasteners. His company manufactured these fasteners and sold them to the B.F. Goodridge Company, who put them on their rubber galoshes (which until then had been fastened the old-fashioned way, with hooks and eyes which, as we all know, only come undone in deep snow). A Goodridge executive called these new boots Zippers. The name of the boot eventually became the name of the fastener.

The word "zipper," however, existed in Canada before it was applied to rubber galoshes. In Kingston Penitentiary in the 1920s, a "zipper" was a home-made device used by inmates to light illicit cigarettes. It consisted of a metal button, a loop of string, a piece of flint, and a square of soft, scorched cloth called the punk. Merilyn Simonds, in her book *The Convict Lover*, has her convict lighting up with a zipper in 1919; she took her reference from *Shackling the Transgressor*, by Oswald C. J. Withrow, a doctor who had been in the Pen in the 1920s. "To see a man grasp one end of the piece of string with his teeth," Withrow wrote, "start the steel revolving, strike a spark or two from the flint, causing a glowing spot in the punk from which his cigarette could catch a light, was one of the sights of the penitentiary." Seasoned inmates could pull a zipper out of its hidey-hole, set it up and have a cigarette lit in a few seconds—hence its name.

Tim Buck (1891–1973), founder of the Communist Party of Canada, was, because of that, an inmate of Kingston Pen in 1933 (the year *Shackling the Transgressor* was published) and claims to have invented the zipper himself when he was working in the prison machine shop. "Somebody had asked me," he recalled in *Yours in the Struggle*, published posthumously in 1977,

> "Could I make something that would strike a spark, enough to light a cigarette?" That was very easy. All I had to do was to take a piece of tooled steel and make a button; drill two holes and put threads through these two holes and spin it so the threads became twisted. Then you could pull the threads in and out.

He used shards from a broken emery wheel instead of a flint, and burnt wool, which he called the poke instead of the punk, but otherwise his apparatus is not significantly different from Merilyn's convict's zipper. As Withrow's account makes clear, the zipper was in the Pen long before Buck was.

Buck, however, didn't call it a zipper, he called it a lighter. He says he "was so busy making these lighters, answering questions about Marxism, and about the reform programme" that he rarely did any work in the machine shop. Buck recorded his memoirs in 1965, but he was writing about the year 1933. The first pair of men's trousers with a zipper in the fly came out in 1935. The first cigarette lighter was patented in the United States in 1934. It worked on almost exactly the same principle as the "zipper" described by Withrow and the "lighter" described by Buck, with the addition of a reservoir of fluid: steel wheel spins, strikes piece of flint, sparks fly to a bit of soft cloth, flame ensues. And it was called the Zippo lighter.

I'm not suggesting that there is any patent disputation to be made between Zippo and the estate of Tim Buck. Such a thing would be philosophically unthinkable: sharing a gadget with a group of fellow inmates is communism; taking a small invention and turning it into a major industry is capitalism. Buck would have had none of it. But I am saying that if Sharon Stone had lit her cheroot with a Zippo lighter instead of having her villain zip up his pants, *The Quick and the Dead* would have been one whole year less anachronistic.